❧ A Journey in the Seaboard Slave States

In the Years 1853–1854

With Remarks on Their Economy

By

Frederick Law Olmsted

[Originally Issued in 1856]

With a Biographical Sketch by

Frederick Law Olmsted, Jr.

And

With an Introduction by

William P. Trent

In Two Volumes

Volume I

G. P. Putnam's Sons

New York   London
27 and 29 W. 23d Street   24 Bedford Street, Strand

The Knickerbocker Press

1904

The Knickerbocker Press, New York

ADVERTISEMENT.

In the year 1853, the author of this work made a journey through the Seaboard Slave States, and gave an account of his observations in the *New York Daily Times*, under the signature of "Yeoman." Those letters excited some attention, and their publication in a book was announced; but before preparing them for the press, the author had occasion to make a second and longer visit to the South. In the light of the experience then gathered, the letters have been revised, and, with much additional matter, are now presented to the public.

PREFACE

THE chief design of the author in writing this book has been, to describe what was most interesting, amusing, and instructive to himself, during the first three of fourteen months' travelling in our Slave States; using the later experience to correct the erroneous impressions of the earlier.

He is aware that it has one fault—it is too fault-finding. He is sorry for it, but it cannot now be helped; so at the outset, let the reader understand that he is invited to travel in company with an honest growler.

But growling is sometimes a duty; and the traveller might well be suspected of being a "dead head," or a sneak, who did not find frequent occasion for its performance, among the notoriously careless, makeshift, impersistent people of the South.

For the rest, the author had, at the outset, of his journey, a determination to see things for himself, as far as possible, and to see them carefully and fairly, but cheerfully and kindly. It was his disposition, also, to search for the causes and extenuating circumstances, past and present, of those phenomena which are commonly reported to the prejudice of the slaveholding community; and especially of those features which are manifestly most to be regretted in the actual condition of the older Slave States.

He protests that he has been influenced by no partisan bias; none, at least, in the smallest degree unfriendly to fair investigation, and honest reporting. At the same time, he avows himself a democrat; not in the technical and partisan, but in the primary and essential sense of that term. As a democrat he went to study the South—its institutions, and its people; more than ever a democrat, he has returned from this labor, and written the pages which follow.

SOUTH-SIDE STATEN ISLAND, Jan. 9, 1856.

"Men are never so likely to settle a question rightly as when they discuss it freely."—*Macaulay.*

"You have among you many a purchased slave,
Which, like your asses, and your dogs, and mules,
You use in abject and in slavish parts,
Because you bought them:

"So do I answer you.
The pound of flesh which I demand of him,
Is dearly bought; 't is mine, and I will have it.
If you deny me, fie upon your law!"—*Shylock.*

"The one idea which History exhibits as evermore developing itself into greater distinctness, is the idea of humanity, the noble endeavor to throw down all barriers erected between men by prejudice and one-sided views, and by setting aside the distinctions of religion, country, and color, to treat the whole human race as one Brotherhood, having one great object — the pure development of our spiritual nature."—*Humboldt's Cosmos.*

CONTENTS

CHAPTER	PAGE
I.—Washington	1
II.—Virginia	18
III.—The Economy of Virginia	183
IV.—The Political Experience of Virginia	241
V.—North Carolina	341

FREDERICK LAW OLMSTED

FREDERICK LAW OLMSTED, born on April 26, 1822, at Hartford, Conn., was the eldest son of John Olmsted, a prosperous merchant of that city, where the family had been living since the settlement of the place in 1636, having come from County Essex, England.

He went to a succession of schools, and was fitted for Yale in 1836, but on account of a weakness of the eyes gave up college, and spent most of the next three years nominally studying engineering with a Rev. Mr. Barton, of Andover, Mass., who was a surveyor as well as a minister, but a large part of his time was spent in the White Mountains.

During his youth and early manhood, he frequently accompanied his father and stepmother on long driving trips through many parts of New England, acquiring a keen power of observation, a warm appreciation of the varieties of New England landscape, and a familiar acquaintance with the conditions and habits of the whole community. The family spent part of nearly every summer at Guilford or some other point on the shore, and he became very fond of cruising in the waters of the Sound in a small sailboat.

In the autumn of 1840, he entered the employ of Benkard & Hutton, dry-goods importers, in New York, and remained in this uncongenial occupation till the spring of 1842, after which for about a year he attended lectures and did a certain amount of reading at Yale, where his younger brother, John Hull Olmsted, was then at college.

In April, 1843, he sailed for Canton as one of the crew of the bark *Ronaldson*, going through with experiences which in many respects resembled those of Richard H. Dana, in his *Two Years before the Mast*. He was attacked by typhus fever while the vessel lay for weeks in the pest-ridden river below Canton, and with the rest of the crew he suffered severely from scurvy on the return voyage. He gave up the sea, with impaired health, but always retained a fondness for ships and an appreciation and mastery of the qualities of that "ship-shape," orderly, and resourceful adaptation of means to ends, which is the ideal of all good seamen and which had produced in those days one of the most beautiful works of man—the American clipper-ship.

After some time spent in recruiting his health, staying a good deal at his Uncle Brooks's farm in Cheshire, Connecticut, and taking more of those carriage cruises about New England with his father, he decided to adopt farming as a regular occupation. The season of 1845 he spent with an intelligent farmer near Waterbury, Connecticut, working hard and learning much, and the next winter was again at Yale taking lectures in chemistry, reading, and enjoying the pleasant society of New Haven. The following season he spent as a workman with another farmer, Mr. Geddes, near Syracuse, N. Y., to whom he had been attracted by his receiving the prize offered by the New York Agricultural Society for the best-ordered farm in the State. Mr. Geddes's father had been prominent in building the Erie Canal, and he was himself an engineer as well as a farmer, and also interested in politics, so that Mr. Olmsted had plenty of stimulus to think while he worked, and in the evening to discuss a wide range of subjects with an intelligent man. Meanwhile he did a great deal of reading.

During 1847, he worked a farm at Sachem's Head, on Long Island Sound, which his father had purchased for him; but it was small and not profitable, and a year later he changed to a farm of 130 acres on Staten Island, N. Y., where he was successful in raising fruit for the New York market.

In 1850, with his brother John and Charles Loring Brace, he made a trip abroad, going very economically and travelling mainly afoot. Although they saw something of France, Switzerland, and Germany, most of their time was spent in England, and after his return Mr. Olmsted wrote out an account of that portion of the trip under the title of *Walks and Talks of an American Farmer in England*. The book was well received, although it never had a very large sale.

At about this time he made the friendship of A. J. Downing, the landscape gardener and writer on horticulture, and was led to do more or less writing for periodicals, mainly on rural subjects.

In 1852, his brother's delicate health suggested the desirability of a warmer climate and he began seriously to consider moving to Virginia. While he was contemplating a visit to Virginia for the selection of a farm for his brother, Mr. Raymond of the New York *Times*, struck by the qualities shown in his book on England, proposed to him to make a tour in the South and write a series of letters to the *Times* upon the economic and social conditions of the Slave States. He at once fell in with the idea, and on December 11, 1852, he started on his first trip. He returned April 6, 1853, having gone as far as New Orleans. It was the letters written to the *Times* while on this trip that formed the principal material for the *Seaboard Slave States*, published in 1856.

On November 10, 1853, again as correspondent of the *Times*, he started, in company with his brother John, on a second trip, which extended to the Mexican boundary. In returning, he parted from his brother at New Orleans and travelled on horseback from there to Richmond, reaching home in the summer of 1854. The letters he wrote during the first part of this trip were compiled and edited by his brother and published in 1857 under the title of *The Texas Journey*, while the material gathered by him on the return journey, alone, forms the major part of *The Back Country*, published in 1860.

A hasty condensation of the three books was published in 1861, at the outbreak of the war, in London and New York, under the title of *The Cotton Kingdom*.

Thus diverted from farming into literary work, Mr. Olmsted moved to New York City, and turned over the farm to his brother. He became one of the editors of *Putnam's Magazine*, and shortly after, with George William Curtis, he entered into partnership with Dix & Edwards, publishers; an ill-judged venture, for the firm proved to be in bad financial condition and soon failed, making Olmsted and Curtis liable for a considerable amount of debts which were finally paid in full.

During 1856, in connection with the publishing business, he was in London for some time and used the opportunity to join his sisters in a little journey through Italy.

He had always been keenly appreciative of the beauty of landscape and had taken much pleasure in quiet contemplation and analysis of its qualities, and this had led him to a close observation not only of the large range of natural scenery through which he had journeyed, but of many public and private parks of Europe; again, he had been a close observer of men, their habits and their social needs; if to these qualities be added his practical experience in farming, it will be seen that he was unconsciously laying a strong foundation for what was to become his chief life work.

In 1856, a Board of Commissioners had been created to lay out the Central Park, New York: the land had already been acquired and its improvement was at once begun under a plan prepared by the Chief Engineer of the Board, Captain (afterward General) Vielé. One of the Commissioners with whom Mr. Olmsted was well acquainted, Charles W. Elliott, met him at a little place near New Haven by chance, late in the summer of 1857, and mentioned that the Commission wanted to get a superintendent to act as assistant to Captain Vielé in handling the large force of men then at work on the park. When asked what kind of man was needed the Commissioner replied: "A man like you—one with your knowledge of farming and your other experience." The failure of Dix & Edwards had left him ready to take up a new enterprise and he returned to New York that night, procured letters of introduction to the several Commissioners, and on September 11, 1857, received the appointment.

The park was "in politics," and the efforts of the new superintendent to introduce good discipline and efficiency in the conduct of the work were hampered at every turn by the exercise of underground and overhead "pulls." By dint of hard work, persistency, and patience, the efficiency of the force was greatly increased, but never in all of Mr. Olmsted's connection with the Central Park was there a cessation of this harassing struggle with the debauchers of the public service. Any one who wishes light on this phase of "practical politics" in the fifties, sixties, and seventies, should read his pamphlet, published in 1882, *The Spoils of the Park; with a Few Leaves from the Deep-laden Note-books of "a Wholly Unpractical Man."*

After some months the Commission, becoming dissatisfied with the plan under which the preliminary work had been done, decided to hold an open competition for a new one. Mr. Olmsted had no intention of going into the competition, and when he was asked by Calvert Vaux, who had been an assistant of A. J. Downing, to collaborate with him in the preparation of a plan, he withheld out of deference to his chief, whose first plan was set aside, and who was going into the competition himself. But when Captain Vielé rather contemptuously expressed his indifference as to whether he entered the competition or not, he accepted Mr. Vaux's proposal. Thirty-three plans were submitted and the award was made to that marked "Greensward," which turned out to be by Olmsted and Vaux, who were thereupon appointed to direct its execution.

"Persistently recasting and retouching their design, consolidating their corps of young engineers and gardeners, managing the thousands of workmen who were often rendered insubordinate by the consciousness of political 'pulls,' and fighting the politicians themselves," the two artists led a difficult life.

"It was a perpetual struggle to obtain the money legally at their disposal, while their steps were dogged by men in search of employment—men often wholly unfit for service, but armed with insistent letters from one 'boss' or another. The extent of this latter annoyance may be read in the fact that it was only by moonlight hours that they could walk about the park to consider what had just been done, and to decide what should next be undertaken."[1]

In June, 1859, Mr. Olmsted married his brother's widow, who, together with her three children, had been under his care since his brother's death at Nice, in 1857; and during the most active period of construction the family lived on the park in the old Convent of the Sacred Heart. In the autumn of 1859, exhausted by the strain

[1] M. G. Van Rensselaer, *Century Magazine*, October, 1893.

of work prosecuted under such harassment from political interference, he was prostrated with a slow fever, and upon recovery went abroad to complete his convalescence, again visiting England and also Paris, where the great works of the Second Empire in laying out and improving the boulevards and parks were then in progress under M. Alphand, who showed many courtesies to his American confrère.

Returning with fresh vigor, he rejoined his partner in their uphill fight for the successful completion of the design and for efficiency, honesty, and economy in the work. A runaway in which his thigh was badly broken kept him on his back for weeks and greatly hampered him in his task at this time, leaving him permanently lame. In spite of all obstacles, however, the greater part of the construction and planting which were necessary to convert eight hundred acres of peculiarly unfavorable, rough, rocky, and swampy land into a highly developed city park were accomplished within the four years 1857–1861.

Very soon after the outbreak of the Civil War, the Rev. Henry W. Bellows, mindful of the terrible suffering of the British troops in the Crimean War from disease and other preventable causes, and of the helplessness of the humane spirit of the people in the face of such suffering without proper organization for its relief, conceived the creation of an independent agency to be supported by voluntary contributions, to be responsible directly to the people, and to serve toward the sick and suffering at the front as the eye of the peo-

ple to see and the hand of the people to relieve. Fully
realizing what a vast field of action such an agency
might be called upon to cover, Dr. Bellows, after consulting with other prominent men in New York, stated
that if he could get Mr. Olmsted to undertake the executive management of such an organization, he would
set his idea on foot.

Incapacitated by his lameness from military service,
Mr. Olmsted gladly seized this opportunity of serving
the country, and with a strong committee which Dr.
Bellows had got together, helped to draw up a project
of organization and aims, which was submitted to President Lincoln who after some hesitation gave his assent.
The United States Sanitary Commission was thereupon
at once organized, with Dr. Bellows as President and
Mr. Olmsted as General Secretary.

The work upon the park was still going on, but Mr.
Vaux, as his contribution to the war, undertook to do
double duty there, still giving his partner his share of
their salary and thus enabling him to serve the Sanitary Commission without pay.

It is impossible to condense into a few words the history of the Sanitary Commission or the work of its
General Secretary, inextricably bound up as it is with
the devoted work of the other members and officers.
In its relation to the army, its primary function was to
inform itself as to conditions affecting the health and
morale of the troops, and simply by advice and suggestion to the officers and medical staff to aid and stimulate
the regular authorities to improve those conditions and

forestall dangers. It was essential to overcome official jealousy and resentment against what was often taken to be meddlesome interference; and to accomplish this while acting with urgent rapidity over an enormous field, and employing a large number of assistants hastily assembled and organized, demanded not only rare executive ability, but the highest tact. That the Commission, which Lincoln feared would be "the fifth wheel of the coach," overcame this fundamental obstacle so successfully, was due in great measure to Mr. Olmsted's management. This work was conducted by the Department of Inspection, the Inspectors being physicians of ability and discretion whose very inquiries in camp and hospital served to call the attention of officers to possibilities of improvement, while suggestions to the Surgeon-General's Department based upon their reports often resulted in orders of far-reaching importance. The volunteer surgeons, drawn from civil practice and entirely inexperienced in campaign conditions, were immensely aided by a series of condensed monographs upon their new problems and duties, and wherever the Inspectors found serious trouble resulting from lack of information upon any subject from camp cooking to the treatment of amputations a systematic general effort was made to supply the information.

A second great department dealt with organizing the means of relief which the whole people was anxious to contribute; instructing the workers at home as to what was most needed; gathering the supplies, and dispatching each thing to the place of most pressing need at the right time. Long before official reserve and distrust were overcome by the tact with which Mr. Olmsted contrived to inspire his lieutenants, the army itself had learned to appreciate the foresight and efficiency which so often brought the means of relief upon the spot at the instant of greatest need. It also became necessary under stress of emergency for the Commission to extend the relief service to include the care of sick and wounded and their transport from the front, the regular hospital service being greatly overtaxed. The emergency became so acute during the Peninsular Campaign that the General Secretary had to take charge of the work at the front in person.

"One thing clearly important was to gain a *system* by which the work could be carried on—the current work disposed of in such a way that everything could be kept clear for an emergency. For this Mr. Olmsted toiled; building unweariedly on shifting sands. . . . Men who ought never to have gone North—who could have got well in ten days, with care—were *rushed* upon the Commission. In vain did Mr. Olmsted protest . . . striving to keep his boats for the essential work. . . . Some of his assistants themselves hardly understood his efforts; but after a while it was seen that, slowly, things were shaping themselves to his moulding, and the time came when the wisdom of it was acknowledged." [1]

A Department of Special Relief was organized for the care of invalid soldiers discharged from hospital in a bewildered and helpless condition to shift for themselves in the turmoil behind the army. It transacted their business, notified their friends, and saw to their transportation to their homes.

[1] Blatchford, *U. S. Sanitary Commission*, Boston, 1863.

The volume of each kind of work accomplished by the Commission was commensurate with the vast size of the war, the number of names on the Commission's Hospital Directory, for example, amounting to 215,221 in 1863.

But the Sanitary Commission had a purpose back of all this activity beyond the mere alleviation of suffering.

"Its projectors were men with strong political purpose, induced to take this means of giving expression to their solicitude for the national life, by discovering that the people of the country had a very much higher sense of the value of the Union, and, above all, of the value of a great common national life, than most of the politicians of the States or the United States Government seemed to recognize; that the women of America had at least half of its patriotism in their keeping, and that a great scheme of practical service, which united men and women, cities and villages, distant States and Territories, in one protracted, systematic, laborious, and costly work—a work of an impersonal character—animated by love for the national cause, the national soldier, and not merely by personal affection or solicitude for their own particular flesh and blood, would develop, purify, and strengthen the imperilled sentiment of nationality, and help to make America sacred in the eyes of the living children of her scattered States.

"The members of the Sanitary Commission were absorbed in this conviction, and under great opposition and immense difficulties, they adhered to it and conquered by it. They would yield nothing to the intense feeling of State and local pride or anxiety which sought to create differences in the administration of their resources. Their plan, with all its methods, was intensely national.

"The education in nationality which the Commission gained in the first year of the war gave it convictions as to the importance of cultivating this sentiment, which over-topped all others. They found in their daily business a perpetual lesson on this theme, and in each other almost the only fully aroused sympathizers with the sentiment. The phrase 'Unconditional

Loyalty,' Mr. Seward said, originated in the Sanitary Commission, and the Government scattered ten thousand copies of a tract with that title through the Army of the Potomac—a tract which the President of the Commission had prepared."[1]

Out of these purposes arose the idea of another agency for strengthening them. Prof. Wolcott Gibbs of the Executive Committee, who first broached the project, turned to Mr. Olmsted for bringing this idea to realization. In the midst of his other labors, Mr. Olmsted then took a leading part in the formation of the Union League Club of New York, an organization the political purpose of which was so quiet in its depth and strength and in the devotion which it inspired that it worked almost unnoticed by the general public beneath the merely social aspect of the Club.

Working under tremendous pressure, often remaining at his desk all night, Mr. Olmsted again impaired his health and in October, 1863, he felt compelled to resign his position as General Secretary of the Sanitary Commission, leaving to his successor a splendid organization for the continuance of the work.

After leaving the Sanitary Commission he was concerned with the earlier stages of a number of projects of public importance: among others that of establishing a weekly review of high standing, for which he desired his friend E. L. Godkin to serve as editor. It was out of this project that soon after sprang *The Nation*, although at the time of its launching Mr. Olmsted had turned it wholly over to Mr. Godkin and was himself

---

[1] H. W. Bellows, The Union League Club, New York, 1897.

in California, whither he had gone to take charge of the mines and other properties of the Frémont estate, which had fallen into a financial confusion from which he was unable to rescue it.

After a sojourn of about two years, during which time he took an active part in the movement to preserve the Yosemite Valley as a public preserve of scenery, he returned from California at the urgent suggestion of Mr. Vaux, who had been asked to plan another great park for Brooklyn, and again entered into partnership with him in landscape architecture. The creation of Prospect Park, together with the completion and development of Central Park, formed their chief work for several years, although numerous other public parks and private estates were planned by them and their several successive partners up to the time when Mr. Olmsted became chiefly engaged upon the Boston parks between 1876 and 1878.

In 1880, he removed his home and office to Brookline, Massachusetts, partly induced by the fact that his friend the architect Richardson had already established himself there.

From 1868 to the time of his retirement through failing health in 1895 his energies were devoted almost exclusively to his profession, and so numerous were the important works of landscape architecture which he designed and the execution of which he directed, many of them in partnership with others, that it is impracticable in so brief a sketch as this to do more than simply enumerate them. After 1875, one partner was always his stepson and nephew, John C. Olmsted, whom he brought up and regarded as a son, and later he was joined by his pupils, H. S. Codman and Charles Eliot, both of whom were soon cut off in their prime. During the twenty years following 1875, he took a controlling part in the design of thirty-seven public pleasure grounds, twelve suburban districts, and four town sites; the grounds of seventeen educational institutions, fifteen public or semi-public buildings, and twelve considerable private estates; and had to do with a large range and number of minor problems. His work was scattered over many parts of the country and has greatly developed popular appreciation of the wholesome enjoyment to be derived from the beauty attainable in the surroundings of daily life through the exercise of foresight, well-balanced intelligence and cultivated taste.

Setting aside the pioneer work on Central Park and Prospect Park, if one were to select examples of the several classes of his work above mentioned, one would naturally call to mind among the grounds of public buildings those of the United States Capitol; among private estates Biltmore, in North Carolina; among the problems involving the grouping of buildings and the treatment of their surroundings, the World's Fair at Chicago; and among public parks, the system of related parks and parkways of the city of Boston.

In all of his professional work he was characterized by breadth of view, by clear insight into conditions, and by a strong common sense in the selection of aims; to which was added that delicacy of feeling in the choice of æsthetic ideals perfectly fitted to the conditions and aims of each problem which is the mark of the great constructive artist. Notable as he was for the masterful executive ability which marked his conduct of large affairs, for the clearness of his observations on social conditions as shown in the present book, and for the statesmanlike qualities which were brought out so clearly in his Sanitary Commission work, he was before all an artist; and he has been called by so eminent a critic as Professor Charles Eliot Norton, "the greatest artist that America has yet produced."

F. L. O.

April 6, 1904.

INTRODUCTION

THAT important statistical journal and organ of pro-slavery propaganda, *De Bow's Commercial Review*, opened its number for August, 1857, with a somewhat cursory article upon the second of Mr. Olmsted's books descriptive of the social and economic features of the South. This article, which was from the pen of Mr. De Bow himself, referred to the prior work of Mr. Olmsted that is here reprinted as "abounding in bitterness and prejudice of every sort," and, after charging him with pandering to abolitionist fanaticism for the sake of gain, continued as follows:

"Here, again, the opportunity is too tempting to be resisted to revile and abuse the men and the society whose open hospitality he undoubtedly enjoyed, and whom, we have no doubt, like every other of his tribe travelling at the South, he found it convenient at the time to flatter and approve."

Mr. Olmsted took occasion later[1] to reply to the aspersions of his critic in a tone of notable moderation. He regretted that the "most able and just-minded statistician in the country" should have condescended to adopt the current partisan practice of attributing unworthy motives to all persons not of his way of thinking with regard to slavery. If Mr. Olmsted had been less modest, he might have called attention to the fact

[1] *A Journey in the Back Country*, p. 399, *seq*.

that Mr. De Bow had found little beyond a rash prediction or two on which to rest his censures, and had thus been thrown back upon general denunciations of the kind just illustrated. It seemed more philanthropical, however, to the downright Northerner to endeavor to open the exuberant Southerner's eyes to the egregiously false assumption he was making with respect to the universal range and the engaging qualities of Southern hospitality. Whether the several pages devoted to this task were convincing to Mr. De Bow may be doubted; they certainly leave upon a modern reader the strong impression that Mr. Olmsted and other Northern travellers whose experiences he cites exchanged more good dollars for bad meals in the newer and rawer portions of the South than would have been possible at that day anywhere else between the Danube and the Mississippi.

The character of Mr. Olmsted's reply to Mr. De Bow is not, however, so much to my purpose as the fact that this reply was incorporated in a later book by Mr. Olmsted, which was dedicated to John Stuart Mill and which has recently been highly praised by no less a person than Mr. John Morley. This book, entitled *Journeys and Explorations in the Cotton Kingdom*, was based upon three former books of its author, *The Seaboard Slave States*, here re-issued, *A Journey through Texas*, the volume reviewed by Mr. De Bow, and *A Journey in the Back Country* (1860), in the second of which, as we have been informed in the Biographical Sketch, Dr. John H. Olmsted had an editorial share. Upon this condensation, and upon the first volume of the series, Mr. Morley, in a footnote to vol. ii., p. 70, of his *Life of Gladstone*, bestowed the high praise that follows:

" . . . the reader who cares to understand the American Civil War should turn to F. L. Olmsted's *Journeys and Explorations in the Cotton Kingdom* (1861) and *A Journey in the Seaboard Slave States* (1856)—as interesting a picture of the South on the eve of its catastrophe as Arthur Young's picture of France on the eve of the revolution."

In these words we have not only the broad view of the world with regard to the value of Mr. Olmsted's books set over against the parochial, polemic view of Mr. De Bow, but also the reason why the first and most interesting of these descriptive works is now, after nearly half a century, given to the public in a new and convenient form. Just as the French Revolution is a cataclysm that will never cease to interest men, so the war between the States is a contest that will continue to attract the attention of successive generations; and just as Arthur Young's famous *Travels in France* is invaluable to the student of the causes of the Revolution, so Mr. Olmsted's "Journeys" are invaluable to the student of the Civil War. Both men were fortunate enough to make fairly leisurely explorations only three or four years before the great catastrophes; both were wide awake, intelligent, and honest observers; and, singularly and appropriately, both were interested in scientific agriculture and were in consequence led to extend their observations over large areas, instead of confining them in the main to urban centres of population.

The genesis of the *Journey in the Seaboard Slave States* has already been given briefly in the sketch of Mr. Olmsted's life and is also to be gathered from the " Advertisement " to the first edition. As he and his son tell us, the book was in the main based on a series of letters written over the signature "Yeoman" to the New York *Times* during a journey which lasted from December, 1852, to April, 1853, and extended as far as New Orleans. The materials gathered on this journey were, however, supplemented by those obtained during the journey of 1853-54, which form the basis of the volumes devoted to Texas and the Back Country. This point is important because it shows that, while the substance of the book before us is mainly due to its author's recorded experiences of his first comparatively short excursion through the Seaboard States, he prepared all his pages for the press in the full light of his subsequent and more ample observations. As his Preface is dated January 9, 1856, it is plain that he utilized not only his wider information, but also the advantages afforded him by eighteen months of reflection and discussion. An additional point to be borne in mind is the fact that this first of his books devoted to a description of the South was not the first of Mr. Olmsted's ventures in this kind of writing—in other words, that he did not make the acquaintance of the Southern States and their peculiar institution as an inexperienced traveller. The volume which secured him Mr. Raymond's invitation to act as correspondent of the *Times* had proved him to possess keen eyes, a clear head, and a very sound heart—in both the primary and the derived meanings of these terms. *Walks and Talks of an American Farmer in England* is a sensible, interesting book that still repays perusal; it owes something to Bayard Taylor, but would surely never prompt any reader to apply to its author the malicious epigram that he had travelled farther and seen less than any one else that ever lived.

In view of the citation already made from Mr. De Bow, it seems needless to dwell upon the views expressed by extreme Southerners upon Mr. Olmsted's calm description of their section. The year of the Brooks-Sumner incident and of the Buchanan-Frémont campaign was not propitious to sound criticism on either side of Mason and Dixon's line—a fact which may absolve us as well from dwelling on the eulogiums passed upon the volume by Northerners of moderate or extreme anti-slavery proclivities. It was not possible, of course, that a book which devoted so many pages to economic topics and to agriculture in its technical aspects should be popular in any extended sense of the term. Its author's Northern birth precluded him from producing such a sensation as was made by Hinton R. Helper of North Carolina with his once famous *Impending Crisis of the South* (1857). But *A Journey in the Seaboard Slave States* must probably rank along with *Uncle Tom's Cabin* and *The Impending Crisis* as one of the three books that did most to open the eyes of the North to the true nature of the plague of slavery and to the inflamed condition of public opinion at the South during the decade preceding the Civil War. And it may be added with little fear of contradiction that the lapse of nearly half a century has shown that of these three books the one which made the least sensation is by far the most valuable to the historian and to the reader interested in reconstructing the past. In the first two volumes of Mr. James Ford Rhodes's *History of the United States from the Compromise of 1850*, the praise of Mr. Olmsted's books and the frequent citations from them are sufficiently marked to impress even the casual reader. In other words, Mr. Rhodes has found no reason to dissent from the favorable opinion with regard to our author's acuteness and honesty of observation expressed by such contemporaries as his friend, George William Curtis and James Russell Lowell, the latter of whom had sufficient prescience to anticipate Mr. Morley's after-the-event comparison with Arthur Young's famous work.

Let us now turn from the reception given *A Journey in the Seaboard Slave States* at the time of its publication to a consideration of the book itself. And first I must disclaim any right to speak authoritatively concerning the fidelity of its descriptions save such as may be granted to a native of the South who for a number of years has been interested in its past and has had opportunities to study its history in a rather formidable mass of books and pamphlets and magazines, and to a less but fairly considerable extent in newspapers and unpublished correspondence. The interesting times of which Mr. Olmsted speaks were times of which *pars nulla fui*. I can neither support nor contradict him in essential matters from direct personal knowledge; but perhaps this disability is counterbalanced by the fact that being of a later generation, I have little temptation to discredit the general faithfulness of the picture he draws of the South on the eve of the Civil War. His picture corresponds in the main with the results of my own independent attempts to reconstruct the Old South imaginatively, save in one important particular.

The particular exception that it seems fair to make to Mr. Olmsted's general picture of the ante-bellum South, or rather to the impressions it appears likely to produce, is based on the comparative absence from his pages of materials from which one can reconstruct the simple, pleasant, ingenuous, and rather dignified life led in both country and town by the older families of well-established social standing. In more than one place in his books Mr. Olmsted admitted freely the attractive qualities of this small but influential element of the population of the South, and it is very clear that he had direct knowledge of its ways; yet it is equally evident that in the main, as was natural with such a traveller, his contact with small farmers, inn-keepers, tradesmen, and passengers in public conveyances made his book valuable as a picture of the Southern masses rather than of the Southern classes. This is a fact not in the least to be regretted, since it was upon the Southern masses that slavery weighed most heavily, and it was these masses that were destined to bear much of the brunt of the Civil War. A book mainly descriptive of social life in the mansions along the James, in the country houses in Fauquier and Botetourt counties, Virginia, in Charleston and Beaufort, or in Savannah and the adjoining region would not have added greatly to our knowledge of that life and would have failed utterly to serve the important purpose of opening the eyes of the North to the blight slavery was casting over the immense region stretching from beyond the Potomac to the Rio Grande. But although the reader of 1856 lost little through the fact that he was not introduced to the more attractive side of Southern life, the reader of 1904 will suffer the disadvantage of being misled unless he remembers that side by side with the unlovely sights witnessed by our traveller flourished many of those social graces and virtues without the existence of which no such characters as George Washington and Robert E. Lee could have brightened the pages of American history.

As to the accuracy or inaccuracy of the vast number of particular statements made in Mr. Olmsted's book, there are few if any men living who could undertake to confirm or correct him with the thoroughness and certainty required of an annotator. He deals with a generation that seems far more remote than it actually is; he writes about topics which fall under such heads as economics, sociology, political history, and the like, each of which is now the province of a group of specialists. One does not read far, however, without feeling that in the main this writer does not need comment or corroboration. He is clear and explicit, cautious and transparently honest, in his statements. What he says he saw was undoubtedly seen with his own eyes, which were not often deliberately averted as on the occasion, described in a later volume, when the overseer flogged the slave girl who had shirked her daily task. What he says he heard may be taken with equal credence, so far as his own accuracy and credibility as a witness are concerned. Whether or not statements which he accepted and wrote down represented fact or fiction, common occurrences or sporadic events of no special significance, must often remain a matter of doubt. Travellers have been liable to confound the false with the true, the concrete and specific with the general, ever since primitive man first ventured beyond the limits of his particular tribe. Doubtless even Mr. Olmsted's acumen did not always save him from being misled by involuntary or deliberate misinformation; but he probably suffered less in this manner than any Northerner that ever journeyed through the Slave States. A conversation heard by him in Texas, and therefore not reported in the present volume, may be taken to illustrate the kind of statement which he sometimes thought it worth while to report, but which to some readers at least will suggest the good story told possibly with the intention of astonishing and taking in a stranger. The talk had turned on runaway negroes, and a man in the company stated that a Georgia slaveowner used to cure his slaves of the disease of *drapetomania*, to use Dr. Cartwright's learned term, by pulling out one toe-nail by the roots and threatening to double the punishment every time the victim sought to gain his liberty by flight. This story seems to bear the label "Made in Texas." It is only fair to add that, although he set it down, Mr. Olmsted made no comments upon it and drew no inferences from it.

But whatever we may think of this or that detail, we must, unless we are wedded to partisanship, accept, however reluctantly, his general picture of Southern conditions. That the Southern masses were far behind those of the North in the comforts of life, that save in exceptional instances the accommodations for travellers were primitive and disagreeable, that houses and farms were not well kept up, that coarse food, surly manners, and crass ignorance were to be found wherever the explorer turned his feet, that slave auctions were disagreeable sights, and that nearly everything he saw of the institution should have seemed to him both revolting and uneconomic—in all this there is nothing that the modern reader can challenge. As we have seen, the more engaging side of Southern life was necessarily left out of the picture, and not a little that is included in it would have been found there even if slavery had not existed; for much of the territory visited by Mr. Olmsted was, as he himself averred, either in or not far removed from the pioneer state. Indeed, slow trains, execrable hotels, vile food, bad manners, and gross ignorance have not, after the lapse of half a century, disappeared entirely from the South, or even from more fortunate sections of this still raw country. It should be remembered also that the thrifty and beautiful Valley of Virginia is not described in this book, that Charleston with its Old World charm receives but slight attention, and that there are evidences of Southern enterprise in spite of slavery which were inaccessible to Mr. Olmsted and are only now being slowly gathered by students of Southern history. But after all these allowances have been made, the picture in its essentials remains true and terribly pathetic. The vast good wrought to the South by the abolition of slavery, even at the cost of the war, of Reconstruction, and of the present agitation of the race question, can be brought home in no better way than by a journey through the New South after a careful study of this book dealing with the Old.

Such a study is made all the easier and more attractive by the fact that Mr. Olmsted was not only an exceptionally intelligent observer, but a good and ready writer. That he did not succeed in removing from his book all traces of its newspaper origin, any more than he could always preserve a perfect poise of temper, cannot, it is true, be denied; but that he wrote clearly and forcibly and interestingly needs scarcely to be affirmed after the testimony of Lowell and Mr. Morley. Perhaps not a few readers will be tempted to skip the numerous pages dealing with technically agricultural matters; but if they do so, they will miss, not only some excellent descriptions of scenery, but also much that is specially characteristic of our author's mind and of his attitude toward social and political life. Probably the strictly historical portions of the book are those that could most readily be spared; yet it would be unfair not to remark that in discussing the economic development of the Southern colonies from the time of their planting, Mr. Olmsted relied on the best authorities then accessible and used them with much discretion. We find him thoroughly posted as to the work of such Southern authorities on agriculture and commerce as Ruffin, De Bow, and Maury. Indeed, this book leaves the impression that its author was almost if not quite as well informed as he was observant. Better still, it leaves the impression that he was a thoroughly just man, a true democrat in the best sense of that ambiguous word, a genuine American. His strictures on slavery and on the backward civilization resulting therefrom were due, not to anti-slavery partisanship, as Mr. De Bow opined, but to real regret that any section of his country should have found itself in such a plight.[1] That he was moderate and scrupulously desirous to be fair in his statements is plain, if only from the infrequency of such manifestations of temper as escaped him in his references to Governor Wise of Virginia. This fact is abundantly clear to any one who has taken the trouble to compare the present book with contemporary fulminations of the anti-slavery press.

To single out for comment special passages and pages

---

[1] See his remarks on this subject in the Preface to *A Journey in the Back Country*, p. vi., from which it is impossible to extract the notion that Mr. Olmsted was an abolitionist.

is a work of supererogation. It is hard, however, to resist calling attention to the description of the negro funeral at Richmond and the solemn preacher.—I have a certain "Uncle Bob" in mind at this moment whose pious language was as distorted as his character was absolutely upright; to the account of the queer antics of a surely unique legislator; to our traveller's amusing difficulties in reaching a gentleman's house near Petersburg; to the interesting pages descriptive of life in the Great Dismal Swamp, which must have appealed to readers of Mrs. Stowe's *Dred*, a book of the same year; to the suggestive comparison of the Southern with the Irish gentry; to the description of the negro divers in North Carolina and of the rice plantations of South Carolina; to the moderation with which the vexed question of cruelty to slaves is treated; to the sentences almost prophetic of the rise of Tilmanism; to the sensible remarks on the use of cheap wines; to the pictures of Creole life; and, finally, to the clear exposure of the gambling element in sugar-planting. This list does not contain a tithe of the passages which the student of the Old South is tempted to note for future use. Nor does it include a number of points on which I should like to comment —for example, the mechanical skill of negroes, which not many years ago I saw remarkably exemplified in the case of one of my own servants, who, however, did not possess sufficient character to make good use of his exceptional talents.

In conclusion, it may not be amiss to say that if any reader is disappointed in not finding Alabama treated so fully as Virginia, the Carolinas, Georgia, and Louisiana, and wishes also to learn something about antebellum conditions in Texas and Mississippi, he has but to turn to Mr. Olmsted's two later volumes in order to satisfy his curiosity. If these books are inaccessible, the second volume of *Journeys and Explorations in the Cotton Kingdom*, hasty compilation though this work is said to have been, will probably serve all purposes.

Here again one finds dozens of things on which one would like to comment. The Northern-born Texas woman with less feeling for her negroes than a matron to the manner born would have had; the young woman who astonished Mr. Olmsted by pouring molasses on a breakfast plate already containing ham and eggs and apple-pie; the reason, amusing though dubious, for the substitution of Montgomery for Tuscaloosa as the capital of Alabama; the clergyman's description of hunting negroes like 'possums; the glimpses of Natchez and of newly rich Mississippians; the things which Mr. Olmsted found and did not find in most of the houses at which he paid for a lodging; his remarks on the burning of negroes, a crime not exclusively the sinister product of our own epoch; and, finally, his already mentioned reply to Mr. De Bow with regard to the assumed universality of Southern hospitality—these and many other topics of interest await the reader who is wise enough to devote a few hours to the remaining volumes of Mr. Olmsted's invaluable series.

W. P. TRENT.

NEW YORK, April 9, 1904.

The Seaboard Slave States

THE SEABOARD SLAVE STATES

CHAPTER I

INNS AND OUTS OF WASHINGTON

GADSBY'S HOTEL, Dec. 10.

To accomplish the purposes which brought me to Washington, it was necessary, on arriving here, to make arrangements to secure food and shelter while I remained. There are two thousand of us visitors in Washington under a similar necessity. There are a dozen or more persons who, for a consideration, undertake to provide what we want. Mr. Dexter is reported to be the best of them, and really seems a very obliging and honestly-disposed person. To Mr. Dexter, therefore, I commit myself.

I commit myself by inscribing my name in a Register. Five minutes after I have done so, Clerk No. 4, whose attention I have been unable to obtain any sooner, suddenly catches the Register by the corner, swings it round with a jerk, and throws a hieroglyphic scrawl at it, which strikes near my name. Henceforth, I figure as Boarder No. 201, (or whatever it may be). Clerk No. 4 whistles ("Boarders, away!"), and throws key, No. 201 upon the table. Turnkey No. 3 takes it, and me, and my travelling bag, up several flights of stairs, along corridors and galleries, and finally consigns me to this little square cell.

I have faith that there is a tight roof above the very much cracked ceiling; that the bed is clean; and that I shall, by-and-by, be summoned, along with hundreds of other persons, to partake, in grandly silent sobriety, of a very sumptuous dinner.

Food and shelter. Therewith should a man be content. It will enable me to accomplish my purpose in coming to Washington. But my perverse nature will not be content: will be wishing things were otherwise. They say this uneasiness—this passion for change—is a peculiarity of our diseased Northern nature. The Southern man finds Providence in all that is: Satan in all that might be. That is good; and, as I am going South, when I have accomplished my purposes at Washington, I will not here restrain the escape of my present discontent.

I have such a shockingly depraved nature that I wish the dinner was not going to be so grand. My idea is that, if it were not, Mr. Dexter would save moneys, which I would like to have him expend in other ways. I wish he had more clerks, so that they would have time to be as polite to an unknown man as I see they are to John P. Hale; and, at least, answer civil questions, when his guests ask them. I don't like such a fearful rush of business as there is down stairs. I wish there were men enough to do the work quietly.

I don't like these cracked and variegated walls; and, though the roof may be tight, I don't like this threatening aspect of the ceiling. It should be kept for people of Damoclesian ambition: I am humble.

I am humble, and I am short, and soon curried; but I am not satisfied with a quarter of a yard of towelling, having an irregular vacancy in its centre, where I am liable to insert my head. I am not proud; but I had rather have something else, or nothing, than these three yards of ragged and faded quarter-ply carpeting. I also would like a curtain to the window, and I wish the glass were not so dusty, and that the sashes did not rattle so in their casements; though, as there is no other ventilation, I suppose I ought not to complain. Of course not; but it is confoundedly cold, as well as noisy. I don't like that broken latch; I don't like this broken chair; I would prefer that this table were not so greasy in its appearance; I would rather the ashes and cinders, and the tobacco juice around the grate, had been removed before I was consigned to the cell.

I wish that less of my two dollars and a half a day went to pay for game for the dinner, and the interest of the cost of the mirrors and mahogany for the public parlors, and of marble for the halls, and more of it for providing me with a private room, which should be more than a barely habitable cell, which should *also* be a little bit tasteful, home-like, and comfortable.

I wish more of it was expended in servants' wages.

Six times I rang the bell; three several times came three different Irish lads; entered, received my demand for a fire, and retired. I was writing, shiveringly, a full hour before the fireman came. Now he has entered, bearing on his head a hod of coal and kindling wood, without knocking. An aged negro, more familiar and more indifferent to forms of subserviency than the Irish lads, very much bent, seemingly with infirmity, an expression of impotent anger in his face, and a look of weakness, like a drunkard's. He does not look at me, but mutters unintelligibly.

"What's that you say?"

"Tink I can make a hundred fires at once?"

"I don't want to sit an hour waiting for a fire, after I have ordered one, and you must not let me again."

"Nebber let de old nigger have no ress—hundred gemmen tink I kin mak dair fires all de same minute; all get mad at an ole nigger; I ain't a goin to stan it— nebber get no ress—up all night—haint got nautin to eat nor drink dis blessed mornin—hunred gemmen—"

"That's not my business; Mr. Dexter should have more servants."

"So he ort ter, master, dat he had, one ole man ain't enough for all dis house, is it master? hundred gemmen—"

"Stop—here's a quarter for you; now I want you to look out that I have a good fire, and keep the hearth clean in my room as long as I stay here. And when I send for you I want you to come immediately. Do you understand?"

"I 'le try, master—you jus look roun and fine me when you want yer fire; I 'll be roun somewhere. You got a newspaper, Sir, I ken take for a minit; I won't hurt it."

I gave him one; and wondered what use he could put it to, that would not hurt it. He opened it to a folio, and spread it before the grate, so the draft held it in place, and it acted as a blower. I asked if there were no blowers? "No." "But have n't you got any brush or shovel?" I inquired, seeing him get down upon his knees again and sweep the cinders and ashes he had thrown upon the floor with the sleeve of his coat, and then take them up with his hands;—no, he said, his master did not give him such things. "Are you a slave?"

"Yes, sir."

"Do you belong to Mr. Dexter?"

"No, sir, he hires me of de man dat owns me. Don't you tink I 'se too ole a man for to be knock roun at dis kind of work, massa?—hundred gemmen all want dair fires made de same minute, and caus de old nigger cant do it all de same minute, ebbery one tinks dey's boun to scold him all de time; nebber no rest for him, no time."

I know the old fellow lied somewhat, for I saw another fireman in Mr. B.'s room. Was that quarter a good investment, or should I have complained at the office? No, they are too busy to listen to me, too busy, certainly, to make better arrangements.

It is time for me to call on Mr. S.; the fire has gone

out, leaving a fine bituminous fragrance in the cell. I will "look round" for the fireman, as I travel the long road to the office, and, if I do not find him, leave an order, in writing, for a fire to be made before two o'clock.

WASHINGTON, Dec. 14th. Called on Mr. C., whose fine farm, from its vicinity to Washington, and its excellent management, as well as from the hospitable habits of its owner, has a national reputation. It is some two thousand acres in extent, and situated just without the District, in Maryland.

The residence is in the midst of the farm, a quarter of a mile from the high road—the private approach being judiciously carried through large pastures which are divided only by slight, but close and well-secured, wire fences. The mansion is of brick, and, as seen through the surrounding trees, has somewhat the look of an old French chateau. The kept grounds are very limited, and in simple but quiet taste; being surrounded only by wires, they merge, in effect, into the pastures. There is a fountain, an ornamental dove-cote, and ice-house, and the approach road, nicely gravelled and rolled, comes up to the door with a fine sweep.

I had dismounted and was standing before the door, when I heard myself loudly hailed from a distance.

"Ef yer wants to see Master, sah, he 's down thar—to the new stable."

I could see no one; and when I was tired of holding my horse, I mounted, and rode on in search of the new stable. I found it without difficulty; and in it Mr. and

Mrs. C. With them were a number of servants, one of whom now took my horse with alacrity. I was taken at once to look at a very fine herd of cows, and afterwards led upon a tramp over the farm, and did not get back to the house till dinner time.

The new stable is most admirably contrived for convenience, labor-saving, and economy of space. (Full and accurate descriptions of it, with illustrations, have been given in several agricultural journals.) The cows are mainly thorough-bred Shorthorns, with a few imported Ayrshires and Alderneys, and some small black "natives." I have seldom seen a better lot of milkers; they are kept in good condition, are brisk and healthy, docile and kind, soft and pliant of skin, and give milk up to the very eve of calving; milking being never interrupted for a day. Near the time of calving the milk is given to the calves and pigs. The object is to obtain milk only, which is never converted into butter or cheese, but sent immediately to town, and for this the Shorthorns are found to be the most profitable breed. Mr. C. believes that, for butter, the little Alderneys, from the peculiar richness of their milk, would be the most valuable. He is, probably, mistaken, though I remember that in Ireland the little black Kerry cow was found fully equal to the Ayrshire for butter, though giving much less milk.

There are extensive bottom lands on the farm, subject to be flooded in freshets, on which the cows are mainly pastured in summer. Indian corn is largely sown for fodder, and, during the driest season, the cows are regularly *soiled* with it. These bottom lands were entirely covered with heavy wood, until, a few years since, Mr. C. erected a steam saw-mill, and has lately been rapidly clearing them, and floating off the sawed timber to market by means of a small stream that runs through the farm.

The low land is much of it drained, underdrains being made of rough boards of any desired width nailed together, so that a section is represented by the inverted letter Λ. Such covered drains have lasted here twenty years without failing yet, but have only been tried where the flow of water was constant throughout the year.

The water collected by the drains can be, much of it, drawn into a reservoir, from which it is forced by a pump, driven by horse-power, to the market-garden, where it is distributed from several fountain-heads, by means of hose, and is found of great value, especially for celery. The celery trenches are arranged in concentric circles, the water-head being in the centre. The water-closets and all the drainage of the house are turned to good account in the same way. Mr. C. contemplates extending his water-pipes to some of his meadow lands. Wheat and hay are the chief crops sold off the farm, and the amount of them produced is yearly increasing.

The two most interesting points of husbandry, to me, were the large and profitable use of guano and bones, and the great extent of turnip culture. Crops of one thousand and twelve hundred bushels of ruta baga to the acre have been frequent, and this year the whole crop of the farm is reckoned to be over thirty thousand bushels; all to be fed out to the neat stock between this time and the next pasture season. The soil is generally a red, stiff loam, with an occasional stratum of coarse gravel, and, therefore, not the most favorable for turnip culture. The seed is always imported, Mr. C.'s experience, in this respect, agreeing with my own: —the ruta baga undoubtedly degenerates in our climate. Bones, guano, and ashes are used in connection with yard-dung for manure. The seed is sown from the middle to the last of July in drills, but not in ridges, in the English way. In both these respects, also, Mr. C. confirms the conclusions I have arrived at in the climate of New York; namely, that ridges are best dispensed with, and that it is better to sow in the latter part of July than in June, as has been generally recommended in our books and periodicals. Last year, turnips sown on the 20th July were larger and finer than others, sown on the same ground, on my farm, about the first of the month. This year I sowed in August, and, by forcing with superphosphate—home manufactured—and guano, obtained a fine crop; but the season was unusually favorable.

Mr. C. always secures a supply of turnips that will allow him to give at least one bushel a day to every cow while in winter quarters. The turnips are sliced, slightly salted, and commonly mixed with fodder and meal. Mr. C. finds that salting the sliced turnip, twelve hours before it is fed, effectually prevents its communicating any taste to the milk. This, so far as I know, is an original discovery of his, and is one of great value to dairymen. In certain English dairies the same result is obtained, where the cows are fed on cabbages, by the expensive process of heating the milk to a certain temperature and then adding saltpetre.

The wheat crop of this district has been immensely increased, by the use of guano, during the last four years. On this farm it has been largely used for five years; and land that had not been cultivated for forty years, and which bore only broom-sedge—a thin, worthless grass—by the application of two hundred weight of Peruvian guano, now yields thirty bushels of wheat to an acre.

Mr. C.'s practice of applying guano differs, in some particulars, from that commonly adopted here. After a deep ploughing of land intended for wheat, he sows the seed and guano at the same time, and harrows both in. The common custom here is to plough in the guano, six or seven inches deep, in preparing the ground for wheat. I believe Mr. C.'s plan is the best. I have myself used guano on a variety of soils for several years with great success for wheat, and I may mention the practice I have adopted from the outset, and with which I am well satisfied. It strikes between the two systems I have mentioned, and I think is philosophically right. After preparing the ground with plough and harrow, I sow wheat and guano together, and plough them in with a gang-plough which covers to a depth, on an average, of three inches.

Clover seed is sowed in the spring following the wheat-sowing, and the year after the wheat is taken off, this — on the old sterile hills — grows luxuriantly, knee-high. It is left alone for two years, neither mown nor pastured; there it grows and there it lies, keeping the ground moist and shady, and improving it on the Gurney principle.

Mr. C. then manures with dung, bones, and guano, and with another crop of wheat lays this land down to grass. What the ultimate effect of this system will be, it is yet too early to say—but Mr. C. is pursuing it with great confidence.

Mr. C. is a large herditary owner of slaves, which, for ordinary field and stable-work, constitute his laboring force. He has employed several Irishmen for ditching, and for this work, and this alone, he thought he could use them to better advantage than negroes. He would not think of using Irishmen for common farm-labor, and made light of their coming in competition with slaves. Negroes at hoeing and any steady field-work, he assured me, would "do two to their one;" but his main objection to employing Irishmen was derived from his experience of their unfaithfulness —they were dishonest, would not obey explicit directions about their work, and required more personal supervision than negroes. From what he had heard and seen of Germans, he supposed they did better than Irish. He mentioned that there were several Germans who had come here as laboring men, and worked for wages several years, who had now got possession of small farms, and were reputed to be getting rich.[1] He was disinclined to converse on the topic of slavery, and I, therefore, made no inquiries about the condition and habits of his negroes, or his management of them. They seemed to live in small and rude log-cabins, scattered in different parts of the farm. Those I saw at work appeared to me to move very slowly and awkwardly, as did also those engaged in the stable. These, also, were very stupid and dilatory in executing any orders given to them, so that Mr. C. would frequently take the duty off their hands into his own, rather than wait for them, or make them correct their blunders: they were much, in these respects, like what our farmers call *dumb Paddies*—that is, Irishmen who do not readily understand the English language, and who are still weak and stiff from the effects of the emigrating voyage. At the entrance-gate was a porter's lodge, and, as I approached, I saw a black face peeping at me from it, but, both when I entered and left, I was obliged to dismount and open the gate myself.

Altogether, it struck me—slaves coming here as they naturally did in direct comparison with free laborers, as

[1] "There is a small settlement of Germans, about three miles from me, who, a few years since (with little or nothing beyond their physical abilities to aid them), seated themselves down in a poor, miserable old field, and have, by their industry, and means obtained by working round among the neighbors, effected a change which is really *surprising and pleasing to behold*, and who will, I have no doubt, become wealthy, provided they remain prudent, as they have hitherto been industrious."—F. A. CLOPPER (Montgomery Co.), Maryland, in Patent Of. Rept., 1851.

commonly employed on my own and my neighbors' farms, in exactly similar duties—that they must be very difficult to direct efficiently, and that it must be very irksome and trying to one's patience, to have to superintend their labor.

WASHINGTON, Dec. 16. Visiting the market-place, early on Tuesday morning, I found myself in the midst of a throng of a very different character from any I have ever seen at the North. The majority of the people were negroes, and, taken as a whole, they appeared inferior in the expression of their face and less well-clothed than any collection of negroes I had ever seen before. All the negro characteristics were more clearly marked in each than they often are in any at the North. In their dress, language, manner, motions—all were distinguishable almost as much as by their color, from the white people who were distributed among them, and engaged in the same occupations—chiefly selling poultry, vegetables, and small country-produce. The white men were, generally, a mean looking people, and but meanly dressed, but differently so from the negroes.

Most of the produce was in small, rickety carts, drawn by the smallest, ugliest, leanest lot of oxen and horses that I ever saw. There was but one pair of horses in over a hundred that were tolerably good—a remarkable proportion of them were maimed in some way. As for the oxen, I do not believe New England and New York together could produce a single yoke so poor as the best of them.

The very trifling quantity of articles brought in and exposed for sale by most of the market-people was noticeable; a peck of potatoes, three bunches of carrots, two cabbages, six eggs and a chicken, would be about the average stock in trade of all the dealers. Mr. F. said that an old negro woman once came to his door with a single large turkey, which she pressed him to buy. Struck with her fatigued appearance, he made some inquiries of her, and ascertained that she had been several days coming from home, had travelled mainly on foot, and had brought the turkey and nothing else with her. "Ole massa had to raise some money somehow, and he could not sell anyting else, so he tole me to catch the big gobbler, and tote um down to Washington and see wot um would fotch."

The prices of garden productions were high, compared even with New York. All the necessaries of life are very expensive in Washington; great complaint is made of exorbitant rents, and building-lots are said to have risen in value several hundred *per cent.* within five or six years.

The population of the city is now over 50,000, and is increasing rapidly. There seems to be a deficiency of tradespeople, and I have no doubt the profits of retailers are excessive. There is one cotton factory in the District of Columbia, employing one hundred and fifty hands, male and female; a small foundry; a distillery; and two tanneries—all not giving occupation to fifty men; less than two hundred, altogether, out of a resident population of nearly 150,000, being engaged in manufactures. Very few of the remainder are engaged in *productive* occupations. There is water-power near the city, superior to that of Lowell, of which, at present, I understand that no use at all is made.

Land may be purchased, within twenty miles of Washington, at from ten to twenty dollars an acre. Most of it has been once in cultivation, and, having been exhausted in raising tobacco, has been, for many years, abandoned, and is now covered by a forest growth. Several New Yorkers have lately speculated in the purchase of this sort of land, and, as there is a good market for wood, and the soil, by the decay of leaves upon it, and other natural causes, has been restored to moderate fertility, have made money by clearing and improving it. By deep ploughing and limeing, and the judicious use of manures, it is made very productive; and, as equally cheap farms can hardly be found in any free State, in such proximity to so high markets for agricultural produce, as those of Washington and Alexandria, there are good inducements for a considerable Northern immigration hither. It may not be long before a majority of the inhabitants will be opposed to Slavery, and desire its abolition within the District. Indeed, when Mr. Seward proposed in the Senate to allow them to decide that matter, the advocates of "popular sovereignty" made haste to vote down the motion.

There are, already, more Irish and German laborers and servants than *slaves*, and, as many of the objections which free laborers have to going further South, do not operate in Washington, the proportion of white laborers is every year increasing. The majority of servants, however, are now *free* negroes, which class constitutes one-fifth of the entire population. The slaves are one fifteenth, but are mostly owned out of the District, and hired annually to those who require their services. In the assessment of taxable property, for 1853, the slaves, owned or hired in the District, were valued at three hundred thousand dollars.

The colored population voluntarily sustain several churches, schools, and mutual assistance and improvement societies, and there are evidently persons among them of no inconsiderable cultivation of mind. Among the Police Reports of the City newspapers, there was lately (April, 1855) an account of the apprehension of twenty-four "genteel colored men" (so they were described), who had been found by a watchman assembling privately in the evening, and been lodged in the watch-house. The object of their meeting appears to have been purely benevolent, and, when they were examined before a magistrate in the morning, no evidence was offered, nor does there seem to have been any suspicion that they had any criminal purpose. On searching their persons, there were found a Bible, a volume of *Seneca's Morals; Life in Earnest;* the printed Constitution of a Society, the object of which was said to be "*to relieve the sick, and bury the dead;*" and a subscription paper *to purchase the freedom of Eliza Howard,* a young woman, whom her owner was willing to sell at $650.

I can think of nothing that would speak higher for the character of a body of poor men, servants and laborers, than to find, by chance, in their pockets, just such things as these. And I cannot value that man as a countryman, who does not feel intense humiliation and indignation, when he learns that such men may not be allowed to meet privately together, with such laudable motives, in the capital city of the United States, without being subject to disgraceful punishment. Washington is, at this time, governed by the Know Nothings, and the magistrate, in disposing of the case, was probably actuated by a well-founded dread of secret conspiracies, inquisitions, and persecutions. One of the prisoners, a slave named Joseph Jones, he ordered to be flogged; four others, called in the papers free men, and named John E. Bennett, Chester Taylor, George Lee, and Aquila Barton, were sent to the Workhouse, and the remainder, on paying costs of court, and fines, amounting, in the aggregate, to one hundred and eleven dollars, were permitted to range loose again.

Had this happened at Naples, and had the men been Protestants, what would the Protestant world have called it? Had it happened at Havana, and the men been American citizens, enrolling offices for volunteers would have been instantly opened in New Orleans and New York.

CHAPTER II

VIRGINIA

Dec. 16th. From Washington to Richmond, Virginia, by the regular great southern route—steamboat on the Potomac to Acquia Creek, and thence direct by rail. The boat makes 55 miles in 3½ hours, including two stoppages (12½ miles an hour); fare $2 (3.6 cents a mile). Flat rail; distance, 75 miles; time, 5½ hours (13 miles an hour); fare, $3.50 (4⅔ cents a mile).

Not more than a third of the country, visible on this route, I should say, is cleared; the rest is mainly a pine forest. Of the cleared land, not more than one-quarter seems to have been lately in cultivation; the rest is grown over with briars and bushes, and a long, coarse grass of no value. But two crops seem to be grown upon the cultivated land—maize and wheat. The last is frequently sown in narrow beds and carefully surface-drained, and is looking remarkably well.

A good many substantial old plantation mansions are to be seen; generally standing in a grove of white oaks, upon some hill-top. Most of them are constructed of wood, of two stories, painted white, and have, perhaps, a dozen rude-looking little log-cabins scattered around them, for the slaves. Now and then, there is one of more pretension, with a large porch or gallery in front, like that of Mount Vernon. These are generally in a heavy, compact style; less often, perhaps, than similar establishments at the North, in markedly bad, or vulgar taste; but seldom elegant, or even neat, and almost always in sad need of repairs.

The more common sort of habitations of the white people are either of logs or loosely-boarded frames, a brick chimney running up outside, at one end: everything very slovenly and dirty about them. Swine, foxhounds, and black and white children, are commonly lying very promiscuously together, on the ground about the doors.

I am struck with the close co-habitation and association of black and white—negro women are carrying black and white babies together in their arms; black and white children are playing together (not going to school together); black and white faces are constantly thrust together out of the doors, to see the train go by.

A fine-looking, well-dressed, and well-behaved colored young man sat, together with a white man, on a seat in the cars. I suppose the man was his master; but he was much the less like a gentleman, of the two. The railroad company advertise to take colored people only in second class trains; but servants seem to go with their masters everywhere. Once, to-day, seeing a lady entering the car at a way-station, with a family behind her, and that she was looking about to find a place where they could be seated together, I rose, and offered her my seat, which had several vacancies around it.

She accepted it, without thanking me, and immediately installed in it a stout negro woman; took the adjoining seat herself, and seated the rest of her party before her. It consisted of a white girl, probably her daughter, and a bright and very pretty mulatto girl. They all talked and laughed together, and the girls munched confectionery out of the same paper, with a familiarity and closeness of intimacy that would have been noticed with astonishment, if not with manifest displeasure, in almost any chance company at the North. When the negro is definitely a slave, it would seem that the alleged natural antipathy of the white race to associate with him is lost.

I am surprised at the number of fine-looking mulattoes, or nearly white colored persons, that I see. The majority of those with whom I have come personally in contact are such. I fancy I see a peculiar expression among these—a contraction of the eyebrows and tightening of the lips—a spying, secretive, and counsel-keeping expression.

But the great mass, as they are seen at work, under overseers, in the fields, appear very dull, idiotic, and brute-like; and it requires an effort to appreciate that they are, very much more than the beasts they drive, our brethren — a part of ourselves. They are very ragged, and the women especially, who work in the field with the men, with no apparent distinction in their labor, disgustingly dirty. They seem to move very awkwardly, slowly, and undecidedly, and almost invariably stop their work while the train is passing.

One tannery and two or three saw-mills afforded the only indications I saw, in seventy-five miles of this old country—settled before any part of Massachusetts—of any industrial occupation other than corn and wheat culture, and fire-wood chopping. At Fredericksburg we passed through the streets of a rather busy, poorly-built town; but, altogether, the country seen from the railroad, bore less signs of an active and prospering people than any I ever travelled through before, for an equal distance.

Richmond, at a glance from adjacent high ground, through a dull cloud of bituminous smoke, upon a lowering winter's day, has a very picturesque appearance, and I was reminded of the sensation produced by a similar *coup d'œil* of Edinburg. It is somewhat similarly situated upon and among some considerable hills, but the moment it is examined at all in detail, there is but one spot, in the whole picture, upon which the eye is at all attracted to rest. This is the Capitol, an imposing Grecian edifice, standing alone, and finely placed on open and elevated ground, in the centre of the town. It was built soon after the Revolution, and the model was obtained by Mr. Jefferson, then Minister to France, from the Maison Carrée.

A considerable part of the town, which contains a population of 28,000, is compactly and somewhat substantially built, but is without any pretensions to architectural merit, except in a few modern private mansions. The streets are not paved, and but few of them are provided with side-walks other than of earth or gravel.

The town is lighted with gas, and furnished with excellent water by an aqueduct.

On a closer view of the Capitol, a bold deviation from the Grecian model is very noticeable. The southern portico is sustained upon a very high blank wall, and is as inaccessible from the exterior as if it had been intended to fortify the edifice from all ingress other than by scaling-ladders. On coming round to the west side, however, which is without a colonnade, a grand entrance, reached by a heavy buttress of stone steps, is found. This incongruity diminishes, in some degree, the usual inconvenience of the Greek temple for modern public purposes, for it gives speedy access to a small central rotunda, out of which doors open into the legislative halls and offices.

If the walling up of the legitimate entrance has caused the impression, in a stranger, that he is being led to a prison or fortress, instead of the place for transacting the public business of a free State by its chosen paid agents, it is not removed when, on approaching this side door, he sees before it an armed sentinel—a meek-looking man in a livery of many colors, embarrassed with a bright bayonetted firelock, which he hugs gently, as though the cold iron, this frosty day, chilled his arm.

He belongs to the Public Guard of Virginia, I am told; a company of a hundred men (more or less), enlisted under an Act of the State, passed in 1801, after a rebellion of the colored people, who, under one "General Gabriel," attempted to take the town, in hopes to gain the means of securing their freedom. Having been betrayed by a traitor, as insurgent slaves almost always are, they were met, on their approach, by a large body of well-armed militia, hastily called out by the Governor. For this, being armed only with scythe-blades, they were unprepared, and immediately dispersed. "General Gabriel" and the other leaders, one after another, were captured, tried, and hanged, the militia in strong force guarding them to execution. Since then, a disciplined guard, bearing the warning motto, "*Sic semper tyrannis!*"[1] has been kept constantly under arms in the capital, and no man can enter the legislative temple of Virginia without being reminded that "Eternal vigilance is the price of ———."

The gentleman who gave me the substance of this information, spoke of the Guard with an admiring and gratulatory tone, as "our little army." "But how is that?" I inquired; "does not our federal Constitution require that no State shall keep troops in time of peace? Is not your little army unconstitutional?"

I could get no satisfactory reply; I fear it was hardly in good taste, under the circumstances, to make such an inquiry of a Virginia democrat.

It was not till I had passed the guard, unchallenged, and stood at the door-way, that I perceived that the imposing edifice, as I had thought it at a distance, was nothing but a cheap stuccoed building; nor would anything short of test by touch, have convinced me that the great State of Virginia would have been so long

---

[1] "So ever to tyrants," the motto on the seal of Virginia.

content with such a parsimonious pretense of dignity as is found in imitation granite and imitation marble.

There is an instance of parsimony, without pretense, in Richmond, which Ruskin, himself, if he were a traveller, could not be expected to applaud. The railroad company which brings the traveller from Washington, so far from being open to the criticism of having provided edifices of a style of architecture only fitted for palaces, instead of a hall suited to conflicts with hackney-coachmen, actually has no sort of stationary accommodations for them at all, but sets them down, rain or shine, in the middle of one of the main streets. The adjoining hucksteries, barbers'-shops, and barrooms, are evidently all the better patronized for this fine simplicity; but I should doubt if the railroad stock would be much advanced in value by it.

In the rotunda of the Capitol stands Houdon's statue of Washington. It was modelled from life, and is said to present the truest similitude of the American Great Man that is retained for posterity. The face has a lofty, serene, slightly saddened expression, as that of a strong, sensible man loaded, but not over-burdened, with cares and anxiety. A self-reliant, brave, able soul, with deep but subdued sympathies, comprehending great duties, calmly and confidently prepared to perform them. There is very little like a king, or a clergyman, or any other professional character-actor in it. In most of the portraits of Washington, he looks as if he were a great tragedian, or a high-priest; but this is a face that would satisfy and encourage one in the engine-driver of a lightning train, or the officer of the deck in a fog off Cape Race; far-seeing, vigilant and fervid, but composed and perfectly controlled—the face of a man, wherever you found him—as a sailor, or a schoolmaster, or a judge, or a general—that you could depend upon to perform his undertakings conscientiously. The figure is not good; it struts, and has an air of nonchalance and ungentlemanly assumption. This was the fashion of the age, however, and education may have given it to the man, though his character, as seen with certainty in his face, is far superior to it.

The grounds about the Capitol are naturally admirable, and have lately been improved with neatness and taste. Their beauty and interest would be greatly increased if more of the fine native trees and shrubs of Virginia, particularly the holly and the evergreen magnolias, were planted in them. I noticed these, as well as the Irish and palmated ivy, growing, with great vigor and beauty, in the private gardens of the town. On some high, sterile lands, of which there are several thousand acres, uninclosed and uncultivated, near the town, I saw a group of exceedingly beautiful trees, having the lively green and all the lightness, gracefulness and beauty of foliage, in the Winter, of the finest deciduous trees. I could not believe, until I came near them, that they were what I found them to be—our common red cedar (*Juniperus Virginiana*). I have frequently noticed that the beauty of this tree is greatly affected by the soil it stands in; in certain localities, on the Hudson river, for instance, and in the lower part of New Jersey, it grows in a perfectly dense, conical, cypress-like form. These, on the other hand, were square-headed, dense, flattened at the top, like the cedar of Lebanon, and with a light and slightly drooping spray, deliciously delicate and graceful, where it cut the light. They stood in a soil of small quartz gravel, slightly bound with red clay. In a soil of similar appearance at the North, cedars are usually thin, stiff, shabby, and dull in color. I notice that they are generally finer here, than we often see them under the best of circumstances; and I presume they are better suited in climate.

On a Sunday afternoon I met a negro funeral procession, and followed after it to the place of burial. There was a decent hearse, of the usual style, drawn by two horses; six hackney coaches followed it, and six well-dressed men, mounted on handsome saddle-horses, and riding them well, rode in the rear of these. Twenty or thirty men and women were also walking together with the procession, on the side-walk. Among all there was not a white person.

Passing out into the country, a little beyond the principal cemetery of the city (a neat, rural ground, well filled with monuments and evergreens), the hearse halted at a desolate place, where a dozen colored people were already engaged heaping the earth over the grave of a child, and singing a wild kind of chant. Another grave was already dug, immediately adjoining that of the child, both being near the foot of a hill, in a crumbling bank—the ground below being already occupied, and the graves advancing in irregular terraces up the hill-side—an arrangement which facilitated labor.

The new comers, setting the coffin—which was neatly made of stained pine—upon the ground, joined in the labor and the singing, with the preceding party, until a small mound of earth was made over the grave of the child. When this was completed, one of those who had been handling a spade, sighed deeply and said,

"Lord Jesus have marcy on us—now! you Jim—*you! see yar;* you jes lay dat yar shovel cross dat grave—so fash—dah—yes, dat's right."

A shovel and a hoe-handle having been laid across the unfilled grave, the coffin was brought and laid upon them, as on a trestle; after which, lines were passed under it, by which it was lowered to the bottom.

Most of the company were of a very poor appearance, rude and unintelligent, but there were several neatly-dressed and very good-looking men. One of these now stepped to the head of the grave, and, after a few sentences of prayer, held a handkerchief before him as if it were a book, and pronounced a short exhortation, as if he were reading from it. His manner was earnest, and the tone of his voice solemn and impressive, except that, occasionally, it would break into a shout or kind of howl at the close of a long sentence. I noticed several women near him, weeping, and one sobbing intensely. I was deeply influenced myself by the unaffected feeling, in connection with the simplicity, natural, rude truthfulness, and absence of all attempt at formal decorum in the crowd.

I never in my life, however, heard such ludicrous language as was sometimes uttered by the speaker. Frequently I could not guess the idea he was intending to express. Sometimes it was evident that he was trying to repeat phrases that he had heard used before, on similar occasions, but which he made absurd by some interpolation or distortion of a word; thus, " We do not see the end here! oh no, my friends! there will be a *putrification* of this body!" the context failing to indicate whether he meant purification or putrefaction, and leaving it doubtful if he attached any definite meaning to the word himself. He quoted from the Bible several times, several times from hymns, always introducing the latter with " in the words of the poet, my brethren;" he once used the same form, before a verse from the New Testament, and once qualified his citation by saying, " I *believe* the Bible says that;" in which he was right, having repeated the words of Job.

He concluded by throwing a handful of earth on the coffin, repeating the usual words, slightly disarranged, and then took a shovel, and, with the aid of six or seven others, proceeded very rapidly to fill the grave. Another man had, in the meantime, stepped into the place he had first occupied at the head of the grave; an old negro, with a very singularly distorted face, who raised a hymn, which soon became a confused chant— the leader singing a few words alone, and the company then either repeating them after him or making a response to them, in the manner of sailors heaving at the windlass. I could understand but very few of the words. The music was wild and barbarous, but not without a plaintive melody. A new leader took the place of the old man, when his breath gave out (he had sung very hard, with much bending of the body and gesticulation), and continued until the grave was filled, and a mound raised over it.

A man had, in the meantime, gone into a ravine near by, and now returned with two small branches, hung with withered leaves, that he had broken off a beech tree; these were placed upright, one at the head, the other at the foot of the grave. A few sentences of prayer were then repeated in a low voice by one of the company, and all dispersed. No one seemed to notice my presence at all. There were about fifty colored people in the assembly, and but one other white man besides myself. This man lounged against the fence, outside the crowd, an apparently indifferent spectator, and I judged he was a police officer, or some one procured to witness the funeral, in compliance with the law which requires that a white man shall always be present at any meeting, for religious exercises, of the negroes, to destroy the opportunity of their conspiring to gain their freedom.

The greater part of the colored people, on Sunday, seemed to be dressed in the cast-off fine clothes of the white people, received, I suppose, as presents, or purchased of the Jews, whose shops show that there must be considerable importation of such articles, probably from the North, as there is from England into Ireland. Indeed, the lowest class, especially among the younger, remind me much, by their dress, of the "lads" of Donnybrook; and when the funeral procession came to its destination, there was a scene precisely like that you may see every day in Sackville-street, Dublin,—a dozen boys in ragged clothes, originally made for tall men, and rather folded round their bodies than worn, striving who should hold the horses of the *gentlemen* when they dismounted to attend the interment of the body. Many, who had probably come in from the farms near the town, wore clothing of coarse gray "negro-cloth," that appeared as if made by contract, without regard to the size of the particular individual to whom it had been allotted, like penitentiary uniforms. A few had a better suit of coarse blue cloth, expressly made for them evidently, for "Sunday clothes."

Some were dressed with laughably foppish extravagance, and a great many in clothing of the most expensive materials, and in the latest style of fashion. In what I suppose to be the fashionable streets, there were many more well-dressed and highly-dressed colored people than white, and among this dark gentry the finest French cloths, embroidered waistcoats, patent-leather shoes, resplendent brooches, silk hats, kid gloves, and *eau de mille fleurs*, were quite as common as among the New York " dry-goods clerks," in their Sunday promenades, in Broadway. Nor was the fairer, or rather the softer sex, at all left in the shade of this splendor. Many of the colored ladies were dressed not only expensively, but with good taste and effect, after the latest Parisian mode. Many of them were quite attractive in appearance, and some would have produced a decided sensation in any European drawing-room. Their walk and carriage was more often stylish and graceful than that of the white ladies who were out. About one-quarter seemed to me to have lost all distinguishingly African peculiarity of feature, and to have acquired, in place of it, a good deal of that voluptuousness of expression which characterizes many of the women of the south of Europe. I was especially surprised to notice the frequency of thin, aquiline noses.

There was no indication of their belonging to a subject race, but that they invariably gave the way to the white people they met. Once, when two of them, engaged in conversation and looking at each other, had not noticed his approach, I saw a Virginia gentleman lift his cane and push a woman aside with it. In the evening I saw three rowdies, arm-in-arm, taking the whole of the sidewalk, hustle a black man off it, giving him a blow, as they passed, that sent him staggering into the middle of the street. As he recovered himself he began to call out to, and threaten them. Perhaps he saw me stop, and thought I should support him, as I was certainly inclined to: " Can't you find anything else to do than to be knockin' quiet people round! You jus' come back here, will you? Here, you! *don't care if you is white*. You jus' come back here and I'll teach you how to behave—knockin' people round!—don't care if I does hab to go to der watch-house." They passed on without noticing him further, only laughing jeeringly—and he continued: "You come back here and I 'll make you laugh; you is jus' three white nigger cowards, dat's what *you* be."

I observe, in the newspapers, complaints of growing insolence and insubordination among the negroes, arising, it is thought, from too many privileges being permitted them by their masters, and from too merciful administration of the police laws with regard to them. Except in this instance, however, I have seen not the slightest evidence of any independent manliness on the part of the negroes towards the whites. As far as I have yet observed, they are treated very kindly and even generously as servants, but their manner to white people is invariably either sullen, jocose, or fawning.

The pronunciation and dialect of the negroes, here, is generally much more idiomatic and peculiar than with us. As I write, I hear a man shouting, slowly and deliberately, meaning to say *there: dah! dah!* DAH!

Yesterday morning, during a cold, sleety storm, against which I was struggling, with my umbrella, to the post office, I met a comfortably-dressed negro leading three others by a rope; the first was a middle-aged man; the second a girl of, perhaps, twenty; and the last a boy, considerably younger. The arms of all three were secured before them with hand-cuffs, and the rope by which they were led passed from one to another; being made fast at each pair of hand-cuffs. They were thinly clad, the girl especially so, having only an old ragged handkerchief around her neck, over a common calico dress, and another handkerchief twisted around her head. They were dripping wet, and icicles were forming, at the time, on the awning bars.

The boy looked most dolefully, and the girl was turning around, with a very angry face, and shouting, "O pshaw! Shut up!"

"What are they?" said I, to a white man, who had also stopped, for a moment, to look at them. "What's he going to do with them?"

"Come in a canal boat, I reckon: sent down here to be sold.—That ar's a likely gall."

Our ways lay together, and I asked further explanation. He informed me that the negro-dealers had confidential servants always in attendance, on the arrival of the railroad trains and canal packets, to take any negroes, that might have come, consigned to them, and bring them to their marts.

Nearly opposite the post office, was another singular group of negroes. They were all men and boys, and each carried a coarse, white blanket, drawn together at the corners so as to hold some articles; probably, extra clothes. They stood in a row, in lounging attitudes, and some of them, again, were quarrelling, or reproving one another. A villainous-looking white man stood in front of them. Presently, a stout, respectable man, dressed in black according to the custom, and without any overcoat or umbrella, but with a large, golden-headed walking-stick, came out of the door of an office, and, without saying a word, walked briskly up the street; the negroes immediately followed, in file; the other white man bringing up the rear. They were slaves that had been sent into the town to be hired out as servants or factory hands. The gentleman in black was, probably, the broker in the business.

Near the post office, opposite a large livery and sale stable, I turned into a short, broad street, in which were a number of establishments, the signs on which indicated that they were occupied by "Slave Dealers," and that "Slaves, for Sale or to Hire," were to be found within them. They were much like Intelligence Offices, being large rooms partly occupied by ranges of forms, on which sat a few comfortably and neatly clad negroes, who appeared perfectly cheerful; each grinning obsequiously, but with a manifest interest or anxiety, when I fixed my eye on them for a moment.

In Chambers' Journal for October, 1853, there is an account of the Richmond slave marts, and the manner of conducting business in them, so graphic and evidently truthful that I omit any further narration of my own observations, to make room for it. I do this, notwithstanding its length, because I did not happen to witness, during fourteen months that I spent in the Slave States, any sale of negroes by auction. This must not be taken as an indication that negro auctions are not of frequent occurrence (I did not, so far as I now recollect, witness the sale of anything else, at auction, at the South). I saw negroes advertised to be sold at auction, very frequently.

"The exposure of ordinary goods in a store is not more open to the public than are the sales of slaves in Richmond. By consulting the local newspapers, I learned that the sales take place by auction every morning in the offices of certain brokers, who, as I understood by the terms of their advertisements, purchased or received slaves for sale on commission.

"Where the street was in which the brokers conducted their business, I did not know; but the discovery was easily made. Rambling down the main street in the city, I found that the subject of my search was a narrow and short thoroughfare, turning off to the left, and terminating in a similar cross thoroughfare. Both streets, lined with brick-houses, were dull and silent. There was not a person to whom I could put a question. Looking about, I observed the office of a commission-agent, and into it I stepped. Conceive the idea of a large shop with two windows, and a door between; no shelving or counters inside; the interior a spacious, dismal apartment, not well swept; the only furniture a desk at one of the windows, and a bench at one side of the shop, three feet high, with two steps to it from the floor. I say, conceive the idea of this dismal-looking place, with nobody in it but three negro children, who, as I entered, were playing at auctioneering each other. An intensely black little negro, of four or five years of age, was standing on the bench, or block, as it is called, with an equally black girl, about a year younger, by his side, whom he was pretending to sell by bids to another black child, who was rolling about the floor.

"My appearance did not interrupt the merriment. The little auctioneer continued his mimic play, and appeared to enjoy the joke of selling the girl, who stood demurely by his side.

"'Fifty dolla for de gal — fifty dolla — fifty dolla — I sell dis here fine gal for fifty dolla,' was uttered with extraordinary volubility by the woolly-headed urchin, accompanied with appropriate gestures, in imitation, doubtless of the scenes he had seen enacted daily in the spot. I spoke a few words to the little creatures, but was scarcely understood: and the fun went on as if I had not been present: so I left them, happy in rehearsing what was likely soon to be their own fate.

"At another office of a similar character, on the opposite side of the street, I was more successful. Here on inquiry, I was respectfully informed, by a person in attendance, that the sale would take place the following morning at half-past nine o'clock.

"Next day I set out accordingly, after breakfast, for the scene of operations, in which there was now a little more life. Two or three persons were lounging about, smoking cigars; and, looking along the street I observed that three red flags were projected from the doors of those offices in which sales were to occur. On each flag was pinned a piece of paper, notifying the articles to be sold. The number of lots was not great. On the first was the following announcement: — 'Will be sold this morning, at half-past nine o'clock, a Man and a Boy.'

"It was already the appointed hour; but as no company had assembled, I entered and took a seat by the fire. The office, provided with a few deal forms and chairs, a desk at one of the windows, and a block accessible by a few steps, was tenantless, save by a gentleman who was arranging papers at the desk, and to whom I had addressed myself on the previous evening. Minute after minute passed, and still nobody entered. There was clearly no hurry in going to business. I felt almost like an intruder, and had formed the resolution of departing, in order to look into the other offices, when the person referred to left his desk, and came and seated himself opposite to me at the fire.

"'You are an Englishman,' said he, looking me steadily in the face; 'do you want to purchase?'

"'Yes,' I replied, 'I am an Englishman; but I do not intend to purchase. I am traveling about for information, and I shall feel obliged by your letting me know the prices at which negro servants are sold.'

"'I will do so with much pleasure,' was the answer; 'do you mean field-hands or house-servants?'

"'All kinds,' I replied; 'I wish to get all the information I can.'

"With much politeness, the gentleman stepped to his desk, and began to draw up a note of prices. This, however, seemed to require careful consideration; and while the note was preparing, a lanky person, in a wide-awake hat, and chewing tobacco, entered, and took the chair just vacated. He had scarcely seated himself, when, on looking towards the door, I observed the subjects of sale — the man and boy indicated by the paper on the red flag — enter together, and quietly walk to a form at the back of the shop, whence, as the day was chilly, they edged themselves towards the fire, in the corner where I was seated. I was now between the two parties — the white man on the right, and the old and young negro on the left — and I waited to see what would take place.

"The sight of the negroes at once attracted the attention of Wide-awake. Chewing with vigor, he kept keenly eying the pair, as if to see what they were good for. Under this searching gaze, the man and boy were a little abashed, but said nothing. Their appearance had little of the repulsiveness we are apt to associate with the idea of slaves. They were dressed in a gray woolen coat, pants, and waistcoat, colored cotton neckcloths, clean shirts, coarse woolen stockings, and stout shoes. The man wore a black hat; the boy was bareheaded. Moved by a sudden impulse, Wide-awake left his seat, and rounding the back of my chair, began to grasp at the man's arms, as if to feel their muscular capacity. He then examined his hands and fingers; and, last of all, told him to open his mouth and show his teeth, which he did in a submissive manner. Having finished these examinations, Wide-awake resumed his seat, and chewed on in silence as before.

"I thought it was but fair that I should now have my turn of investigation, and accordingly asked the elder negro what was his age. He said he did not know. I next inquired how old the boy was. He said he was seven years of age. On asking the man if the boy was his son, he said he was not — he was his cousin. I was going into other particulars, when the office-keeper approached, and handed me the note he had been preparing; at the same time making the observation that the market was dull at present, and that there never could be a more favorable opportunity of buying. I thanked him for the trouble which he had taken; and now submit a copy of his price-current:

"'Best Men, 18 to 25 years old,   1200 to 1300 dollars.
    Fair do.   do.   do.,   950 to 1050   "
    Boys, 5 feet,   850 to 950   "
    Do., 4 feet 8 inches,   700 to 800   "
    Do., 4 feet 5 inches,   500 to 600   "
    Do., 4 feet,   375 to 450   "
    Young Women,   800 to 1000   "
    Girls, 5 feet,   750 to 850   "
    Do., 4 feet 9 inches,   700 to 750   "
    Do., 4 feet,   350 to 452   "
            (Signed)   ⎯⎯⎯⎯⎯⎯⎯,
                                    Richmond, Virginia.'

"Leaving this document for future consideration, I pass on to a history of the day's proceedings. It was now ten minutes to ten o'clock, and Wide-awake and I being alike tired of waiting, we went off in quest of sales further up the street. Passing the second office, in which also nobody was to be seen, we were more fortunate at the third. Here, according to the announcement on the paper stuck to the flag, there were to be sold, 'A woman and three children; a young woman, three men, a middle-aged woman, and a little boy.' Already a crowd had met, composed, I should think, of persons mostly from the cotton-plantations of the south. A few were seated near a fire on the right-hand side, and others stood round an iron stove in the middle of the apartment. The whole place had a dilapidated appearance. From a back-window, there was a view into a ruinous court-yard; beyond which, in a hollow, accessible by a side-lane, stood a shabby brick-house, on which the word *Jail* was inscribed in large black letters on a white ground. I imagined it to be a dépôt for the reception of negroes.

"On my arrival, and while making these preliminary observations, the lots for sale had not made their appearance. In about five minutes afterwards they were ushered in, one after the other, under the charge of a mulatto, who seemed to act as principal assistant. I saw no whips, chains, or any other engine of force. Nor did such appear to be required. All the lots took their seats on two long forms near the stove; none showed any signs of resistance; nor did any one utter a word. Their manner was that of perfect humility and resignation.

"As soon as all were seated, there was a general examination of their respective merits, by feeling their arms, looking into their mouths, and investigating the quality of their hands and fingers—this last being evidently an important particular. Yet there was no abrupt rudeness in making these examinations—no coarse or domineering language was employed. The three negro men were dressed in the usual manner—in gray woolen clothing. The woman, with three children, excited my peculiar attention. She was neatly attired, with a colored handkerchief bound around her head, and wore a white apron over her gown. Her children were all girls, one of them a baby at the breast, three months old, and the others two and three years of age respectively, rigged out with clean white pinafores. There was not a tear or an emotion visible in the whole party. Everything seemed to be considered as a matter of course; and the change of owners was possibly looked forward to with as much indifference as ordinary hired servants anticipate a removal from one employer to another.

"While intending-purchasers were proceeding with personal examinations of the several lots, I took the liberty of putting a few questions to the mother of the children. The following was our conversation :—

"'Are you a married woman?'

"'Yes, sir.'

"'How many children have you had?'

"'Seven.'

"'Where is your husband?'

"'In Madison county.'

"'When did you part from him?'

"'On Wednesday—two days ago.'

"'Were you sorry to part from him?'

"'Yes, sir,' she replied, with a deep sigh; 'my heart was a'most broke.'

"'Why is your master selling you?'

"'I don't know—he wants money to buy some land—suppose he sells me for that.'

"There might not be a word of truth in these answers, for I had no means of testing their correctness; but the woman seemed to speak unreservedly, and I am inclined to think that she said nothing but what, if necessary, could be substantiated. I spoke, also, to the young woman who was seated near her. She, like the others, was perfectly black, and appeared stout and healthy, of which some of the persons present assured themselves by feeling her arms and ankles, looking into her mouth, and causing her to stand up. She told me she had several brothers and sisters, but did not know where they were. She said she was a house-servant, and would be glad to be bought by a good master—looking at me, as if I should not be unacceptable.

"I have said that there was an entire absence of emotion in the party of men, women, and children, thus seated preparatory to being sold. This does not correspond with the ordinary accounts of slave-sales, which are represented as tearful and harrowing. My belief is, that none of the parties felt deeply on the subject, or at least that any distress they experienced was but momentary—soon passed away, and was forgotten. One of my reasons for this opinion rests on a trifling incident which occurred. While waiting for the commencement of the sale, one of the gentlemen present amused himself with a pointer-dog, which, at command, stood on its hind-legs, and took pieces of bread from his pocket. These tricks greatly entertained the row of negroes, old and young; and the poor woman, whose heart three minutes before was almost broken, now laughed as heartily as any one.

"'Sale is going to commence—this way, gentlemen,' cried a man at the door to a number of loungers outside; and all having assembled, the mulatto assistant led the woman and her children to the block, which he helped her to mount. There she stood with her infant at the breast, and one of her girls at each side. The auctioneer, a handsome, gentlemanly personage, took his place, with one foot on an old deal chair with a broken back, and the other raised on the somewhat more elevated block. It was a striking scene.

"'Well, gentlemen,' began the salesman, 'here is a capital woman and her three children, all in good health—what do you say for them? Give me an offer. (Nobody speaks.) I put up the whole lot at 850 dollars—850 dollars—850 dollars (speaking very fast)—850 dollars. Will no one advance upon that? A very extraordinary bargain, gentlemen. A fine, healthy baby. Hold it up. (Mulatto goes up the first step of the block; takes the baby from the woman's breast and holds it aloft with one hand, so as to show that it was a veritable sucking baby.) That will do. A woman, still young, and three children, all for 850 dollars. An advance, if you please, gentlemen. (A voice bids 860.) Thank you, sir, 860; any one bids more? (A second voice says, 870; and so on the bidding goes as far as 890 dollars, when it stops.) That won't do, gentlemen. I cannot take such a low price. (After a pause, addressing the mulatto): She may go down.' Down from the block the woman and her children were therefore conducted by the assistant, and, as if nothing had occurred, they calmly resumed their seats by the stove.

"The next lot brought forward was one of the men. The mulatto, beckoning to him with his hand, requested him to come behind a canvas screen, of two leaves, which was standing near the back window. The man placidly rose, and having been placed behind the screen, was ordered to take off his clothes, which he did without a word or look of remonstrance. About a dozen gentlemen crowded to the spot while the poor fellow was stripping himself, and as soon as he stood on the floor, bare from top to toe, a most rigorous scrutiny of his person was instituted. The clear black skin, back and front, was viewed all over for sores from disease; and there was no part of his body left unexamined. The man was told to open and shut his hands, asked if he could pick cotton, and every tooth in his head was scrupulously looked at. The investigation being at an end, he was ordered to dress himself; and having done so, was requested to walk to the block.

"The ceremony of offering him for competition was gone through as before, but no one would bid. The other two men, after undergoing similar examinations behind the screen, were also put up, but with the same result. Nobody would bid for them, and they were all sent back to their seats. It seemed as if the company had conspired not to buy anything that day. Probably some imperfections had been detected in the personal qualities of the negroes. Be this as it may, the auctioneer, perhaps a little out of temper from his want of success, walked off to his desk, and the affair was so far at an end.

"'This way, gentlemen — this way!' was heard from a voice outside, and the company immediately hived off to the second establishment. At this office there was a young woman, and also a man, for sale. The woman was put up first at 500 dollars; and possessing some recommendable qualities, the bidding for her was run as high as 710 dollars, at which she was knocked down to a purchaser. The man, after the customary examination behind the screen, was put up at 700 dollars; but a small imperfection having been observed in his person, no one would bid for him; and he was ordered down.

"'This way, gentlemen, this way — down the street, if you please!' was now shouted by a person in the employment of the first firm, to whose office all very willingly adjourned — one migratory company, it will be perceived, serving all the slave auctions in the place. Mingling in the crowd, I went to see what should be the fate of the man and boy, with whom I had already had some communication.

"There the pair, the two cousins, sat by the fire, just where I had left them an hour ago. The boy was put up first.

"'Come along, my man — jump up; there's a good boy!' said one of the partners, a bulky and respectable-looking person, with a gold chain and bunch of seals; at the same time getting on the block. With alacrity the little fellow came forward, and, mounting the steps, stood by his side. The forms in front were filled by the company; and as I seated myself, I found that my old companion, Wide-awake, was close at hand, still chewing and spitting at a great rate.

"'Now, gentlemen,' said the auctioneer, putting his hand on the shoulder of the boy, 'here is a very fine boy, seven years of age, warranted sound — what do you say for him? I put him up at 500 dollars — 500 dollars (speaking quick, his right hand raised up, and coming down on the open palm of his left) — 500 dollars. Any one say more than 500 dollars? (560 is bid.) 560 dollars. Nonsense! Just look at him. See how high he is. (He draws the lot in front of him, and shows that the little fellow's head comes up to his breast.) You see he is a fine, tall, healthy boy. Look at his hands.'

"Several step forward, and cause the boy to open and shut his hands — the flexibility of the small fingers, black on the one side, and whitish on the other, being well looked to. The hands, and also the mouth, having given satisfaction, an advance is made to 570, then to 580 dollars.

"'Gentlemen, that is a very poor price for a boy of this size. (Addressing the lot) — Go down, my boy, and show them how you can run.'

"The boy, seemingly happy to do as he was bid, went down from the block, and ran smartly across the floor several times; the eyes of every one in the room following him.

"'Now that will do. Get up again. (Boy mounts the block, the steps being rather deep for his short legs; but the auctioneer kindly lends him a hand.) Come, gentlemen, you see this is a first-rate lot. (590—600—610—620—630 dollars are bid.) I will sell him for 630 dollars. (Right hand coming down on left.) Last call. 630 dollars, once — 630 dollars, twice. (A pause; hand sinks.) Gone!'

"The boy having descended, the man was desired to come forward; and after the usual scrutiny behind a screen, he took his place on the block.

"'Well, now, gentlemen,' said the auctioneer, 'here is a right prime lot. Look at this man; strong, healthy, able-bodied; could not be a better hand for field-work. He can drive a wagon, or anything. What do you say for him? I offer the man at the low price of 800 dollars — he is well worth 1200 dollars. Come, make an advance, if you please. 800 dollars said for the man (a bid), thank you; 810 dollars—810 dollars—810 dollars (several bids)—820—830—850—860—going at 860—going. Gentlemen, this is far below his value. A strong-boned man, fit for any kind of heavy work. Just take a look at him. (Addressing the lot): Walk down. (Lot dismounts, and walks from one side of the shop to the other. When about to reascend the block, a gentleman, who is smoking a cigar, examines his mouth with his fingers. Lot resumes his place.) Pray, gentlemen, be quick (continues the auctioneer); I must sell him, and 860 dollars are only bid for the man—860 dollars. (A fresh run of bids to 945 dollars.) 945 dollars, once, 945 dollars, twice (looking slowly round, to see if all were done), 945 dollars, going—going—(hand drops)—gone!'

"Such were a forenoon's experiences in the slave-market of Richmond. Everything is described precisely as it occurred, without passion or prejudice. It would not have been difficult to be sentimental on a subject which appeals so strongly to the feelings; but I have preferred telling the simple truth. In a subsequent chapter, I shall endeavor to offer some general views of slavery in its social and political relations.
"W. C."

This morning I visited a farm, some account of which will give a good idea of the more advanced mode of agriculture in Eastern Virginia. It is situated on the bank of James River, and has ready access, by water or land-carriage, to the town of Richmond.

The soil of the greater part is a red, plastic, clayey loam, of a medium or low fertility, with a large intermixture of small quartz pebbles. On the river bank is a tract of low alluvial land, varying from an eighth to a quarter of a mile in breadth. The soil of this is a sandy loam, of the very finest quality in every respect, and it has been discovered, in some places, to be over ten feet in thickness; at which depth the sound trunk of a white oak has been found, showing it to be a recent deposit. I was assured that good crops of corn, wheat, and clover, had been taken from it, without its giving any indications of "wearing out," although no manure, except an occasional dressing of lime, had ever been returned to it. Maize, wheat, and clover for two years, usually occupy the ground, in succession, both on upland and lowland, herd's-grass (red-top of New York), sometimes taking the place of the clover, or being grown with it for hay, in which case the ground remains in sward for several years. Oats are sometimes also introduced, but the yield is said to be very small.

Hay always brings a high price in Richmond, and is usually shipped to that market from the eastward. This year, however, it is but a trifle above New York prices, and the main supply is drawn from this vicinity. I notice that oats, in the straw, are brought, in considerable quantity, to Richmond, for horse-feed, from the surrounding country. It is often pressed in bales, like hay, and sells for about the same price. At present, hay, brought from New York in bales, is selling at $1.25 to $1.50 per cwt.; oats, in straw, the same; oats, by the bushel, 40 to 50 cents; maize, 66 to 70 cents; wheat straw, 75 cents per cwt.; maize leaves ("corn fodder"), 75 cents per cwt.

Wheat, notwithstanding these high prices of forage crops, is considered the most important crop of the farm. The practice is to cut the maize (which is grown on much the same plan as is usual in New York) at the root, stook it in rows upon the field, plough the lands between the rows (one way) and drill in wheat with a horse drilling machine: then remove the stooks of maize into the sown ground, and prepare the intervening lands in like manner. The maize is afterwards husked in the field, at leisure, and carted off, with the stalks, when the ground is frozen. Sometimes the seed-wheat is sown by hand on the fresh-ploughed ground, and harrowed in. In the spring, clover-seed is sown by hand. The wheat is reaped by either Hussey's or M'Cormick's machine, both being used on the farm, but Hussey's rather preferred, as less liable to get out of order, and, if slightly damaged, more readily repaired by the slave blacksmith on the farm.

Lime is frequently applied, commonly at the time of wheat-sowing, at the rate of from twenty-five to fifty bushels an acre. It is brought, by sea, from Haverstraw, New York, at a cost, delivered on the farm, of 7¼ to 7½ cents a bushel. Plaster (sulphate of lime) has been tried, with little or no perceptible effect on the crops.

Dung, largely accumulated from the farm stock, is applied almost exclusively to the maize crops. Guano is also largely used as an application for wheat. After trying greater and less quantities, the proprietor has arrived at the conclusion that 200 lbs. to the acre is most profitable. It will, hereafter, be applied, at that rate, to all the wheat grown upon the farm. It has also been used with advantage for ruta baga. For corn, it was not thought of much value; the greatest advantage had been obtained by applying it to the *poorest land of the farm, some of which was of so small fertility, and at such a distance from the cattle quarters and the river, that it could not be profitably cultivated, and had been at waste for many years. I understand this may be the case with half the land included in the large farms or plantations of this part of the country.* Two hundred weight of Peruvian guano to the acre brought fifteen bushels of wheat; and a good crop of clover was perfectly sure to follow, by which the permanent improvement of the soil could be secured. This the proprietor esteemed to be the greatest benefit he derived from guano, and he is pursuing a regular plan for bringing all his more sterile upland into the system of Convertible husbandry by its aid.

This plan is, to prepare the ground, by fallowing, for wheat; spread two hundred pounds of guano, broadcast, on the harrowed surface, and turn it under, as soon as possible after the sowers, with a "two-shovel plough" (a sort of large two-shared cultivator, which could only be used, I should think, on very light, clean soils), the wheat either being sown and covered with the guano, or, immediately afterwards, drilled in with a horse-machine. In the spring, clover is sown. After the wheat is harvested, the clover is allowed to grow, without being pastured or mown, for twelve months. The ground is then limed, clover ploughed in, and, in October, again guanoed, two hundred weight to the acre, and wheat sown, with clover to follow. The clover may be pastured the following year, but in the year succeeding that, it is allowed to grow unchecked until August, when it is ploughed in, the ground again guanoed, and wheat sown with herd's grass (red-top) and clover, which is to remain, for mowing and pasture, as long as the ground will profitably sustain it.

The labor of this farm was entirely performed by slaves. I did not inquire their number, but I judged there were from twenty to forty. Their "quarters" lined the approach-road to the mansion, and were well-made and comfortable log-cabins, about thirty feet long by twenty wide, and eight feet wall, with a high loft and shingle roof. Each, divided in the middle, and having a brick chimney outside the wall at each end, was intended to be occupied by two families. There were square windows, closed by wooden ports, having a single pane of glass in the centre. The house-servants were neatly dressed, but the field-hands wore very coarse and ragged garments.

During three hours, or more, in which I was in company with the proprietor, I do not think there were ten consecutive minutes uninterrupted by some of the slaves requiring his personal direction or assistance. He was even obliged, three times, to leave the dinner-table.

"You see," said he, smiling, as he came in the last time, "a farmer's life, in this country, is no sinecure." This turning the conversation to Slavery, he observed, in answer to a remark of mine, "I only wish your philanthropists would contrive some satisfactory plan to relieve us of it; the trouble and the responsibility of properly taking care of our negroes, you may judge, from what you see yourself here, is anything but enviable. But what can we do that *is better*? Our free negroes—and, I believe it is the same at the North as it is here—are a miserable set of vagabonds, drunken, vicious, worse off, it is my honest opinion, than those who are retained in slavery. I am satisfied, too, that our slaves are better off, as they are, than the majority of your free laboring classes at the North."

I expressed my doubts.

"Well, they certainly are better off than the English agricultural laborers or, I believe, those of any other Christian country. Free labor might be more profitable to us: I am inclined to think it would be. The slaves are excessively careless and wasteful, and, in various ways—which, without you lived among them, you could hardly be made to understand—subject us to very annoying losses.

"To make anything by farming, here, a man has got to live a hard life. You see how constantly I am called upon—and, often, it is about as bad at night as by day. Last night I did not sleep a wink till near morning; I am quite worn out with it, and my wife's health is failing. But I cannot rid myself of it."

I asked why he did not employ an overseer.

"Because I do not think it right to trust to such men as we have to use, if we use any, for overseers."

"Is the general character of overseers bad?"

"They are the curse of this country, sir; the worst men in the community. . . . But lately, I had another sort of fellow offer—a fellow like a dancing-master, with kid gloves, and wrist-bands turned up over his coat-sleeves, and all so nice, that I was almost ashamed to talk to him in my old coat and slouched hat. Half a bushel of recommendations he had with him, too. Well, he was not the man for me—not half the gentleman, with all his airs, that Ned here is"—(a black servant, who was bursting with suppressed laughter, behind his chair).

"Oh, they are interesting creatures, sir," he continued, "and, with all their faults, have many beautiful traits. I can't help being attached to them, and I am sure they love us." In his own case, at least, I did not doubt it; his manner towards them was paternal—familiar and kind; and they came to him like children who have been given some task, and constantly are wanting to be encouraged and guided, simply and confidently. At dinner, he frequently addressed the servant familiarly, and drew him into our conversation as if he were a family friend, better informed, on some local and domestic points, than himself.

He informed me that able-bodied field-hands were hired out, in this vicinity, at the rate of one hundred dollars a year, and their board and clothing. Four able-bodied men, that I have employed the last year, on my farm in New York, I pay, on an average, one hundred and five dollars each, and board them; they clothe themselves at an expense, I think, of twenty dollars a year;— probably, slaves' clothing costs twice that. They constitute all the force of my farm, hired by the year (except a boy, who goes to school in Winter), and, in my absence, have no overseer except one of themselves, whom I appoint. I pay the fair wages of the market, more than any of my neighbors, I believe, and these are no lower than the average of what I have paid for the last five years. It is difficult to measure the labor performed in a day by one, with that of the other, on account of undefined differences in the soil, and in the bulk and weight of articles operated upon. But, here, I am shown tools that no man in his senses, with us, would allow a laborer, to whom he was paying wages, to be encumbered with; and the excessive weight and clumsiness of which, I would judge, would make work at least ten per cent. greater than those ordinarily used with us. And I am assured that, in the careless and clumsy way they must be used by the slaves, anything lighter or less rude could not be furnished them with good economy, and that such tools as we constantly give our laborers, and find our profit in giving them, would not last out a day in a Virginia corn-field — much lighter and more free from stones though it be than ours.

So, too, when I ask why mules are so universally substituted for horses on the farm, the first reason given, and confessedly the most conclusive one, is, that horses cannot bear the treatment that they always *must* get from negroes; horses are always soon foundered or crippled by them, while mules will bear cudgelling, and lose a meal or two now and then, and not be materially injured, and they do not take cold or get sick if neglected or overworked. But I do not need to go further than to the window of the room in which I am writing, to see, at almost any time, treatment of cattle that would insure the immediate discharge of the driver, by almost any farmer owning them at the North.

Yesterday I visited a coal-pit: the majority of the mining laborers are slaves, and uncommonly athletic and fine-looking negroes; but a considerable number of white hands are also employed, and they occupy all the responsible posts. The slaves are, some of them, owned by the Mining Company; but the most are hired of their owners, at from $120 to $200 a year, the company boarding and clothing them. (I have the impression that I heard it was customary to give them a certain allowance of money and let them find their own board.)

The white hands are mostly English or Welchmen.

One of them, with whom I conversed, told me that he had been here several years; he had previously lived some years at the North. He got better wages here than he had earned at the North, but he was not contented, and did not intend to remain. On pressing him *for the reason of his discontent*, he said, after some hesitation, that he had rather live where he could be more free; a man had to be too "*discreet*" here: if one happened to say anything that gave offense, they thought no more of drawing a pistol or a knife upon him, than they would of kicking a dog that was in their way. Not long since, a young English fellow came to the pit, and was put to work along with a gang of negroes. One morning, about a week afterwards, twenty or thirty men called on him, and told him that they would allow him fifteen minutes to get out of sight, and if they ever saw him in those parts again, they would "give him hell." They were all armed, and there was nothing for the young fellow to do but to move "right off."

"What reason did they give him for it?"

"They did not give him any reason."

"But what had he done?"

"Why I believe they thought he had been too free with the niggers; he was n't used *to them, you see*, sir, and he talked to 'em free like, and they thought he 'd make 'em think too much of themselves."

He said the slaves were very well fed, and well treated —not worked over hard. They were employed night and day, in relays.

The coal from these beds is of special value for gas manufacture, and is shipped, for that purpose, to all the large towns on the Atlantic sea-board, even to beyond Boston. It is delivered to shipping at Richmond, at fifteen cents a bushel: about thirty bushels go to a ton.

The hotel at which I am staying, "the American," Milberger Smith, from New York, proprietor, is a very capital one. I have never, this side the Atlantic, had my comforts provided for better, in my private room, with so little annoyance from the servants. The chamber-servants are negroes, and are accomplished in their business; (the dining-room servants are Irish). A man and a woman attend together upon a few assigned rooms, in the hall adjoining which they are constantly in waiting; your bell is answered immediately, your orders are quickly and quietly followed, and your particular personal wants anticipated as much as possible, and provided for, as well as the usual offices performed, when you are out. The man becomes your servant while you are in your room; he asks, at night, when he comes to request your boots, at what time he shall come in the morning, and then, without being very exactly punctual, he comes quietly in, makes your fire, sets the boots before it, brushes and arranges your clothes, lays out your linen, arranges your washing and dressing gear, asks if you want anything else of him before breakfast, opens the shutters, and goes off to the next room. I took occasion to speak well of him to my neighbor one day, that I might judge whether I was particularly favored.

"Oh yes," he said, "Henry was a very good boy, very—valuable servant—quite so—would be worth two thousand dollars, if he was a little younger—easy."

At dinner, a respectable looking, gray-headed man asked another:

"Niggers are going high now, ain't they?"

"Yes, sir."

"What would you consider a fair price for a woman thirty years old, with a young-one two years old?"

"Depends altogether on her physical condition, you know.—Has she any other children?"

"*Yes; four*."

"——Well—I reckon about seven to eight hundred."

"I bought one yesterday—gave six hundred and fifty."

"Well, sir, if she's tolerable likely, you did well."

What is most remarkable in the appearance of the people of the better class, is their invariably *high-dressed* condition; look down the opposite side of the table, even at breakfast, and you will probably see thirty men drinking coffee, all in full funeral dress, not an easy coat amongst them. It is the same in the street, and the same with ladies as with gentlemen; silk and satin, under umbrellas, rustle along the sidewalk, or skip across it between carriages and the shops, as if they were going to a dinner-party, at eleven o'clock in the morning. The last is only New York repeated, to be sure, but the gentlemen carry it further than in New York, and seem never to indulge in undress.

I have rarely seen a finer assemblage of people than filled the theatre one night, at the benefit of the Bateman children, who are especial favorites of the public here. As the Legislature is in session, I presume there was a fair representation of the Virginians of all parts of the State. A remarkable proportion of the men were very tall and of animated expression—and of the women, fair, refined, and serene. The men, however, were very deficient in robustness, and the women, though graceful and attractive, had none of that dignity and stateliness for which the dames of Virginia were formerly much distinguished.

In *manners*, I notice that, between man and man, more ceremony and form is sustained, in familiar conversation, than well-bred people commonly use at the North.

Among the people you see in the streets, full half, I should think, are more or less of negro blood, and a very decent, civil people these seem, in general, to be; more so than the laboring class of whites, among which there are many very ruffianly looking fellows. There is a considerable population of foreign origin, generally of the least valuable class; very dirty German Jews, especially, abound, and their characteristic shops (with their characteristic smells, quite as bad as in Cologne), are thickly set in the narrowest and meanest streets, which seem to be otherwise inhabited mainly by negroes.

Immense wagons, drawn by six mules each, the teamster always riding on the back of the near-wheeler, are a characteristic feature of the streets. Another is the wood-carts; small trucks loaded with about a cord of pine wood, drawn by three mules or horses, one in shafts, and two others, abreast, before him, a negro always riding the shaft-horse and guiding the leaders with a single rein, one pull to turn them to the right, and two to the left, with a great deal of the whip whichever way they go. The same guiding apparatus, a single line, with branches to each bit, is used altogether upon the long wagon teams. On the canal, a long, narrow, canoe-like boat, perhaps fifty feet long and six wide, and drawing but a foot or two of water, is nearly as common as the ordinary large boats, such as are used on our canals. They come out of some of the small, narrow, crooked streams, connected with the canals, in which a difficult navigation is effected by poling. They are loaded with tobacco, flour, and a great variety of raw country produce. The canal boatmen of Virginia seem to be quite as rude, insolent, and riotous a class as those of New York, and every facility is evidently afforded them, at Richmond, for indulging their peculiar appetites and tastes. A great many low eating, and, I should think, drinking shops are frequented chiefly by the negroes. Dancing and other amusements are carried on in these at night.

From reading the comments of Southern statesmen and newspapers on the crime and misery which sometimes result from the accumulation of poor and ignorant people, with no intelligent masters to take care of them, in our Northern towns, one might get the impression that Southern towns—especially those not demoralized by foreign commerce—were comparatively free from a low and licentious population. From what I have seen, however, I should be now led to think that there was at least as much vice, and of what we call rowdyism, in Richmond, as in any Northern town of its size.[1]

The train was advertised to leave at 3.30 P.M. At that hour the cars were crowded with passengers, and the engineer, punctually at the minute, gave notice that he was at his post, by a long, loud whistle of the locomotive. Five minutes afterwards he gave us an impatient jerk; ten minutes afterwards we advanced three rods; twelve minutes afterwards, returned to first position: continued, "backing and filling" upon the bridge over the rapids of the James river, for half an hour. At precisely four o'clock, crossed the bridge and fairly started for Petersburg.

Ran twenty miles in exactly an hour and thirty minutes, (thirteen miles an hour; mail train, especially recommended by advertisement as "fast"). Brakes on, three times, for cattle on the track; twenty minutes spent at way-stations. Flat rail. Locomotive built at Philadelphia. I am informed that most of those used

---

[1] SAD PICTURE.—A gentleman informs the *Richmond* (Va.) *Dispatch* that, while taking a stroll on one of the islands in James river, not far from Mayo's Bridge, last Sunday morning, he counted as many as twenty-two boys, from ten to fifteen years of age, engaged in gaming with cards and dice for money. In some of the parties he saw grown men and small boys playing bluff, and cursing, swearing, and drinking.—*Southern Newspaper*.

on the road—perhaps all those of the *slow* trains—are made at Petersburg.

At one of the stoppages, smoke was to be seen issuing from the truck of a car. The conductor, on having his attention called to it, nodded his head sagely, took a morsel of tobacco, put his hands in his pocket, looked at the truck as if he would mesmerize it, spat upon it, and then stept upon the platform and shouted "All right! Go ahead!" At the next stoppage, the smoking was furious; conductor bent himself over it with an evidently strong exercise of his will, but not succeeding to tranquilize the subject at all, he suddenly relinquished the attempt, and, deserting Mesmer for Preisnitz, shouted, "Ho! boy! bring me some water here." A negro soon brought a quart of water in a tin vessel.

"Hain't got no oil, Columbus?"

"No, sir."

"Hum—go ask Mr. Smith for some: this yer's a screaking so, I durstn't go on. You Scott! get some salt. And look here, some of you boys, get me some more water. D'ye hear?"

Salt, oil, and water, were crowded into the box, and, after five minutes longer delay, we went on, the truck still smoking, and the water and oil boiling in the box, until we reached Petersburg. The heat was the result, I suppose, of a neglect of sufficient or timely oiling. While waiting, in a carriage, for the driver to get my baggage, I saw a negro oiling all the trucks of the train; as he proceeded from one to the other, he did not give himself the trouble to elevate the outlet of his oiler, so that a stream of oil, costing probably a dollar and a half a gallon, was poured out upon the ground the whole length of the train.

While on the bridge at Richmond, the car in which I was seated was over-full—several persons standing; among them, one considerably "excited," who informed the company that he was a Member of the House of Delegates, and that he would take advantage of this opportune collection of the people, to expose an atrocious attempt, on the part of the minority, to jump a Bill through the Legislature, which was not in accordance with true Democratic principles. He continued for some time to address them in most violent, absurd, profane, and meaningless language; the main point of his oration being, to demand the popular gratitude for himself, for having had the sagacity and courage to prevent the accomplishment of the nefarious design. He afterwards attempted to pass into the ladies' car, but was dissuaded from doing so by the conductor, who prevailed on a young man to give him his seat. Having taken it, he immediately lifted his feet upon the back of the seat before him, resting them upon the shoulders of its occupant. This gentleman turning his head, he begged his pardon; but, hoping it would not occasion him inconvenience, he said he would prefer to keep them there, and did so; soon afterwards falling asleep.

There were, in the train, two first-class passenger cars, and two freight cars. The latter were occupied by about forty negroes, most of them belonging to traders who were sending them to the cotton States to be sold. Such kind of evidence of activity in the slave trade of Virginia is to be seen every day; but particulars and statistics of it are not to be obtained by a stranger here. Most gentlemen of character seem to have a special disinclination to converse on the subject; and it is denied, with feeling, that slaves are often reared, as is supposed by the Abolitionists, with the intention of selling them to the traders. It appears to me evident, however, from the manner in which I hear the traffic spoken of incidentally, that the cash value of a slave for sale, above the cost of raising it from infancy to the age at which it commands the highest price, is generally considered among the surest elements of a planter's wealth. Such a nigger is worth such a price, and such another is too old to learn to pick cotton, and such another will bring so much, when it has grown a little more, I have frequently heard people say, in the street, or the public-houses. That a slave woman is commonly esteemed least for her laboring qualities, most for those qualities which give value to a broodmare is, also, constantly made apparent.[1]

By comparing the average decennial ratio of slave in-

[1] A slaveholder writing to me with regard to my cautious statements on this subject, made in the *Daily Times*, says:—
"In the States of Maryland, Virginia, North Carolina, Kentucky, Tennessee, and Missouri, as much attention is paid to the breeding and growth of negroes as to that of horses and mules. Further South, we raise them both for use and for market. Planters command their girls and women (married or unmarried) to have children; and I have known a great many

crease in all the States with the difference in the number of the actual slave-population of the slave-breeding States, as ascertained by the census, it is apparent that the number of slaves exported to the cotton States is considerably more than twenty thousand a year.

While calling on a gentleman occupying an honorable official position at Richmond, I noticed upon his table a copy of Professor Johnson's Agricultural Tour in the United States. Referring to a paragraph in it, where some statistics of the value of the slaves raised and annually exported from Virginia were given, I asked if he knew how these had been obtained, and whether they were reliable. "No," he replied; "I don't know anything about it; but if they are anything unfavorable to the institution of slavery, you may be sure they are false." This is but an illustration, in extreme, of the manner in which I find a desire to obtain more correct but *definite* information, on the subject of slavery, is usually met, by gentlemen otherwise of enlarged mind and generous qualities.

A gentleman, who was a member of the "Union Safety Committee" of New York, during the excitement which attended the discussion of the Fugitive Slave Act of 1850, told me that, as he was passing through Virginia this winter, a man entered the car in which he was seated, leading in a negro girl, whose manner and expression of face indicated dread and

negro girls to be sold off, because they did not have children. A breeding woman is worth from one-sixth to one-fourth more than one that does not breed."

grief. Thinking she was a criminal, he asked the man what she had done:

"Done? Nothing."

"What are you going to do with her?"

"I 'm taking her down to Richmond, to be sold."

"Does she belong to you?"

"No; she belongs to——; he raised her."

"Why does he sell her — has she done anything wrong?"

"Done anything? No: she 's no fault, I reckon."

"Then, what does he want to sell for?"

"Sell her for! Why should n't he sell her? He sells one or two every year; wants the money for 'em, I reckon."

The irritated tone and severe stare with which this was said, my friend took as a caution not to pursue his investigation.

A gentleman, with whom I was conversing on the subject of the cost of slave labor, in answer to an inquiry—what proportion of all the stock of slaves of an old plantation might be reckoned upon to do full work?—answered, that he owned ninety-six negroes; of these, only thirty-five were field-hands, the rest being either too young or too old for hard work. He reckoned his whole force as only equal to twenty-one strong men, or "*prime* field-hands." But this proportion was somewhat smaller than usual, he added, "because his women were uncommonly good breeders; he did not suppose there was a lot of women anywhere that bred faster than his; he never heard of babies coming so fast as they did on his plantation; it was perfectly surprising; and every one of them, in his estimation, was worth two hundred dollars, as negroes were selling now, the moment it drew breath."

I asked what he thought might be the usual proportion of workers to slaves, supported on plantations, throughout the South. On the large cotton and sugar plantations of the more Southern States, it was very high, he replied; because their hands were nearly all bought and *picked for work;* he supposed, on these, it would be about one-half; but, on any old plantation, where the stock of slaves had been an inheritance, and none had been bought or sold, he thought the working force would rarely be more than one-third, at most, of the whole number.

This gentleman was out of health, and told me, with frankness, that such was the trouble and annoyance his negroes occasioned him—although he had an overseer—and so wearisome did he find the lonely life he led on his plantation, that he could not remain upon it; and, as he knew everything would go to the dogs if he did not, he was seriously contemplating to sell out, retaining only his foster-mother and a body-servant. He thought of taking them to Louisiana and Texas, for sale; but, if he should learn that there was much probability that Lower California would be made a slave State, he supposed it would pay him to wait, as probably, if that should occur, he could take them there and sell them for twice as much as they would now bring in New Orleans. He knew very well, he said, that, as they were, raising corn and tobacco, they were paying nothing at all like a fair interest on their value.[1]

Some of his best hands he now rented out, to work in a furnace, and for the best of these he had been offered, for next year, two hundred dollars. He did not know whether he ought to let them go, though. They were worked hard, and had too much liberty, and were acquiring bad habits. They earned money, by overwork, and spent it for whiskey, and got a habit of roaming about and *taking care of themselves;* because, when they were not at work in the furnace, nobody looked out for them.

I begin to suspect that the great trouble and anxiety of Southern gentlemen is:—How, without quite destroying the capabilities of the negro for any work at all, to prevent him from learning to take care of himself.

PETERSBURG, Dec. 28.—It was early in a fine, mild, bright morning, like the pleasantest we ever have in March, that I alighted, from a train of cars, at a country station. Besides the shanty that stood for a station-house, there was a small, comfortable farm-house on the right, and a country store on the left, and around them, perhaps, fifty acres of cleared land, now much flooded with muddy water;—all environed by thick woods.

[1] Mr. Wise is reported to have stated, in his electioneering tour, when candidate for Governor, in 1855, that, if slavery were permitted in California, negroes would sell for $5,000 apiece.

A few negro children, staring as fixedly and posed as lifelessly as if they were really figures "carved in ebony," stood, lay, and lounged on the sunny side of the ranks of locomotive-firewood; a white man, smoking a cigar, looked out of the door of the store, and another, chewing tobacco, leaned against a gate-post in front of the farm-house; I advanced to the latter, and asked him if I could hire a horse in the neighborhood.

"How d'ye do, sir?" he replied; "I have some horses—none on 'em very good ones, though—rather hard riders; reckon, perhaps, they would n't suit you very well."

"Thank you; do you think I could find anything better about here?"

"Colonel Gillin, over there to the store, 's got a right nice saddle-horse, if he 'll let you take her. I 'll go over there with you, and see if he will. . . . Mornin', Colonel;—here 's a gentleman that wants to go to Thomas W.'s: could n't you let him have your saddle-horse?"

"How do you do, sir; I suppose you 'd come back to-night?"

"That 's my intention, but I might be detained till to-morrow, unless it would be inconvenient to you to spare your horse."

"Well, yes, sir, I reckon you can have her;—Tom! —Tom!—*Tom!* Now, has that devilish nigger gone again! Tom! *Oh,* Tom! saddle the filly for this gentleman.——Have you ever been to Mr. W.'s, sir?"

"No, I have not."

"It is n't a very easy place for strangers to go to from here; but I reckon I can direct you, so you 'll have no difficulty."

He accordingly began to direct me; but, the way appeared so difficult to find, I asked him to let me make a written memorandum, and, from this memorandum, I now repeat the directions he gave me.

"You take this road here—you 'll see where it 's most travelled, and it 's easy enough to keep on it for about a mile; then there 's a fork, and you take the right; pretty soon, you 'll cross a creek and turn to the right—the creek 's been up a good deal lately, and there 's some big trees fallen along there, and, if they ha'n't got them out of the way, you may have some difficulty in finding where the road is; but you keep bearing off to the right, where it 's the most open (*i. e.*, the wood), and you 'll see it again pretty soon. Then you go on, keeping along in the road—you 'll see where folks have travelled before—for maybe quarter of a mile, and you 'll find a cross-road; you must take that to the left; pretty soon you 'll pass two cabins; one of 'em 's old and all fallen in, the other one 's new, and there 's a white man lives into it: you can't mistake it. About a hundred yards beyond it, there 's a fork, and you take the left—it turns square off, and it 's fenced for a good bit; keep along by the fence, and you can't miss it. It 's right straight beyond that till you come to a school-house, there 's a gate opposite to it, and off there there 's a big house—but I don't reckon you 'll see it neither, for the woods. But somewhere, about three hundred yards beyond the school-house, you 'll find a little road running off to the left through an old field; you take that and keep along in it, and in less than half a mile you 'll find a path going square off to the right; you take that, and keep on it till you pass a little cabin in the woods; ain't nobody lives there now: then it turns to the left, and when you come to a fence and gate, you 'll see a house there, that 's Mr. George Rivers' plantation—it breaks in two, and you take the right, and when you come to the end of the fence, turn the corner—don't keep on, but turn there. Then it 's straight, till you come to the creek again—there 's a bridge there; don't go over the bridge, but turn to the left and keep along nigh the creek, and pretty soon you 'll see a meeting-house in the woods; you go to that, and you 'll see a path bearing off to the right—it looks as if it was going right away from the creek, but you take it, and pretty soon it 'll bring you to a saw-mill on the creek, up higher a piece; you just cross the creek there, and you 'll find some people at the mill, and they 'll put you right straight on the road to Mr. W.'s."

"How far is it all, sir?"

"I reckon it 's about two hours' ride, when the roads are good, to the saw-mill. Mr. W.'s gate is only a mile or so beyond that, and then you 've got another mile, or better, after you get to the gate, but you 'll see some nigger-quarters—the niggers belong to Mr. W., and I reckon ther 'll be some of 'em round, and they 'll show you just where to go."

After reading over my memorandum, and finding it correct, and agreeing with him that I should pay two dollars a day for the mare, we walked out, and found her saddled and waiting for me.

I remarked that she was very good-looking.

"Yes, sir; she a'n't a bad filly; out of a mare that came of Lady Rackett by old Lord-knows-who, the best horse we ever had in this part of the country: I expect you have heard of him. Oh! she's maybe a little playful, but you'll find her a pleasant riding-horse."

The filly was just so pleasantly playful, and full of well-bred life, as to create a joyful, healthy, sympathetic, frolicsome heedlessness in her rider—walking rapidly, and with a sometimes irresistible inclination to dance and bound; making believe she was frightened at all the burnt stumps, and flashes of sun-light on the ice, and, every time a hog lifted himself up before her, starting back in the most ridiculous manner, as if she had never seen a hog before; bounding over the fallen trees as easily as a life-boat over a billow; and all the time gracefully playing tricks with her feet, and her ears, and her tail, and evidently enjoying herself just like any child in a half-holiday ramble through the woods, yet never failing to answer to every motion of my hand or my knees, as if she were a part of myself. In fact, there soon came to be a real good understanding, if not even something like a merging of identity, between Jane and me (the filly's name was Jane Gillin); if *her* feet were not in the stirrups, I am sure I had all the sensation of tripping it on the ground with mine, half the time, and we both entered into each other's feelings, and moved, and were moved, together, in a way which a two hours' lecture, by a professor of psychology, would be insufficient, satisfactorily, to explain to people who never—but all that's of no consequence, except that, of course, we soon lost our way.

We were walking along slowly, quietly, musingly—I was fondling her with my hand under her mane, when it suddenly came into my mind: "Why Jane! it's a long time since I 've thought anything about the road—I wonder where we 've got to." We stopped and tried to work up our dead-reckoning.

First, we picked our way from the store down to the brook, through a deeply corrugated clay-road; then there was the swamp, with the fallen trees and thick underwood, beaten down and barked in the miry parts by wagons, making a road for themselves, no traces of which could we find in the harder, pebbly ground. At length when we came on to drier land, and among pine trees, we discovered a clear way cut through them, and a distinct road before us again; and this brought us soon to an old clearing, just beginning to be grown over with pines, in which was the old cabin of rotten logs, one or two of them falling out of rank on the door-side, and the whole concern having a dangerous lurch to one corner, as if too much whiskey had been drank in it: then a more recent clearing, with a fenced field and another cabin, the residence of that white man we were told of probably. No white people, however, were to be seen, but two negroes sat in the mouth of a wigwam, husking maize, and a couple of hungry hounds came bounding over the zig-zag, gateless fence, as if they had agreed with each other that they would wait no longer for the return of their master, but would straightway pull down the first traveller that passed, and have something to eat before they were quite famished. They stopped short, however, when they had got within a good cart-whip's length of us, and contented themselves with dolefully *youping* as long as we continued in sight. We turned the corner, following some slight traces of a road, and shortly afterwards met a curious vehicular establishment, probably belonging to the master of the hounds. It consisted of an axle-tree and wheels, and a pair of shafts made of unbarked saplings, in which was harnessed, by attachments of raw-hide and rope, a single small black ox. There was a bit, made of telegraph-wire, in his mouth, by which he was guided, through the mediation of a pair of much knotted rope-reins, by a white man—a dignified sovereign, wearing a brimless crown—who sat upon a two-bushel sack, (of meal, I trust, for the hounds' sake,) balanced upon the axle-tree, and who saluted me with a frank "How are you?" as we came opposite each other.

Soon after this, we reached a small grove of much older and larger pines than we had seen before, with long and horizontally stretching branches, and duller and thinner foliage. In the middle of it was another log-cabin, with a door in one of the gable-ends, a stove-pipe, half-rusted away, protruding from the other, and, in the middle of one of the sides, a small square port-hole, closed by a wooden shutter. This must have been the school-house, but there were no children then about it, and no appearance of there having been any lately. Near it was a long string of fence and a gate and lane, which gave entrance, probably, to a large plantation, though there was no cultivated land within sight of the road.

I could remember hardly anything after this, except a continuation of pine trees, big, little, and medium in size, and hogs, and a black, crooked, burnt sapling, that we had made believe was a snake springing at us and had jumped away from, and then we had gone on at a trot—it must have been some time ago, that—and then I was paying attentions to Jane, and finally my thoughts had gone wool-gathering, and we must have travelled some miles out of our way and—"never mind," said Jane, lifting her head, and turning in the direction we had been going, "I don't think it's any great matter if we are lost; such a fine day—so long since I've been out; if you don't care, I'd just as lief be lost as not; let's go on and see what we shall come to."

"Very well, my dear, you know the country better than I do; go where you like; if you'll risk your dinner, I'm quite ready to go anywhere in your company. It's quite certain we have not passed any meeting-house, or creek, or saw-mill, or negro-quarters, and, as we have been two hours on the road, it's evident we are not going straight to Mr. W.'s; I'll try at least to take note of what we *do pass after this,*" and I stood up in the stirrups as we walked on, to see what the country around us was.

"Old fields"—a coarse, yellow, sandy soil, bearing scarce anything but pine trees and broom-sedge. In some places, for acres, the pines would not be above five feet high—that was land that had been in cultivation, used up and "turned out," not more than six or eight years before; then there were patches of every age; sometimes the trees were a hundred feet high. At long intervals, there were fields in which the pine was just beginning to spring in beautiful green plumes from the ground, and was yet hardly noticeable among the dead brown grass and sassafras bushes and blackberry-vines, which nature first sends to hide the nakedness of the impoverished earth.

Of living creatures, for miles, not one was to be seen (not even a crow or a snow-bird), except hogs. These —long, lank, bony, snake-headed, hairy, wild beasts— would come dashing across our path, in packs of from three to a dozen, with short, hasty grunts, almost always at a gallop, and looking neither to right nor left, as if they were in pursuit of a fox, and were quite certain to catch him in the next hundred yards; or droves of little pigs would rise up suddenly in the sedge, and scamper off squealing into cover, while their heroic mothers would turn around and make a stand, looking fiercely at us, as if they were quite ready to fight if we advanced any further, but always breaking, as we came near, with a loud *boosch!*

Once I saw a house, across a large, new old-field, but it was far off, and there was no distinct path leading towards it out of the wagon-track we were following; so we did not go to it, but continued walking steadily on through the old-fields and pine woods for more than an hour longer.

We then arrived at a grove of tall oak trees, in the midst of which ran a brook, giving motion to a small grist-mill. Back of the mill were two log cabins, and near these a number of negroes, in holiday clothes, were standing in groups among the trees. When we stopped one of them came towards us. He wore a battered old hat, of the cylindrical fashion, stiffly starched shirt-collar, cutting his ears, a red cravat, and an old black dress coat, thread-bare and a little ragged, but adorned with new brass buttons. He knew Mr. Thomas W., certainly he did; and he reckoned I had come about four miles (he did not know but it might be eight, if I thought so) off the road I had been directed to follow. But that was of no consequence, because he could show me where to go by a straight road —a cross cut—from here, that would make it just as quick for me as if I had gone the way I had intended.

"How far is it from here?" I asked.

"Oh, 'taint far, sar."

"How far do you think?"

"Well, massa, I spec—I spec—(looking at my horse) I spec massa, ef you goes de way, sar, dat I shows you, sar, I reckon it 'll take you—"

"How far is it—how many miles?"

"How many miles, sar? ha! masser, I don 'zactly reckon I ken tell ou—not 'cisely, sar—how many miles it is, not 'zactly, 'cisely, sar."

"How is that—you don't what?"

"I don't 'zactly reckon I can give you de drection excise about de miles, sar."

"Oh! but how many miles do you think it is; is it two miles?"

"Yes, sar; as de roads is now, I tink it is just about two miles. Dey's long ones, dough, I reckon."

"Long ones? you think it's more than two miles, don't you, then?"

"Yes, sar, I reckon its four or five miles."

"Four or five! four or five long ones or short ones do you mean?"

"I don 'zactly know, sar, wedder dey is short ones or long ones, sar, but I reckon you find em middlin' long; I spec you 'll be about two hours 'fore you be done gone all de way to mass W.'s."

He walked on with us a few rods upon a narrow path, until we came to a crossing of the stream; pointing to where it continued on the other side, he assured me that it went right straight to Mr. W.'s plantation. "You juss keep de straight road, master," he repeated several times, "and it 'll take you right dar, sar."

He had been grinning and bowing, and constantly touching his hat, or holding it in his hand during our conversation, which I understood to mean, that he would thank me for a dime. I gave it to him, upon which he repeated his contortions and his form of direction—"keep de straight road." I rode through the brook, and he called out again—"you keep dat road right straight and it 'll take you right straight dar." I rode up the bank and entered the oak wood, and still again heard him enjoining me to "keep dat road right straight."

Within less than quarter of a mile, there was a fork in the road to the left, which seemed a good deal more travelled than the straight one; nevertheless I kept the latter, and was soon well satisfied that I had done so. It presently led me up a slope out of the oak woods into a dark evergreen forest; and though it was a mere bridle-path, it must have existed, I thought, before the trees began to grow, for it was free of stumps, and smooth and clean as a garden walk, and the pines grew thickly up, about four feet apart, on each side of it, their branches meeting, just clear of my head, and making a dense shade. There was an agreeable, slightly balsamic odor in the air; the path was covered with a deep, elastic mat of pine leaves, so that our footstep could hardly be heard; and for a time we greatly enjoyed going along at a lazy, pacing walk of Jane's. It was noon-day, and had been rather warmer than was quite agreeable on the open road, and I took my hat off, and let the living pine leaves brush my hair. But, after a while, I felt slightly chilly; and when Jane, at the same time, gave a little sympathizing caper, I bent my head down, that the limbs might not hit me, until it nearly rested on her neck, dropped my hands and pressed my knees tightly against her. Away we bounded!

What a glorious gallop Jane had inherited from her noble grandfather!

Out of the cool, dark-green alley, at last, and soon with a more cautious step, down a steep, stony declivity, set with deciduous trees—beech, ash, oak, gum—"gum," beloved of the "minstrels." A brawling shallow brook at the bottom, into which our path descended, though on the opposite shore was a steep high bank, faced by an impenetrable brake of bush and briar.

Have we been following a path only leading to a watering-place, then? I see no continuance of it. Jane does not hesitate at all; but, as if it was the commonest thing here to take advantage of nature's engineering in this way, walking into the water, turns her head up stream.

For more than a mile we continued following up the brook, which was all the time walled in by insurmountable banks, overhung by large trees. Sometimes it swept strongly through a deep channel, contracted by boulders; sometimes purled and tinkled over a pebbly slope; and sometimes stood in broad, silent pools, around the edges of which remained a skirt of ice, held there by bushes and long, broken water-grasses. Across the end of one of these, barring our way, a dead trunk had lately fallen. Jane walked up to it and turned her head to the right. "No," said I, "let's go over." She turned, and made a step left—"No!

over," said I, drawing her back, and touching her with my heels.

Over we went, landing with such a concussion that I was nearly thrown off. I fell forward upon Jane's neck; she threw up her head, spurning my involuntary embrace; and then, with swollen nostrils and flashing eyes, walked on rapidly.

"Hope you are satisfied," said she, as I pulled my coat down; "if not, you had better spur me again."

"Why, my dear girl, what's the matter? It was nothing but leather—calf-skin—that I touched you with. I have no spurs—don't you see?" for she was turning her head to bite my foot. "Now, don't be foolish."

"Well, well," said she, "I'm a good-tempered girl, if I am blood; let's stop and drink."

After this, we soon came to pine woods again. Jane was now for leaving the brook. I let her have her own way, and she soon found a beaten track in the woods. It certainly was not the "straight road" we had been directed to follow; but its course was less crooked than that of the brook, and after some time it led us out into a more open country, with young pines and inclosed fields. Eventually we came to a gate and lane, which we followed till we came to another cross-lane, leading straight to a farm-house.

As soon as we turned into the cross-lane, half-a-dozen little negro boys and girls were seen running towards the house, to give alarm. We passed a stable, with a cattle-pen by its side, opposite which was a vegetable garden, enclosed with split palings; then across a running stream of water; then by a small cabin on the right; and a corn-crib and large pen, with a number of fatting hogs in it, on the left; then into a large, irregular yard, in the midst of which was the farm-house, before which were now collected three white children, six black ones, two negro women, and an old lady with spectacles.

"How dy do, sir?" said the old lady, as we reined up, bowed, and lifted our hat, and put our black foot foremost.

"Thank you, madam, quite well; but I have lost my way to Mr. Thomas W.'s, and will trouble you to tell me how to go from here to get to his house."

By this time a black man came cautiously walking in from the field back of the house, bringing an axe; a woman, who had been washing clothes in the brook, left her work and came up on the other side, and two more girls climbed up on to a heap of logs that had been thrown upon the ground, near the porch, for fuel. The swine were making a great noise in their pen, as if feeding-time had come; and a flock of turkeys were gobbling so incessantly and loudly that I was not heard. The old lady ordered the turkeys to be driven away, but nobody stirred to do it, and I rode nearer and repeated my request. No better success. "Can't you shew away them turkeys?" she asked again; but nobody "shewed." A third time I endeavored to make myself understood. "Will you please direct me how to go to Mr. W.'s."

"No, sir—not here."

"Excuse me—I asked if you would direct me to Mr. W.'s."

"If some of you niggers don't shew them turkeys, I'll have you all whipped as soon as your mass John comes home," exclaimed the old lady, now quite excited. The man with the axe, without moving towards them at all, picked up a billet of wood and threw it at the biggest cock-turkey, who immediately collapsed; and the whole flock scattered, chased by the two girls who had been on the log-heap.

"An't dat Colonel Gillin's mare, master?" asked the black man, coming up on my left.

"You want to go to Thomas W.'s?" asked the old lady.

"Yes, madam."

"It's a good many years since I have been to Thomas W.'s, and I reckon I can't tell you how to go there now."

"If master'll go over to Missy Abler's, I reckon dey ken tell 'em dah, sar."

"And how shall I go to Mrs. Abler's?"

"You want to go to Missy Abler's; you take dat path right over 'yond dem bars, dar, by de hog-pen, dat runs along by dat fence into de woods, and dat'll take you right straight dar."

"Is you come from Colonel Gillin's, massa?" asked the washwoman.

"Yes."

"Did you see a black man dar, dey calls Tom, sar?"

"Yes."

"Tom's my husband, massa; if you's gwine back dah, wish you'd tell um, ef you please, sar, dat I wants to see him *particklar;* will ou, massa?"

"Yes."

"Tank you, massa."

I bowed to the old lady, and, in turning to ride off, saw two other negro boys who had come out of the woods, and were now leaning over the fence, and staring at us, as if I was a giant and Jane was a dragoness.

We trotted away, found the path, and in course of a mile had our choice of at least twenty forks to go "straight to Mrs. Abler's." At length, cleared land again, fences, stubble-fields, and a lane, that took us to a little cabin, which fronted, much to my surprise, upon a broad and well-travelled road. Over the door of the cabin was a sign, done in black, upon a hogshead stave, showing that it was a "GROSERY," which, in Virginia, means the same thing as in Ireland—a dram-shop.

I hung the bridle over a rack before the door, and walked in. At one end of the interior was a range of shelves, on which were two decanters, some dirty tumblers, a box of crackers, a canister, and several packages in paper; under the shelves were a table and a barrel. At the other end of the room was a fireplace; near this, a chest, and another range of shelves, on which stood plates and cooking utensils: between these and the grocery end were a bed and a spinning-wheel. Near the spinning-wheel sat a tall, bony, sickly, sullen young woman, nursing a languishing infant.

The faculty would not have discouraged either of them from trying hydropathic practice. In a corner of the fire-place sat a man, smoking a pipe. He rose, as I entered, walked across to the grocery-shelves, turned a chair round at the table, and asked me to take a seat. I excused myself, and requested him to direct me to Mr. W.'s. He had heard of such a man living somewhere about there, but he did not know where. He repeated this, with an oath, when I declined to "take" anything, and added, that he had not lived here long, and he was sorry he had ever come here. It was the worst job, for himself, ever he did, when he came here, though all he wanted was to just get a living.

I rode on till I came to another house, a very pleasant little house, with a steep, gabled roof, curving at the bottom, and extending over a little gallery, which was entered, by steps, from the road; back of it were stables and negro-cabins, and by its side was a small garden, and beyond that a peach-orchard. As I approached it, a well-dressed young man, with an intelligent and pleasant face, came out into the gallery. I asked him if he could direct me to Mr. W.'s. "Thomas W.'s?" he inquired.

"Yes, sir."

"You are not going in the right direction to go to Mr. W.'s. The shortest way you can take to go there is, to go right back to the Court House."

I told him I had just come out of the lane by the grocery on to the road. "Ah! well, I'll tell you; you had better turn round, and keep right straight upon this road till you get to the Court House, and anybody can tell you, there, how to go."

"How far is it, sir?"

"To the Court House?—not above a mile."

"And to Mr. W.'s?"

"To Mr. W.'s, I should think it was as much as ten miles, and long ones, too."

I rode to the Court House, which was a plain brick building in the centre of a small square, around which there were twenty or thirty houses, two of them being occupied as stores, one as a saddler's shop, one had the sign of "Law Office" upon it, two were occupied by physicians, one other looked as if it might be a meeting-house or school-house, or the shop of any mechanic needing much light for his work, and two were "Hotels." At one of these we stopped, to dine; Jane had "corn and fodder" (they had no oats or hay in the stable), and I had ham and eggs (they had no fresh meat in the house). I had several other things, however, that were very good, besides the company of the landlady, who sat alone with me, at the table, in a long, dining hall, and was very pretty, amiable, and talkative.

In a course of apologies, which came in the place of soup, she gave me the clue to the assemblage of negroes I had seen at the mill. It was Christmas week; all the servants thought they must go for at least, one day, to have a frolic, and to-day (as luck would have it, when I was coming,) her cook was off with some others; she did not suppose they 'd be back till to-morrow, and then, likely as not, they 'd be drunk. She did not think this custom, of letting servants go so, at Christmas, was a good one; niggers were not fit to be let to take care of themselves, anyhow. It was very bad for them, and she did n't think it was *right*. Providence had put the servants into our hands to be looked out for, and she did n't believe it was intended they should be let to do all sorts of wickedness, if Christmas did n't come but once a year. She wished, for her part, it did not come but once in ten years.

(The negroes, that were husking maize near the cabin where the White-man lived, were, no doubt, slaves, who had hired themselves out by the day, during the holiday-week, to earn a little money on their own account.)

In regard to the size of the dining hall, and the extent of sheds in the stable-yard, the landlady told me that though at other times they very often did not have a single guest in a day, at "Court time" they always had more than they could comfortably accommodate. I judged, also, from her manners, and the general appearance of the house, as well as from the charges, that, at such times, the company was of a rather respectable character. The appearance of the other public-house indicated that it expected a less select patronage.

When I left, my direction was to keep on the main road until I came to a fork, about four miles distant, then take the left, and keep *the best travelled road*, until I came to a certain house, which was so described that

I should know it, whère I was advised to ask further directions.

The sky was now clouding over; it was growing cold; and we went on, as fast as we conveniently could, until we reached the fork in the road. The direction, to keep the best travelled road, was unpleasantly prominent in my mind; it was near sunset, I reflected, and, however jolly it might be at twelve o'clock at noon, it would be quite another thing to be knocking about among those fierce hogs in the pine-forest, if I should be lost, at twelve o'clock at night. Besides, as the landlady said about her negroes, I did not think it was *right* to expose Jane to this danger, unnecessarily. A little beyond the fork, there was a large, gray, old house, with a grove of tall poplars before it; a respectable, country-gentleman-of-the-old-school look it had.—These old Virginians are proverbially hospitable.—It's rather impudent; but I hate to go back to the Court House, and I am——I will ride on, and look it in the face, at any rate.

Zig-zag fences up to a large, square yard, growing full of Lombardy poplar sprouts, from the roots of eight or ten old trees, which were planted some fifty years ago, I suppose, in a double row, on two sides of the house. At the further end of this yard, beyond the house, a gate opened on the road, and out of this was just then coming a black man.

I inquired of him if there was a house, near by, at which I could get accommodations for the night. Reckoned his master 'd take me in, if I 'd ask him.

Where was his master? In the house: I could go right in here (at a place where a panel of the paling had fallen over) and see him, if I wanted to. I asked him to hold my horse, and went in.

It was a simple, two-story house, very much like those built by the wealthier class of people in New England villages, from fifty to a hundred years ago, except that the chimneys were carried up outside the walls. There was a porch at the front door, and a small wing at one end, in the rear; from this wing to the other end extended a broad gallery.

A dog had been barking at me after I dismounted; and just as I reached the steps of the gallery, a vigorous, middle-aged man, with a rather sullen and suspicious expression of face, came out without any coat on, to see what had excited him.

Doubting whether he was the master of the house, I told him that I had come in to inquire if it would be convenient to allow me to spend the night with them. He asked where I came from, where I was going to, and various other questions, until I had given him an epitome of my day's wanderings and adventures; at the conclusion of which he walked to the end of the gallery to look at my horse; then, without giving me any answer, but muttering indistinctly something about servants, walked into the house, shutting the door behind him!

Well, thought I, this is not very overwhelmingly hospitable. What can it mean?

While I was considering whether he expected me to

go without any further talk — his curiosity being, I judged, satisfied — he came out again, and said, "Reckon you can stay, sir, if you'll take what we'll give you." (The good man had been in to consult his wife.) I replied that I would do so, thankfully, and hoped they would not give themselves any unnecessary trouble, or alter their usual family arrangements. I was then invited to come in, but I preferred to see my horse taken care of first. My host called for "Sam," two or three times, and then said he reckoned all his "people" had gone off, and he would attend to my horse himself. I offered to assist him, and we walked out to the gate, where the negro, not being inclined to wait for my return, had left Jane fastened to a post. Our host conducted us to an old square log-cabin, which had formerly been used for curing tobacco, there being no room for Jane, he said, in the stables proper.

The floor of the tobacco-house was covered with lumber, old ploughs, scythes and cradles, a part of which had to be removed to make room for the filly to stand. She was then induced, with some difficulty, to enter it through a low, square door-way; saddle and bridle were removed, and she was fastened in a corner by a piece of old plough-line. We then went to a fodder-stack, and pulled out from it several small bundles of maize leaves. Additional feed and water were promised when "some of the niggers" came in; and, after righting up an old door that had fallen from one hinge, and setting a rail against it to keep it in its place, we returned to the house.

My host (whom I will call Mr. Newman) observed that his buildings and fences were a good deal out of order. He had owned the place but a few years, and had not had time to make much improvement about the house yet.

Entering the mansion, he took me to a large room on the first floor, gave me a chair, went out and soon returned (now wearing a coat) with two negro girls, one bringing wood and the other some flaming brands. A fire was made with a great deal of trouble, scolding of the girls, bringing in more brands, and blowing with the mouth. When the room had been suffocatingly filled with smoke, and at length a strong bright blaze swept steadily up the chimney, Mr. Newman again went out with the girls, and I was left alone for nearly an hour, with one interruption, when he came in and threw some more wood upon the fire, and said he hoped I would make myself comfortable.

It was a square room, with a door from the hall on one side, and two windows on each of the other sides. The lower part of the walls was wainscoted, and the upper part, with the ceiling, plastered and whitewashed. The fire-place and mantle-piece were somewhat carved, and were painted black; all the other wood-work, lead color. Blue paper curtains covered the windows; the floor was uncarpeted, and the only furniture in the room was some strong plain chairs, painted yellow, and a Connecticut clock, which did not run. The house had evidently been built for a family of some wealth, and, after having been deserted by them, had been bought at a bargain by the present resident, who either had not the capital or the inclination to furnish and occupy it appropriately.

When my entertainer called again, he merely opened the door and said, in the words of an order, but in a tone of advice, "Come! get something to eat!" I followed him out into the gallery, and thence through a door at its end into a room in the wing—a family room, and a very comfortable, homely room. A most bountifully spread supper-table stood in the centre, at which was sitting a very neat, pretty little woman, of as silent habits as her husband, but neither bashful nor morose. A very nice little girl sat at her right side, and a peevish, ill-behaved, whining glutton of a boy at her left. I was requested to be seated adjoining the little girl, and the master of the house sat opposite me. The fourth side of the table was unoccupied, though a plate and chair were placed there, as if some one else had been expected.

The two negro girls waited at table, and a negro boy was in the room, who, when I asked for a glass of water, was sent to get it. An old negro woman also frequently came in from the kitchen, with hot biscuit and corn-cake. There was fried fowl, and fried bacon and eggs, and cold ham; there were preserved peaches, and preserved quinces and grapes; there was hot wheaten biscuit, and hot short-cake, and hot corn-cake, and hot griddle cakes, soaked in butter; there was coffee, and there was milk, sour or sweet, whichever I preferred to drink. I really ate more than I wanted, and extolled the corn-cake and the peach preserve, and asked how they were made; but I evidently disappointed my pretty hostess, who said she was afraid there was n't anything that suited me,—she feared there was n't anything on the table I could eat; and she was sorry I could n't make out a supper. And this was about all she would say. I tried to get a free conversation started, but I have myself but poor endowments for such a purpose, and I could obtain little more than very laconic answers to my questions.

Except from the little girl at my side, whose confidence I gained by taking an opportunity, when her mother was engaged, with young hopeful t'other side the coffee-pot, to give her a great lot of quince and grape, and by several times pouring molasses very freely on her cakes and bacon; and finally by feeding Pink out of my hand. (Hopeful had done this first, and then kicked him away, when he came round to Martha and me.) She told me her name, and that she had got a kitten, and that she hated Pink; and that she went to a Sunday-school at the Court House, and that she was going to go to an every-day school next winter—she was n't big enough to walk so far now, but she would be then. But Billy said he did n't mean to go, because he did n't like to, though Billy was bigger nor she was, a heap. She reckoned when Billy saw Wash. Baker going past every day, and heard how much fun he had every day with the other boys at the school, he would want to go too, would n't he? etc., etc. When supper was ended, I set back my chair to the wall, and took her on my knee; but after she had been told twice not to trouble the gentleman, and I had testified that she did n't do it, and after several mild hints that I would perhaps find it pleasanter in the sitting-room—(the chairs in the supper-room were the easiest, being country-made, low, and seated with undressed calf-skin), she was called to, out of the kitchen, and Mr. Newman, in the form of advice, but with the tone of command, said—going to the door and opening it for me—"Reckon you 'd better walk into the sittin'-room, sir."

I walked out at this, and said I would go and look at the filly. Mr. Newman called "Sam" again, and Sam, having at that moment arrived at the kitchen-door, was ordered to go and take care of this gentleman's horse. I followed Sam to the tobacco-house, and gave him to know that he would be properly remembered for any attentions he could give to Jane. He watered her, and brought her a large supply of oats in straw, and some maize on the cob; but he could get no litter, and declared there was no straw on the plantation, though the next morning I saw a large quantity in a heap (not a stack), at a little greater distance than he was willing to go for it, I suppose, at a barn on the opposite side of the road. Having seen her rubbed clean and apparently well contented with her quarters and her supper, I bade her good-night, and returned to the house.

I did not venture again into the supper-room, but went to the sitting-room, where I found Miss Martha

Ann and her kitten; I was having a very good time with her, when her father came in and told her she was "troubling the gentleman;" I denied it, and he took a seat by the fire with us, and I soon succeeded in drawing him into a conversation on farming, and the differences in our methods of work at the North and those he was accustomed to.

I learned that there were no white laboring men here who hired themselves out by the month. The poor white people that had to labor for their living, never would work steadily at any employment. "They mostly followed boating"—hiring as hands on the bateaus that navigate the small streams and canals, but never for a longer term at once than a single trip of a boat, whether that might be long or short. At the end of the trip they were paid by the day. Their wages were from fifty cents to a dollar, varying with the demand and individual capacities. They hardly ever worked on farms except in harvest, when they usually received a dollar a day, sometimes more. In harvest-time, most of the rural mechanics closed their shops and hired out to the farmers at a dollar a day, which would indicate that their ordinary earnings are considerably less than this. At other than harvest-time, the poor white people, who had no trade, would sometimes work for the farmers by the job; not often at any regular agricultural labor, but at getting rails or shingles, or clearing land.

He did not know that they were particular about working with negroes, but no white man would ever do certain kinds of work (such as taking care of cattle, or getting water or wood to be used in the house), and if you should ask a white man you had hired, to do such things, he would get mad and tell you he was n't a nigger. Poor white girls never hired out to do servants' work, but they would come and help another white woman about her sewing or quilting, and take wages for it. But these girls were not very respectable generally, and it was not agreeable to have them in your house, though there were some very respectable ladies that would go out to sew. Farmers depended almost entirely upon their negroes; it was only when they were hard pushed by their crops, that they got white hands to help them any.

Negroes had commanded such high wages lately, to work on railroads and in tobacco-factories, that farmers were tempted to hire out too many of their people, and to undertake to do too much work with those they retained, and thus they were often driven to employ white men, and to give them very high wages by the day, when they found themselves getting much behindhand with their crops. He had been driven very hard in this way this last season; he had been so unfortunate as to lose one of his best women, who died in child-bed just before harvest. The loss of the woman and her child, for the child had died also, just at that time, came very hard upon him. He would not have taken a thousand dollars of any man's money for them. He had had to hire white men to help him, but they were very poor sticks and would be half the time drunk, and you never know what to depend upon with them. One fellow that he had hired, who had agreed to work for him all through harvest, got him to pay him some wages in advance, (he said it was to buy him some clothes with, so he could go to meeting, Sunday, at the Court-House,) and went off the next day, right in the middle of harvest, and he never had seen him since. He had heard of him—he was on a boat—but he did n't reckon he should ever get his money again.

Of course, he did not see how white laborers were ever going to come into competition with negroes here, at all. You never could depend on white men, and you could n't *drive* them any; they would n't stand it. Slaves were the only reliable laborers—you could command them and *make* them do what was right.

From the manner in which he always talked of the white laboring people, it was evident that, although he placed them in some sort on an equality with himself, and that in his intercourse with them he would n't think of asserting for himself any superior dignity, or even feel himself to be patronizing them in not doing so, yet he, all the time, recognized them as a distinct and a rather despicable class, and wanted to have as little to do with them as he conveniently could.

I have been once or twice told that the poor white people, meaning those, I suppose, who bring nothing to market to exchange for money but their labor, although they may own a cabin and a little furniture, and cultivate land enough to supply themselves with (maize) bread, are worse off in almost all respects than the slaves. They are said to be extremely ignorant and immoral, as well as indolent and unambitious. That their condition is not as unfortunate by any means as that of negroes, however, is most obvious, since from among them, men *sometimes* elevate themselves to positions and habits of usefulness, and respectability. They are said to "corrupt" the negroes, and to encourage them to steal, or to work for them at night and on Sundays, and to pay them with liquor, and also to constantly associate licentiously with them. They seem, nevertheless, more than any other portion of the community, to hate and despise the negroes.

In the midst of our conversation, one of the black girls had come into the room and stood still with her head dropped forward, staring at me from under her brows, without saying a word. When she had waited, in this way, perhaps two minutes, her master turned to her and asked what she wanted.

"Miss Matty says Marta Ann go to bed now."

But Martha Ann refused to budge; after being told once or twice by her father to go with Rose, she came to me and lifted up her hands, I supposed to kiss me and go, but when I reached down, she took hold of my shoulders and climbed up on to my knees. Her father seemed to take no notice of this proceeding, but continued talking about guano; Rose went to a corner of the fire-place, dropped down upon the floor and presently was asleep, leaning her head against the wall. In about half an hour, the other negro girl came to the door, when Mr. Newman abruptly called out, "girl! take that child to bed!" and immediately got up himself and walked out. Rose roused herself and lifted Martha Ann out of my arms, and carried her off fast asleep. Mr. Newman returned holding a small candle in his hand, and, without entering the room, stood at the door and said, "I'll show you your bed if you are ready, sir." As he evidently meant, "I am ready to show you to bed if you will not refuse to go," I followed him up stairs.

Into a large room, again, with six windows, with a fire-place, in which a few brands were smoking, with some wool spread thinly upon the floor in a corner; with a dozen small bundles of tobacco leaves; with a lady's saddle; with a deep feather-bed, covered with a bright patch-work quilt, on a maple bedstead, and without a single item of any other furniture whatever. Mr. Newman asked if I wanted the candle to undress by, I said yes, if he pleased, and waited a moment for him to set it down: as he did not do so I walked towards him, lifting my hand to take it. "No—I'll hold it," said he, and I then perceived that he had no candle-stick, but held the lean little dip in his hand: I remembered also that no candle had been brought into the "sitting-room," and that while we were at supper only one candle had stood upon the table, which had been immediately extinguished when we rose, the room being lighted only from the fire.

I very quickly undressed and hung my clothes upon a bed-post: Mr. Newman looked on in silence until I had got into bed, when, with an abrupt "good-night, sir," he went out and shut the door.

It was not until after I had consulted Sam the next morning, that I ventured to consider that my entertainment might be taken as a mere business transaction, and not as "genuine planter's hospitality," though this had become rather a ridiculous view of it, after a repetition of the supper, in all respects, had been eaten for breakfast, with equal moroseness on the part of my host and equal quietness on the part of his kind-looking little wife. I was, nevertheless, amused at the promptness with which he replied to my rather hesitating inquiry—what I might pay him for the trouble I had given him—"I reckon a dollar and a quarter will be right, sir."

I have described, perhaps with tedious prolixity, what adventures befell me, and what scenes I passed through in my first day's random riding, for the purpose of giving an idea of the uncultivated and unimproved—rather, sadly worn and misused—condition of some parts, and I judge, of a very large part, of all Eastern Virginia, and of the isolated, lonely, and dissociable aspect of the dwelling places of a large part of the people.

Much the same general characteristics pervade the Slave States, everywhere, except in certain rich regions, or on the banks of some rivers, or in the vicinity of some great routes of travel and transportation, which have occasioned closer settlement or stimulated public spirit. For hours and hours one has to ride through the unlimited, continual, all-shadowing, all-embracing forest, following roads, in the making of which no more labor has been given than was necessary to remove the timber which would obstruct the passage of wagons; and even for days and days he may sometimes travel, and see never two dwellings of mankind within sight of each other; only, at long distances, often several miles asunder, these isolated plantation patriarchates. If a traveller leaves the main road to go any distance, it is not to be imagined how difficult it is for him to find his way from one house to any other in particular; his only safety is in the fact that, unless there are mountains or swamps in the way, he is not likely to go many miles upon any wagon or horse track without coming to some white man's habitation.

The country passed through, in the early part of my second day's ride, was very similar in general characteristics to that I have already described; only that a rather larger portion of it was cleared, and plantations were more frequent. About eleven o'clock I crossed a bridge and came to the meeting-house I had been expecting to reach by that hour the previous day. It was in the midst of the woods, and the small clearing around it was still dotted with the stumps of the trees out of whose trunks it had been built; for it was a log structure. In one end there was a single square port, closed by a sliding shutter, in the other end were two doors, both standing open. In front of the doors, a rude scaffolding had been made of poles and saplings, extending out twenty feet from the wall of the house, and this had been covered with boughs of trees, the leaves now withered; a few benches, made of split trunks of trees, slightly hewn with the axe, were arranged under this arbor, as if the religious service was sometimes conducted on the outside in preference to the interior of the edifice. Looking in, I saw that a gallery or loft extended from over the doors, across about one-third the length of the house, access to which was had by a ladder. At the opposite end was a square, unpainted pulpit, and on the floor were rows of rude benches. The house was sufficiently lighted by crevices between the upper logs.

Half an hour after this I arrived at the negro-quarters—a little hamlet of ten or twelve small and dilapidated cabins. Just beyond them was a plain farm-gate, at which several negroes were standing; one of them, a well-made man, with an intelligent countenance and prompt manner, directed me how to find my way to his owner's house. It was still nearly a mile distant; and yet, until I arrived in its immediate vicinity, I saw no cultivated field, and but one clearing. In the edge of this clearing, a number of negroes, male and female, lay stretched out upon the ground near a small smoking charcoal pit. Their master afterwards informed me that they were burning charcoal for the plantation blacksmith, using the time allowed them for holidays—from Christmas to New Year's—to earn a little money for themselves in this way. He paid them by the bushel for it. When I said that I supposed he allowed them to take what wood they chose for this purpose, he replied that he had five hundred acres covered with wood, which he would be very glad to have any one burn, or clear off in any way. Cannot some Yankee contrive a method of concentrating some of the valuable properties of this old-field pine, so that they may be profitably brought into use in more cultivated regions? Charcoal is now brought to New York from Virginia; but when made from pine it is not very valuable, and will only bear transportation from the banks of the navigable rivers, whence it can be shipped, at one movement, to New York. Turpentine does not flow in sufficient quantity from this variety of the pine to be profitably collected, and for lumber it is of very small value.

Mr. W.'s house was an old family mansion, which he had himself remodeled in the Grecian style, and furnished with a large wooden portico. An oak forest had originally occupied the ground where it stood; but this having been cleared and the soil worn out in cultivation by the previous proprietors, pine woods now surrounded it in every direction, a square of a few acres only being kept clear immediately about it. A number of the old oaks still stood in the rear of the house, and, until Mr. W. commenced his improvements, there had been some in its front. These, however, he had cut away, as interfering with the symmetry of his grounds, and in place of them had planted ailanthus trees in parallel rows.

On three sides of the outer part of the cleared square there was a row of large and comfortable-looking negro-quarters, stables, tobacco-houses, and other offices, built of logs.

Mr. W. was one of the few large planters, of his vicinity, who still made the culture of tobacco their principal business. He said there was a general prejudice against tobacco, in all the tidewater region of the State, because it was through the culture of tobacco that the once fertile soils had been impoverished; but he did not believe that, at the present value of negroes, their labor could be applied to the culture of grain, with any profit, except under peculiarly favorable circumstances. Possibly, the use of guano might make wheat a paying crop, but he still doubted. He had not used it, himself. Tobacco required fresh land, and was rapidly exhausting, but it returned more money, for the labor used upon it, than anything else; enough more, in his opinion, to pay for the wearing out of the land. If he was well-paid for it, he did not know why he should not wear out his land.

His tobacco-fields were nearly all in a distant and lower part of his plantation; land which had been neglected before his time, in a great measure, because it had been sometimes flooded, and was, much of the year, too wet for cultivation. He was draining and clearing it, and it now brought good crops.

He had had an Irish gang draining for him, by contract. He thought a negro could do twice as much work, in a day, as an Irishman. He had not stood over them and seen them at work, but judged entirely from the amount they accomplished: he thought a good gang of negroes would have got on twice as fast. He was sure they must have "trifled" a great deal, or they would have accomplished more than they had. He complained much, also, of their sprees and quarrels. I asked why he should employ Irishmen, in preference to doing the work with his own hands. "It's dangerous work (unhealthy?), and a negro's life is too valuable to be risked at it. If a negro dies, it's a considerable loss, you know."

He afterwards said that his negroes never worked so hard as to tire themselves—always were lively, and ready to go off on a frolic at night. He did not think they ever did half a fair day's work. They could not be made to work hard: they never would lay out their strength freely, and it was impossible to make them do it.

This is just what I have thought when I have seen slaves at work—they seem to go through the motions of labor without putting strength into them. They keep their powers in reserve for their own use at night, perhaps.

Mr. W. also said that he cultivated only the coarser and lower-priced sorts of tobacco, because the finer sorts required more pains-taking and discretion than it was possible to make a large gang of negroes use. "You can make a nigger work," he said, "*but you cannot make him think.*"

Although Mr. W. was very wealthy (or, at least, would be considered so anywhere at the North), and was a gentleman of education, his style of living was very farmer-like, and thoroughly Southern. On their plantations, generally, the Virginia gentlemen seem to drop their full-dress and constrained town-habits, and to live a free, rustic, shooting-jacket life. We dined in a room that extended out, rearwardly, from the house, and which, in a Northern establishment, would have been the kitchen. The cooking was done in a detached log-cabin, and the dishes brought some distance, through the open air, by the servants. The outer door was left constantly open, though there was a fire in an enormous old fire-place, large enough, if it could have been distributed sufficiently, to have lasted a New York seamstress the best part of the winter. By the door, there was indiscriminate admittance to negro-children and fox-hounds, and, on an average, there were four of these, grinning or licking their chops, on either side of my chair, all the time I was at the table. A stout woman acted as head waitress, employing two handsome little mulatto boys as her aids in communicating with the kitchen, from which relays of hot corn-bread, of an excellence quite new to me, were brought at frequent intervals.[1] There was no other bread, and but one vegetable served—sweet potato, roasted in ashes,

---

[1] There is probably some choice in the sort of corn used. The best corn-bread that I have eaten was made simply by wetting coarse meal with pure water, adding only a little salt, and baking in the form of a breakfast-roll. The addition of milk, butter, or eggs, damages it. I speak now from experience—having been, in my second journey in the South, often obliged to make my own bread. The only care required, except not to burn it, is to make sure, if possible—which it was not, generally, in Texas—that the corn is not mouldy.

and this, I thought, was the best sweet potato, also, that I ever had eaten; but there were four preparations of swine's flesh, besides fried fowls, fried eggs, cold roast turkey, and opossum, cooked, I know not how, but it somewhat resembled baked sucking-pig. The only beverages on the table were milk and whiskey.

I was pressed to stay several days with Mr. W., and should have been glad to have accepted such hospitality, had not another engagement prevented. When I was about to leave, an old servant was directed to get a horse, and go with me, as guide, to the railroad station at Col. Gillin's. He followed behind me, and I had great difficulty in inducing him to ride near enough to converse with me. I wished to ascertain from him how old the different stages of the old-field forest-growth, by the side of our road, might be; but, for a long time, he was, or pretended to be, unable to comprehend my questions. When he did so, the most accurate information he could give me was, that he reckoned such a field (in which the pines were now some sixty feet high) had been planted with tobacco the year his old master bought him. He thought he was about twenty years old then, and that now he was forty. He had every appearance of being seventy.

He frequently told me there was no need for him to go any further, and that it was a dead, straight road to the station, without any forks. As he appeared very eager to return, I was at length foolish enough to allow myself to be prevailed upon to dispense with his guidance; gave him a quarter of a dollar for his time that I had employed, and went on alone. The road, which for a short distance further was plain enough, soon began to ramify, and, in half an hour, we were stumbling along a dark wood-path, looking eagerly for a house. At length, seeing one across a large clearing, we went through a long lane, opening gates and letting down bars, until we met two negroes, riding a mule, who were going to the plantation near the school-house, which we had seen the day before. Following them thither, we knew the rest of the way (Jane gave a bound and neighed, when we struck the old road, showing that she had been lost, as well as I, up to the moment).

It was twenty minutes after the hour given in the time-table for the passage of the train, when I reached the station, but it had not arrived; nor did it make its appearance for a quarter of an hour longer; so I had plenty of time to deliver Tom's wife's message and take leave of Jane. I am sorry to say she appeared very indifferent, and seemed to think a good deal more of Tom than of me. Mr. W. had told me that the train would, probably, be half an hour behind its advertised time, and that I had no need to ride with haste, to reach it. I asked Col. Gillin if it would be safe to always calculate on the train being half an hour late: he said it would not; for, although usually that much behind the time-table, it was sometimes half an hour ahead of it. So those, who would be safe, had commonly to wait an hour. People, therefore, who wished to go not more than twenty miles from home, would find it more convenient, and equally expeditious, taking all things into account, to go in their own conveyances—there being but few who lived so near the station that they would not have to employ a horse and servant to get to it.

———————, ———. I have been visiting a farm, cultivated entirely by free-labor. The proprietor told me that he was first led to disuse slave-labor, not from any economical considerations, but because he had become convinced that there was an essential wrong in holding men in forced servitude with any other purpose than to benefit them alone, and because he was not willing to allow his own children to be educated as slave-masters. His father had been a large slave-holder, and he felt very strongly the bad influence it had had on his own character. He wished me to be satisfied that Jefferson uttered a great truth when he asserted that slavery was more pernicious to the white race than the black. Although, therefore, a chief part of his inheritance had been in slaves, he had liberated them all.

Most of them had, by his advice, gone to Africa. These he had frequently heard from. Except a child that had been drowned, they were, at his last account, all alive, in general good health, and satisfactorily prospering. He had lately received a letter from one of them, who told him that he was "*trying* to preach the Gospel," and who had evidently greatly improved, both intellectually and morally, since he left here. With regard to those going North, and the common opinion that they encountered much misery, and would be much better off here, he said that it entirely depended on the general character and habits of the individual; it was true of those who were badly brought up, and who had acquired indolent and vicious habits, especially if they were drunkards, but, if of some intelligence and well-trained, they generally represented themselves to be successful and contented.

He mentioned two remarkable cases, that had come under his own observation, of this kind. One was that of a man who had been free, but, by some fraud and informality of his papers, was reënslaved. He ran away, and afterwards negotiated, by correspondence, with his master, and purchased his freedom. This man he had accidentally met, fifteen years afterwards, in a Northern city; he was engaged in profitable and increasing business, and showed him, by his books, that he was possessed of property to the amount of ten thousand dollars. He was living a great deal more comfortably and wisely than ever his old master had done. The other case was that of a colored woman, who had obtained her freedom, and who became apprehensive that she also was about to be fraudulently made a slave again. She fled to Philadelphia, where she was nearly starved, at first. A little girl, who heard her begging in the streets to be allowed to work for bread, told her that her mother was wanting some washing done, and she followed her home. The mother, not knowing her, was afraid to trust her with the articles to be washed. She prayed so earnestly for the job, however—suggesting that she might be locked into a room until she had completed it—that it was given her.

So she commenced life in Philadelphia. Ten years afterwards he had accidentally met her there; she recognized him immediately, recalled herself to his recollection, manifested the greatest joy at seeing him, and asked him to come to her house, which he found a handsome three-story building, furnished really with elegance; and she pointed out to him, from the window, three houses in the vicinity that she owned and rented. She showed great anxiety to have her children well educated, and was employing the best instructors for them which she could procure in Philadelphia.

This gentleman, notwithstanding his anti-slavery sentiments, by no means favors the running away of slaves, and thinks the Abolitionists have done immense harm to the cause they have at heart. He wishes Northerners would mind their business, and leave Slavery alone, say but little about it—nothing in the present condition of affairs at the South—and never speak of it but in a kind and calm manner. He would not think it right to return a fugitive slave; but he would never assist one to escape. He has several times purchased slaves, generally such as his neighbors were obliged to sell, and who would otherwise have been taken South. This he had been led to do by the solicitation of some of their relatives. He had retained them in his possession until their labor had in some degree returned their cost to him, and he could afford to provide them with the means of going to Africa or the North, and a small means of support after their arrival.

Having received some suitable training in his family, they had, without exception, been successful, and had frequently sent him money to purchase the freedom of relatives or friends they had left in slavery.

He considered the condition of slaves to have much improved since the Revolution, and very perceptibly during the last twenty years. The original stock of slaves, the imported Africans, he observed, probably required to be governed with much greater severity, and very little humanity was exercised or thought of with regard to them. The slaves of the present day are of a higher character; in fact, he did not think more than half of them were full-blooded Africans. Public sentiment condemned the man who treated his slaves with cruelty. The owners were mainly men of some cultivation, and felt a family attachment to their slaves, many of whom had been the playmates of their boyhood. Nevertheless, they were frequently punished severely, under the impulse of temporary passion, often without deliberation, and on unfounded suspicion. This was especially the case where they were left to overseers, who, though sometimes men of intelligence and piety, were more often coarse, brutal, and licentious; drinking men, wholly unfitted for the responsibility imposed on them.

He had read "Uncle Tom's Cabin;" mentioned several points in which he thought it wrong — that Uncle Tom was too highly painted, for instance; that such a character could not exist in, or spring out of Slavery, and that no gentleman of Kentucky or Virginia would have allowed himself to be in the position with a slave-dealer in which Mr. Shelby is represented—but he acknowledged that cases of cruelty and suffering, equal to any described in it, might be found. In his own neighborhood, some time ago, a man had been whipped to death; and he recollected several that had been maimed for life, by harsh and hasty punishment; but the whole community were indignant when such things occurred, and any man guilty of them would be without associates, except of similar character.

The opinions of this gentleman must not, of course, be considered as representative of those of the South in general, by any means; but as to facts, he is a competent, and, I believe, a wholly candid and unprejudiced witness. He is much respected, and on terms of friendship with all his neighbors, though they do not like his views on this subject. He told me, however, that one of them, becoming convinced of their correctness some time ago, freed his slaves, and moved to Ohio. As to "Uncle Tom," it is generally criticised very severely, and its representations of Slavery indignantly denied. I observe that it is not placarded outside the booksellers' stores, though the whole fleet of gunboats that have been launched after it show their colors bravely. It must, however, be a good deal read here, as I judge from the frequent allusions I hear made to it.

With regard to the value of slave-labor, this gentleman is confident that, at present, he has the advantage in employing freemen instead of it. It has not been so until of late, the price of slaves having much advanced within ten years, while immigration has made free white laborers more easy to be procured.

He has heretofore had some difficulty in obtaining hands when he needed them, and has suffered a good deal from the demoralizing influence of adjacent slave-labor, the men, after a few months' residence, inclining to follow the customs of the slaves with regard to the amount of work they should do in a day, or their careless mode of operation. He has had white and black Virginians, sometimes Germans, and latterly Irish. Of all these, he has found the Irish on the whole the best. The poorest have been the native white Virginians; next, the free blacks: and though there have been exceptions, he has not generally paid these as high as one hundred dollars a year, and has thought them less worth their wages than any he has had. At present, he has two white natives and two free colored men, but both the latter were brought up in his family, and are worth twenty dollars a year more than the average. The free black, he thinks, is generally worse than the slave, and so is the poor white man. He also employs, at present, four Irish hands, and is expecting two more to arrive, who have been recommended to him, and sent for by those he has. He pays the Irishmen $120 a year, and boards them. He has had them for $100; but these are all excellent men, and well worth their price. They are less given to drinking than any men he has ever had; and one of them first suggested improvements to him in his farm, that he is now carrying out with prospects of considerable advantage. House-maids, Irish girls, he pays $3 and $6 a month.

He does not apprehend that in future he shall have any difficulty in obtaining steady and reliable men, that will accomplish much more work than any slaves. There are some operations, such as carting and spreading dung, and all work with the fork, spade, or shovel, at which his Irishmen will do, he thinks, over fifty per cent. more in a day than any negroes he has ever known. On the whole, he is satisfied that at present free-labor is more profitable than slave-labor, though his success is not so evident that he would be willing to have attention particularly called to it. His farm, moreover, is now in a transition state from one system of husbandry to another, and appearances are temporarily more unfavorable on that account.

The wages paid for slaves, when they are hired for agricultural labor, do not differ at present, he says, from those which he pays for his free laborers. In both cases the hiring party boards the laborer, but, in addition to money and board, the slave-employer has to furnish clothing, and is subject, without redress, to any losses which may result from the carelessness or malevolence of the slave. He also has to lose his time if he is unwell, or when from any cause he is absent or unable to work.

The slave, if he is indisposed to work, and especially if he is not treated well, or does not like the master who has hired him, will sham sickness—even make himself sick or lame—that he need not work. But a more serious loss frequently arises, when the slave, thinking he is worked too hard, or being angered by punishment or unkind treatment, "getting the sulks," takes to "the swamp," and comes back when he has a mind to. Often this will not be till the year is up for which he is engaged, when he will return to his owner, who, glad to find his property safe, and that it has not died in the swamp, or gone to Canada, forgets to punish him, and immediately sends him for another year to a new master.

"But, meanwhile, how does the negro support life in the swamp?" I asked.

"Oh, he gets sheep and pigs and calves, and fowls and turkeys; sometimes they will kill a small cow. We have often seen the fires, where they were cooking them, through the woods, in the swamp yonder. If it is cold, he will crawl under a fodder-stack, or go into the cabins with some of the other negroes, and in the same way, you see, he can get all the corn, or almost anything else he wants."

"He steals them from his master?"

"From any one; frequently from me. I have had many a sheep taken by them."

"It is a common thing, then?"

"Certainly, it is, very common, and the loss is sometimes exceedingly provoking. One of my neighbors here was going to build, and hired two mechanics for a year. Just as he was ready to put his house up, the two men, taking offense at something, both ran away, and did not come back at all, till their year was out, and then their owner immediately hired them out again to another man."

These negroes "in the swamp," he said, were often hunted after, but it was very difficult to find them, and, if caught, they would run again, and the other negroes would hide and assist them. Dogs to track them he had never known to be used in Virginia.

SATURDAY, Dec. 25. From Christmas to New-Year's Day, most of the slaves, except house servants, enjoy a freedom from labor; and Christmas is especially holiday, or Saturnalia, with them. The young ones began last night firing crackers, and I do not observe that they are engaged in any other amusement to-day; the older ones are generally getting drunk, and making business for the police. I have seen large gangs coming in from the country, and these contrast much in their general appearance with the town negroes. The latter are dressed expensively, and frequently more elegantly than the whites. They seem to be spending money freely, and I observe that they, and even the slaves that wait upon me at the hotel, often have watches, and other articles of value.

The slaves have a good many ways of obtaining "spending money," which, though in law belonging to their owner, as the property of a son under age does to his father, they are never dispossessed of, and use for their own gratification, with even less restraint than a wholesome regard for their health and moral condition may be thought to require. A Richmond paper, complaining of the liberty allowed to slaves in this respect, as calculated to foster an insubordinate spirit, speaks of their "champagne suppers." The police broke into a gambling cellar a few nights since, and found about twenty negroes at "high play," with all the usual accessories of a first-class " Hell." It is mentioned that, among the number taken to the watchhouse, and treated with lashes the next morning, there were some who had previously enjoyed a high reputation for piety, and others of a very elegant or foppish appearance.

Passing two negroes in the street, I heard the following:

"—— Workin' in a tobacco factory all de year roun', an' come Christmas, only twenty dollars! Workin' mighty hard, too—up to 12 o'clock o' night very often —an' then to hab a nigger oberseah!"

" A nigger!"

"Yes—dat's it, yer see. Would n't care if 't warnt for dat. Nothin' but a dirty nigger! orderin' 'round, jes' as if he was a wite man!"

It is the custom of tobacco manufacturers to hire slaves and free negroes at a certain rate of wages per year. A task of 45 lbs. per day is given them to work up, and all that they choose to do more than this they are paid for—payment being made once a fortnight; and invariably this over-wages is used by the slave for himself, and is usually spent in drinking, licentiousness and gambling. The man was grumbling that he had saved but $20 to spend at the holidays. One of the manufacturers offered to show me, by his books, that nearly all gained by overwork $5 a month, many $20, and some as much as $28.

Sitting with a company of smokers last night, one of them, to show me the manner in which a slave of any ingenuity or cunning would manage to avoid working for his master's profit, narrated the following anecdote. He was executor of an estate in which, among other negroes, there was one very smart man, who, he knew perfectly well, ought to be earning for the estate $150 a year, and who could do it if he chose, yet whose wages for a year, being let out by the day or job, had amounted to but $18, while he had paid for medical attendance upon him $45. Having failed in every other way to make him earn anything, he proposed to him that he should purchase his freedom and go to Philadelphia, where he had a brother. He told him if he would earn a certain sum ($400 I believe), and pay it over to the estate for himself, he would give him his free papers. The man agreed to the arrangement, and by his overwork in a tobacco factory, and some assistance from his free brother, soon paid the sum agreed upon, and was sent to Philadelphia. A few weeks afterwards he met him in the street, and asked him why he had returned. "Oh, I don't like dat Philadelphy, massa; ant no chance for colored folks dere; spec' if I 'd been a runaway, de wite folks dere take care o' me; but I could n't git anythin' to do, so I jis borrow ten dollar of my broder, and cum back to old Virginny."

"But you know the law forbids your return. I

wonder that you are not afraid to be seen here; I should think Mr. —— (an officer of police) would take you up."

"Oh! I look out for dat, Massa, I juss hire myself out to Mr. —— himself, ha! ha! He tink I your boy."

And so it proved; the officer, thinking that he was permitted to hire himself out, and tempted by the low wages at which he offered himself, had neglected to ask for his written permission, and had engaged him for a year. He still lived with the officer, and was an active, healthy, good servant to him.

A well-informed capitalist and slave-holder remarked, that negroes could not be employed in cotton factories. I said that I understood they were so in Charleston, and some other places at the South.

"It may be so, *yet*," he answered, "but they will have to give it up."

The reason was, he said, that the negro could never be trained to exercise judgment; he cannot be made to use his mind; he always depends on machinery doing its own work, and cannot be made to watch it. He neglects it until something is broken or there is great waste. "We have tried reward and punishments, but it makes no difference. It's his nature and you cannot change it. All men are indolent and have a disinclination to labor, but this is a great deal stronger in the African race than in any other. In working niggers, we must always calculate that they will not labor at all except to avoid punishment, and they will never do more than just enough to save themselves from being punished, and no amount of punishment will prevent their working carelessly and indifferently. It always seems on the plantation as if they took pains to break all the tools and spoil all the cattle that they possibly can, even when they know they 'll be directly punished for it.''

As to rewards, he said, "They only want to support life, they will not work for anything more; and in this country it would be hard to prevent their getting that.'' I thought this opinion of the power of rewards was not exactly confirmed by the narrative we had just heard, but I said nothing. "If you could move,'' he continued, "all the white people from the whole seaboard district of Virginia and give it up to the negroes that are on it now, just leave them to themselves, in ten years time there would not be an acre of land cultivated, and nothing would be produced, except what grew spontaneously.''

The Hon. Willoughby Newton, by the way, seems to think that if it had not been for the introduction of guano, a similar desolation would have soon occurred without the Africanization of the country. He is reported to have said:

"I look upon the introduction of guano, and the success attending its application to our barren lands, in the light of a special interposition of Divine Providence, to save the northern neck of Virginia from reverting entirely into its former state of wilderness and utter desolation. Until the discovery of guano—more valuable to us than the mines of California—I looked upon the possibility of renovating our soil, of ever bringing it to a point capable of producing remunerating crops, as utterly hopeless. Our up-lands were all worn out, and our bottom-lands fast failing, and if it had not been for guano, to revive our last hope, a few years more and the whole country must have been deserted by all who desired to increase their own wealth, or advance the cause of civilization by a proper cultivation of the earth."

"But are they not *improving?*" said I; "that is a point in which I am much interested, and I should be glad to know what is your observation? Have they not, as a race, improved during the last hundred years, do you not think?"

"Oh, yes indeed, very greatly. During my time—I can remember how they were forty years ago—they have improved *two thousand per cent.!* Don't you think so?" he asked another gentleman.

"Yes; certainly."

"And you may find them now, on the isolated old plantations in the back country, just as I recollect them when I was a boy, stupid and moping, and with no more intelligence than when they first came from Africa. But all about where the country is much settled their condition is vastly ameliorated. They are treated much better, they are fed better, and they have much greater educational privileges."

"Educational privileges?" I asked, in surprise.

"I mean by preaching and religious instruction. They have the Bible read to them a great deal, and there is preaching for them all over the country. They have preachers of their own; right smart ones they are, too, some of them."

"Do they?" said I. "I thought that was not allowed by law."

"Well, it is not—that is, they are not allowed to have meetings without some white man is present. They must not preach unless a white man hears what they say. However, they do. On my plantation, they always have a meeting on Sundays, and I have sometimes, when I have been there, told my overseer,—'You must go up there to the meeting, you know the law requires it;' and he would start as if he was going, but would just look in and go by; he was n't going to wait for them."

He then spoke of a minister, whom he owned, and described him as a very intelligent man. He knew almost the whole of the Bible by heart. He was a fine-looking man—a fine head and a very large frame. He had been a sailor, and had been in New Orleans and New York, and many foreign ports. "He could have left me at any time for twenty years, if he had wished to," he said. "I asked him once how he would like to live in New York? Oh, he did not like New York at all! niggers were not treated well there—there was more distinction made between them and white folks than there was here. 'Oh, dey ain't no place in de worl like Ole Virginny for niggers, massa,' says he."

Another gentleman gave similar testimony.

I said I supposed that they were much better off,

more improved intellectually, and more kindly treated in Virginia than further South. He said I was mistaken in both respects—that in Louisiana, especially, they were more intelligent, because the amalgamation of the races was much greater, and they were treated with more familiarity by the whites; besides which, the laws of Louisiana were much more favorable to them. For instance, they required the planter to give slaves 200 pounds of pork a year: and he gave a very apt anecdote, showing the effect of this law, but which, at the same time, made it evident that a Virginian may be accustomed to neglect providing sufficient food for his force, and that they sometimes suffer greatly for want of it. I was assured, however, that this was very rare—that, generally, the slaves were well provided for—always allowed a sufficient quantity of meal, and, generally, of pork—were permitted to raise pigs and poultry, and in summer could always grow as many vegetables as they wanted. It was observed, however, that they frequently neglect to provide for themselves in this way, and live mainly on meal and bacon. If a man does not provide well for his slaves, it soon becomes known, he gets the name of a "nigger killer," and loses the respect of the community.

The general allowance of food was thought to be a peck and a half of meal, and three pounds of bacon a week. This, it was observed, is as much meal as they can eat, but they would be glad to have more bacon; sometimes they receive four pounds, but it is oftener that they get less than three. It is distributed to them on Saturday nights; or, on the better managed plantations, sometimes, on Wednesday, to prevent their using it extravagantly, or selling it for whiskey on Sunday. This distribution is called the "drawing," and is made by the overseer to all the heads of families or single negroes. Except on the smallest plantations, where the cooking is done in the house of the proprietor, there is a cook-house, furnished with a large copper for boiling, and an oven. Every night the negroes take their "mess," for the next day's breakfast and dinner, to the cook, to be prepared for the next day. Custom varies as to the time it is served out to them; sometimes at morning and noon, at other times at noon and night. Each negro marks his meat by cuts, so that he shall know it from the rest, and they observe each other's rights with regard to this, punctiliously.

After breakfast has been eaten early in the cabins, at sunrise or a little before in winter, and perhaps a little later in summer, they go to the field. At noon dinner is brought to them, and, unless the work presses, they are allowed two hours' rest. Very punctually at sunset they stop work and are at liberty, except that a squad is detached once a week for shelling corn, to go to the mill for the next week's drawing of meal. Thus they work in the field about eleven hours a day on an average. Returning to the cabins, wood "ought to have been" carted for them; but if it has not been, they then go to the woods and "tote" it home for themselves. They then make a fire—a big, blazing fire at this season, for the supply of fuel is unlimited—and cook their own supper, which will be a bit of bacon fried, often with eggs, corn-bread baked in the spider after the bacon, to absorb the fat, and perhaps some sweet potatoes roasted in the ashes. Immediately after supper they go to sleep, often lying on the floor or a bench in preference to a bed. About two o'clock they very generally rouse up and cook and eat, or eat cold, what they call their " mornin' bit;" then sleep again till breakfast.

I think the slaves generally (no one denies that there are exceptions) have plenty to eat; probably are fed better than the proletarian class of any other part of the world. I think that they generally save from their ration of meal. My informant said that commonly as much as five bushels of meal was sent to town by his hands every week, to be sold for them. Upon inquiry, he almost always found that it belonged to only two or three individuals, who had traded for it with the rest; he added, that too often the exchange was for whiskey, which, against his rules, they obtained of some rascally white people in the neighborhood, and kept concealed. They were very fond of whiskey, and sometimes much injured themselves with it.

To show me how well they were supplied with eggs, he said that once a vessel came to anchor, becalmed, off his place, and the captain came to him and asked leave to purchase some eggs of his people. He gave him permission, and called the cook to collect them for him. The cook asked how many she should bring. " Oh, all you can get," he answered—and she returned after a time, with several boys assisting her, bringing nearly two bushels, all the property of the slaves, and which they were willing to sell at four cents a dozen.

One of the smokers explained to me that it is very bad economy, not to allow an abundant supply of food to "a man's force." The negroes are fond of good living, and, if not well provided for, know how to provide for themselves. It is, also, but simple policy to have them well lodged and clothed. If they do not have comfortable cabins and sufficient clothing, they will take cold, and be laid up. He lost a very valuable negro, once, from having neglected to provide him with shoes.

The houses of the slaves are usually log-cabins, of various degrees of comfort and commodiousness. At one end there is a great open fire-place, which is exterior to the wall of the house, being made of clay in an inclosure, about eight feet square and high, of logs. The chimney is sometimes of brick, but more commonly of lath or split sticks, laid up like log-work and plastered with mud. They enjoy great roaring fires, and, as the common fuel is pitch pine, the cabin, at night when the door is open, seen from a distance, appears like a fierce furnace. The chimneys often catch fire, and the cabin is destroyed. Very little precaution can be taken against this danger.[1] Several cabins are

---

[1] "AN INGENIOUS NEGRO.—In Lafayette, Miss., a few days ago, a negro, who, with his wife and three children, occupied a hut upon the plantation of Col. Peques, was very much annoyed by fleas. Believing that they congregated in great numbers beneath the house, he resolved to destroy them by fire; and

placed near together, and they are called "the quarters." On a plantation of moderate size there will be but one "quarters." The situation chosen for it has reference to convenience of obtaining water from springs and fuel from the woods. On some of the James River plantations there are larger houses, boarded and made ornamental. In these, eight families, each having a distinct sleeping-room and lock-up closets, and every two having a common kitchen or living-room, are accommodated.

As to the clothing of the slaves on the plantations, they are said to be usually furnished by their owners or masters, every year, each with a coat and trousers, of a coarse woollen or woollen and cotton stuff (mostly made, especially for this purpose, in Providence, R. I.), for Winter, trousers of cotton osnaburghs for Summer, sometimes with a jacket also of the same; two pairs of strong shoes, or one pair of strong boots and one of lighter shoes for harvest; three shirts; one blanket, and one felt hat.

The women have two dresses of striped cotton, three shifts, two pairs of shoes, etc. The women lying-in are kept at knitting short sacks, from cotton which, in Southern Virginia, is usually raised, for this purpose, on the farm, and these are also given to the negroes.

accordingly, one night when his family were asleep, he raised a plank in the floor of the cabin, and, procuring an armful of shucks, scattered them on the ground beneath, and lighted them. The consequence was, that the cabin was consumed, and the whole family, with the exception of the man who lighted the fire, was burned to death."—*Journal of Commerce.*

They also purchase clothing for themselves, and, I notice especially, are well supplied with handkerchiefs which the men frequently, and the women nearly always, wear on their heads. On Sundays and holidays they usually look very smart, but when at work, very ragged and slovenly.

At the conclusion of our bar-room session, some time after midnight, as we were retiring to our rooms, our progress up stairs and along the corridors was several times impeded, by negroes lying fast asleep, in their usual clothes only, upon the floor. I asked why they were not abed, and was answered by a gentleman, that negroes never wanted to go to bed; they always preferred to sleep upon the floor.

As I was walking in the outskirts of the town this morning, I saw squads of negro and white boys together, pitching pennies and firing crackers in complete fraternization. The white boys manifested no superiority, or assumption of it, over the dark ones.

An old, palsied negro-woman, very thinly and very raggedly clad, met me and spoke to me. I could not, from the trembling incoherency of her voice, understand what she said, but she was evidently begging, and I never saw a more pitiable object of charity at the North. She was, perhaps, a free person, with no master and no system to provide for her.

I saw, for the first time in my life, two or three young white women smoking tobacco in clay pipes. From their manner it was evidently a well-formed habit, and one which they did not suspect there was occasion for them to practice clandestinely, or be ashamed of.

With regard to the moral and religious condition of the slaves, I cannot, either from what I observe, or from what is told me, consider it in any way gratifying. They are forbidden by law to meet together for worship, or for the purpose of mutual improvement. In the cities, there are churches especially for them, in which the exercises are conducted by white clergymen. In the country, there is usually a service, after that for the whites especially, in all the churches, which, by the way, are not very thickly scattered. In one parish, about twenty miles from Richmond, I was told that the colored congregation in the afternoon is much smaller than that of the whites in the morning; and it was thought not more than one-fifth of the negroes living within a convenient distance were in the habit of attending it; and of these many came late, and many more slept through the greater part of the service.

A goodly proportion of them, I am told, "profess religion," and are received into the fellowship of the churches; but it is evident, of the greater part even of these, that their idea of religion, and the standard of morality which they deem consistent with a "profession" of it, is very degraded. That they are subject to intense excitements, often really maniacal, which they consider to be religious, is true; but as these are described, I cannot see that they indicate anything but a miserable system of superstition, the more painful that it employs some forms and words ordinarily connected with true Christianity.

A Virginia correspondent of the *N. Y. Times*, writing upon the general religious condition of the State, and of the comparative strength and usefulness of the different churches, says:

"The Baptists also number (in Eastern Virginia) 44,000 colored members. This makes a great difference. Negroes join the church—perhaps in a great majority of cases—with no ideas of religion. I have but little confidence in their religious professions. Many of them I hope are very pious; but many of them are great scoundrels—perhaps the great majority of them—regardless of their church profession as a rule of conduct. They are often baptized in great numbers, and the Baptist Church (so exemplary in so much) is to blame, I fear, in the ready admission it gives to the negroes.

"The Baptist Church generally gets the negroes—where there are no Baptists, the Methodist. *Immersion* strikes their fancy. It is a palpable, overt act, that their imagination can take hold of. The ceremony mystically impresses them, as the ceremonies of Romanism affect the devotees of that connection. They come up out of the water, and believe they see 'the Lord.' In their religion, negroes are excessively superstitious. They have all sorts of 'experiences,' and enjoy the most wonderful revelations. Visions of the supernatural are of nightly occurrence, and the most absurd circumstances are invested with some marvellous significance. I have heard that the great ordeal, in their estimation, a 'seeker' had to pass, was being *held over the infernal flames by a thread or a hair*. If the thread does not break, the suspendee is 'in the Lord.'

"It is proper, therefore, I think, to consider this circumstance, in estimating the strength of a Church, whose communicants embrace such a number of negroes. Of the Methodists, in Eastern Virginia, some six or seven thousand are colored."

This condition of the slaves is not necessarily a reproach to those whose duty it more particularly is to instruct and preach the true Gospel to them. It is, in a great degree, a necessary result of the circumstances of their existence. The possession of arbitrary power has always, the world over, tended irresistibly to destroy humane sensibility, magnanimity, and truth. Look at the sovereigns of Europe in our day. There is not one, having sovereign power, that would not, over and over again, for acts of which he is notoriously and undeniably guilty, under our laws, be confined with the most depraved of criminals. It is, I have no doubt, utterly impossible, except as a camel shall enter the eye of a needle, for a man to have the will of others habitually under his control, without its impairing his sense of justice, his power of sympathy, his respect for manhood, and his worshipful love of the Infinite Father.

But it is much more evident that involuntary subjection directly tends to turpitude and demoralization. True, it may tend also to the encouragement of some beautiful traits, to meekness, humility, and a kind of generosity and unselfishness. But where has it not ever been accompanied by the loss of the nobler virtues of manhood, especially of the noblest, the most essential of all, that without which all others avail nothing for good: TRUTH. What is the matter with the Irish? No one can rely on them—they cannot rely on one another. Though sensitive to duty, and in their way conscientious, they absolutely are not able to comprehend a rule, a law; and that a man can be fixed by his promise they have never thought. A promise with them signifies merely an expressed intention. Irishmen that have long associated with us, we can depend on, for we have their confidence; but to a stranger still, their word is not worth a farthing. They are inveterate falsifiers, on the general principle that no man can want information of them but for his own good, and that good can only exist to their injury. What is the cause of this? their religion?—that to which it is attributed in their religion is the effect of it, more than the cause. It is the subjection of generations of this people to the will of landlords, corrupted to fiendish insensibility by the long continued possession of nearly arbitrary power. The capacity of mind for truth and reliance has been all but lost, by generations of unjust subjection.

It is the same—only in some respects better, and some far worse—even already, with the African slave of the South. Every Virginian acknowledges it. Religion, to call that by the name which they do, has become subject to it. "They will lie in their very prayers to God."

I find illustrations of the trouble that this vice occasions on every hand here. I just heard this, for instance, from a lady. A house-maid, who had the reputation of being especially devout, was suspected by her mistress of having stolen from her bureau several trinkets. She was charged with the theft, and vociferously denied it. She was watched, and the articles discovered openly displayed on her person as she went to church. She still, on her return, denied having them — was searched, and they were found in her pockets. When reproached by her mistress, and lectured on the wickedness of lying and stealing, she replied with the confident air of knowing the ground she stood upon, "Law, mam, don't say I's wicked; ole Aunt Ann says it allers right for us poor colored people to 'popiate whatever of de wite folk's blessins de Lord puts in our way." Old Aunt Ann was a sort of mother in the colored Israel of the town.

It is told me as a singular fact, that everywhere on the plantations, the agrarian notion has become a fixed point of the negro system of ethics: that the result of labor belongs of right to the laborer, and on this ground, even the religious feel justified in using "Massa's" property for their own temporal benefit. This they term "taking," and it is never admitted to be a reproach to a man among them that he is charged with it, though "stealing," or taking from another than their master, and particularly from one another, is so. They almost universally pilfer from the household stores when they have a safe opportunity. Thieving, by the way, is not a national vice of the Irish, because the opportunities and temptations for it have been too small to have bred the habit.

Jefferson says of the slaves:

"Whether further observation will or will not verify the conjecture, that nature has been less bountiful to them in the endowments of the head, I believe that in those of the heart she will have done them justice. That disposition to theft, with which they have been branded, must be ascribed to their situation, and not to any depravity of the moral sense. The man in whose favor no laws of property exist, probably feels himself less bound to respect those made in favor of others. When arguing for ourselves, we lay it down as fundamental, that laws, to be just, must give a reciprocation of right; that without this, they are mere arbitrary rules, founded in force, and not in conscience, and it is a problem which I give to the master to solve, whether the religious precepts against the violation of property were not framed for him as well as his slave? and whether the slave may not as justifiably take a little from one who has taken all from him, as he may slay one who would slay him? That a change of the relations in which a man is placed should change his ideas of moral right and wrong, is neither new, nor peculiar to the color of the blacks. Homer tells us it was so, 2,600 years ago:

"'Jove fixed it certain, that whatever day
Makes man a slave, takes half his worth away.'"

The following is a specimen of the most careful kind of preaching, ordinarily addressed by the white clergy to the black sheep of their flocks. It is by Bishop Meade, of the Church of England in Virginia, and is copied from a published volume of sermons, recommended by him to masters and mistresses of his diocese, for use in their households.

"And think within yourselves what a terrible thing it would be, after all your labors and sufferings in this life, to be turned into hell in the next life, and, after wearing out your bodies in service here, to go into a far worse slavery when this is over, and your poor souls be delivered over into the possession of the devil, to become his slaves forever in hell, without any hope of ever getting free from it! If, therefore, you would be God's freemen in heaven, you must strive to be good, and serve him here on earth. Your bodies, you know, are not your own; they are at the disposal of those you belong to; but your precious souls are still your own, which nothing can take from you, if it be not your own fault. Consider well, then, that, if you lose your souls by leading idle, wicked lives here, you have got nothing by it in this world, and you have lost your all in the next. For your idleness and wickedness are generally found out, and your bodies suffer for it here; and what is far worse, if you do not repent and amend, your unhappy souls will suffer for it hereafter.

"Having thus shown you the chief duties you owe to your great Master in heaven, I now come to lay before you the duties you owe to your masters and mistresses here upon earth. And for this you have one general rule, that you ought always to carry in your minds; and that is, to do all service for them as if you did it for God himself.

"Poor creatures! you little consider, when you are idle and neglectful of your masters' business, when you steal, and waste, and hurt any of their substance, when you are saucy and impudent, when you are telling them lies and deceiving them, or when you prove stubborn and sullen, and will not do the work you are set about without stripes and vexation,—you do not consider, I say, that what faults you are guilty of towards your masters and mistresses are faults done against God himself, who hath set your masters and mistresses over you in his own stead, and expects that you would do for them just as you would do for him. And pray do not think that I want to deceive you when I tell you that your masters and mistresses are God's overseers, and that, if you are faulty towards them, God himself will punish you severely for it in the next world, unless you repent of it, and strive to make amends by your faithfulness and diligence for the time to come; for God himself hath declared the same.

"And in the first place, you are to be obedient and subject to your masters in all things. * * * And Christian ministers are commanded to 'exhort servants to be obedient unto their own masters, and to please them well in all things, not answering them again, or gainsaying.' * * * You are to be faithful and honest to your masters and mistresses, not purloining or wasting their goods or substance, but showing all good fidelity in all things. * * * Do not your masters, under God, provide for you? And how shall they be able to do this, to feed and to clothe you, unless you take honest care of everything that belongs to them? Remember that God requires this of you; and if you are not afraid of suffering for it here, you cannot escape the vengeance of Almighty God, who will judge between you and your masters, and make you pay severely, in the next world, for all the injustice you do them here. And though you could manage so cunningly as to escape the eyes and hands of man, yet think what a dreadful thing it is to fall into the hands of the living God, who is able to cast both soul and body into hell."

That wicked historian, Volney, "shows up" this sort of preaching, in the following suppositious debate, which, no doubt, has often been realized in the minds of the slaves:

"Then the Spiritual Governors said: 'There is no other way. As the People is superstitious, it is necessary to frighten them by the name of God and Religion.' So they said:

"'Our dear brothers—our children! God has appointed us to govern you.'

"S. 'Show us your heavenly authority.'

"M. 'You must have faith: Reason deceives.'

"S. 'Do you rule us without Reason?'

"M. 'God wishes Peace: Religion prescribes Obedience.'

"S. 'Peace supposes Justice: Obedience wishes to know the Law.'

"M. 'One is here below only to suffer.'

"S. 'Show us an example!'

"M. 'Do you wish to live without God and without Kings?'

"S. 'We would live without Tyrants.'"

[My aunt, who, on account of my habitual carelessness—"not to suggest occasional approach to something like vulgarity"—of style, is good enough to assist me in reading proofs, thinks that I ought not to make use of a quotation from this heterodox historian, without a clearer indication of my own opinions. The Episcopalians, in the words of a certain un-eminent Southern divine, "are a high-sailin' set," and easily offended, and *The Churchman*, she thinks, will be sure to suggest doubts of my rigid orthodoxy.]

A great many bad things have been furnished with props out of Scripture, by bad men, and a great many more by mistaken men, and the venerable Virginia prelate is not infallible. Exactly what such passages as he quotes were intended to teach, it is not for me to define and limit; but that they were meant to encourage any men, immortal and accountable, under all circumstances and forever, to submit, in acquiescent stupefaction, to Slavery, I venture to discredit. Because it is contrary to nature and to common sense, and I think it takes a more hair-splitting mind, than negroes are generally endowed with, to think otherwise. Because it seems to me that, to do so, it is necessary that a man should acquire a more debased condition of soul than to be a schismatic, a fanatic, or a murderer. Suppose the bishop had been consigned to my cell at Gadsby's, and had found it not only wanting in comfort, but possessed by vermin, and stenches, and damp, and Mr. Dexter had been ready with 1 Tim. vi., 8, and ordered him, on the strength of it, to shut up and go to bed, when he mildly objected to the arrangements, would he have meekly resigned himself to certain bronchitis, and a probability of acute laryngitis and speedy transfer to the eternal mansions? I respect him too much to believe it. The relation between an impostor and one who carelessly and slothfully allows himself to be imposed upon, is the same as that between a thief and a receiver of stolen goods. Indolent acquiescence in that which is unjust and harmful to us, is as wrong as a revengeful or an unforgiving spirit; and if the Apostles had had to travel by our railroads, and rest at our hotels, and employ our hackney-coachmen, I believe they would have said so in so many words.

The bishop seems to me to teach, by implication, the doctrine of the Divine Right of Kings; for what else, except in name, is this divine right of oversight with which he invests the slave's master, and for disloyalty to which he threatens corresponding torment eternal? In doing so, is he not disloyal and rebellious to his own sovereign, "the Good People of Virginia," for their sovereignty is based in treason, and in denial of this divine right of government of one man over another? If the bishop does not repent, where does he expect to go to?

My aunt thinks that, before I venture to object to the preaching of a bishop, I should be ready to say what should be preached to slaves, while the necessity of keeping them in Slavery continues. I don't admit this; yet I may say, in general, that I should think that it would be encouragement to them, to so conduct and train themselves that this necessity should be removed as rapidly as possible; the supposition being always maintained, that this necessity rested on the extraordinary stupidity and vicious proclivities of the slaves themselves, and would be happily removed by their enlightenment and growth in grace.

What says the learned and pious father Gregory, bishop of the sixth century of Christianity?

Quum redemptor noster, totius conditor creaturæ, ad hoc propitiatus humanam voluint carnem assumere, ut divinitatis suæ gratia, dirupto quo tenebamur captivi vinculo, servitatis, pristinæ nos restituerit libertati salubriter agitur si homines quos ab initio natura liberos protulit, et jus gentium jugo substituit servitatis, in ea qua nati sunt, manumittentis beneficie, libertate reddantur.

Decret. Grat. P. II. *Caus. XII. Quæst.* 2.[1]

I had an idea that a good deal was done, with some reference to the future freedom of the slaves; but I can't hear that such is the case, in the Episcopal or any other Christian organization. The Church of England form of worship is, in my opinion, the best calculated to encourage their elevation, of any used at the South; and the slaves who habitually attend and commune in the Episcopal church are, as a general rule, much more intelligent and elevated in their religious nature than any others. The ceremony and pomp, the frequent responses and chants, in which negroes are expected and encouraged to unite, in unison with the whites, and the liturgical system of instruction in religious truth, are all favorable to the improvement in character of the negro, and admirably adapted to the idiosyncrasies of his nature.

The Baptist and Methodist clergy, when addressing negro congregations, are said to spend most of their

[1] Now, as our Redeemer and the Creator of every creature, was willing to assume a human body, in order that by the grace of his divinity he might break the bonds of servitude, wherein we were held captive, and restore us to our freedom; so it is a good and salutary thing when those who, by nature, were created free, and whom the laws of men have reduced to slavery, are, by the benefaction of manumission, restored to that liberty in which they were born.

force in arguing against each other's doctrines, and the negroes are represented to have a great taste for theological controversy.

As an illustration of the way in which a great many negroes understood a certain tenet of the Baptists, a gentleman narrated the following circumstance:

A slave, who was "a professor," plagued his master very much by his persistence in certain immoral practices, and he requested a clergyman to converse with him and try to reform him. The clergyman did so, and endeavored to bring the terrors of the law to bear upon his conscience. "Look yeah, massa," said the backslider, "don't de Scriptur say, 'Dem who believes an is baptize shall be save?'" "Certainly," the clergyman answered; and went on to explain and expound the passage: but directly the slave interrupted him again.

"Jus you tell me now, massa, don't de good book say dese word: 'Dem as believes and is baptize, shall be save;' want to know dat."

"Yes; but—"

"Dat's all I want to know, sar; now wat's de use o' talkin to me? You aint a goin to make me bleve wat de blessed Lord says, an't so, not ef you tries forever."

The clergyman again attempted to explain, but the negro would not allow him, and as often as he got back to the judgment-day, or charging him with sin, and demanding reformation, he would interrupt him in the same way.

"De Scriptur say, if a man believe and be baptize

he shall—he *shall*, be save. Now, massa minister, I *done* believe and I *done* baptize, an *I shall be save suah.* —Dere 's no use talkin, sar."

My remarks in this letter, upon the religious and moral condition of the slaves, are to be considered as my first impressions from what I see and hear. There appears to be a great difference of opinion among those who have had better opportunities of judging than I, on the subject, and it is fair that I should say, that some assure me they have no doubt the religious character of the slaves, who are members of churches, is as high as that of the white members, and that it is better than that of the lower class of whites. Opinions as to the general standard of morality among the slaves are strongly contradictory. My own impression has, therefore, been derived from facts that I hear, and from general observation of the manners and conversation of the slaves. It is true that a great deal of religious phraseology and much Scripture language is used by them; but the very levity and inappropriateness with which it is applied, shows a want of a right appreciation of it. It is not at all improbable, however, that I shall find occasion to modify this early formed opinion, as I see and hear further. Of the frequently elevated religious and moral as well as cultivated and refined intellectual character of the more favored household servants of many excellent families, there can be no room for doubt. I have hardly less doubt, however, of the almost heathenish condition of the slaves on many of the large plantations.

"Slavery is such an atrocious debasement of human nature, that its very extirpation, if not performed with solicitous care, may sometimes open a source of serious evils."—BENJAMIN FRANKLIN.

During forty-five years, according to Howison, the number of white convicts in the Virginia penitentiaries was in the ratio of 1 to about 328 of the whole population; the number of colored convicts, 1 in 67. "The free negroes and mulattoes are, unquestionably," says this historian, "the most vicious and corrupting of the varied materials composing our social system." "The criminal law, as to free colored persons and slaves, differs widely from that applied to whites. The free negroes occupy an equivocal and most unhappy position between the whites and slaves, and the laws affecting them partake of this peculiarity. Capital punishment is inflicted on them for offences more lightly punished in whites. They are entitled to trial by jury in cases of homicide and in all capital cases, but, for all other crimes, they are tried by justices' courts of Oyer and Terminer, who must be unanimous in order to convict. They are subjected to restraint and surveillance in points beyond number."

To show their poverty and the benevolence of providing for the race by slavery, I am told that in one county, a few years ago, an inventory and estimate of the value of their property was made by order of the magistracy. With one exception, the highest value placed upon the property of an individual was two dollars and a half ($2.50). The person excepted owned one hundred and fifty acres of land, a cabin upon it, a mule and some implements. He had a family of nine. Of provisions for its support, there were in the house, at the time of the visit of the appraisers, a peck and a half of Indian meal and part of a herring. The man was then absent to purchase some more meal, but had no money, and was to give his promise to pay in wood, which he was to cut from his farm. And this was in winter.

That this poverty is not the result of want of facilities or security of accumulating property, is proved by the exceptional instances of considerable wealth existing among them. An account of the death of a free colored man, who devised by will property to the amount of thirty thousand dollars, has lately been in the newspapers. I am assured, by one who knew the man very well, of the general accuracy of the narration, though one somewhat important circumstance was omitted. It was stated that the man preferred that his children should continue in the condition of slaves, and gave his property to a man who was to be their master. He gave as a reason for this, that he had personally examined the condition of the free blacks in Philadelphia and Boston, as well as in Virginia, and he preferred that his children should remain slaves, knowing that their master would take better care of them than they were capable of exercising for themselves. This was substantially correct. He had been, however, for a long time before his death, in a low state of health, and it is not known how sound, or uninfluenced by others, his mind might have been. The circumstance omitted was, that these were illegitimate children, by a slave woman, and that he simply left them in the condition in which they were born, in the care of their legal owner, having himself no legal right to dispose of them in any other way. It is a general custom of white people here to leave their illegitimate children, by slaves (and they are *very* common), in slavery. The man was himself a mulatto.

A man of wealth and station, who enjoys the friendship of the best and most respected people, lately sold his own half-brother, an intelligent, and of course "valuable," young man, to the traders, to be sent South, because he had attempted to run away to the Free States. So I am informed by his neighbor and friend.

At the present rate of wages, any free colored man might accumulate property more rapidly in Virginia than almost any man, depending solely on his labor, can at the North. In the tobacco-factories in Richmond and Petersburg, slaves are, at this time, in great demand, and are paid one hundred and fifty to two hundred dollars, and all expenses, for a year. These slaves are expected to work only to a certain extent for their employers; it having been found that they could not be "driven" to do a fair day's work so easily as they could be stimulated to it by the offer of a bonus for all they would manufacture above a certain number of pounds. This quantity is so easily exceeded, that the slaves earn for themselves from five to twenty dollars a month. Freemen are paid for all they do, at rates which make their labor equally profitable, and can earn, if they give but moderate attention and diligence to the labor, very large sums. One man's wages amounted last year, as I am informed by his employer, to over nine hundred dollars; but he is supposed to have laid up none of it. Nearly all the negroes, slave and free, it is said, spend their money as fast as they receive it. And nearly all of it goes in a manner to do them injury.

Formerly, it is said, the slaves were accustomed to amuse themselves, in the evening and on holidays, a great deal in dancing, and they took great enjoyment in this exercise. It was at length, however, preached against, and the "professors" so generally induced to use their influence against it, as an immoral practice, that it has greatly gone "out of fashion," and, in place of it, the young ones have got into the habit of gambling, and worse occupations, for the pastime of their holidays and leisure hours. I have not seen any dancing during these holidays, nor any recreation engaged in by the blacks, that is not essentially gross, dissipating, or wasteful, unless I except the firing of crackers.

Improvidence is generally considered here a natural trait of African character; and by none is it more so than by the negroes themselves. I think it is a mistake. Negroes, as far as I have observed at the North, although suffering from the contamination of habits acquired by themselves or their fathers in Slavery, are more provident than whites of equal educational advantages. Much more so than the newly-arrived Irish, though the Irish, soon after their immigration, are usually infected with the desire of accumulating wealth and acquiring permanent means of comfort. This opinion is confirmed by the experience of our City Missionaries — one of whom has informed me that where the very poorest classes of New York reside, black and white in the same house, the rooms occupied by the blacks are generally much less bare of furniture and the means of subsistence than those of the whites.

I observed that the negroes themselves follow the notion of the whites here, and look upon the people of their race as naturally unfitted to look out for themselves far ahead. Accustomed, like children, to have all their necessary wants provided for, their whole energies and powers of mind are habitually given to obtaining the means of temporary ease and enjoyment. Their masters and the poor or "mean" whites acquire somewhat of the same habits from early association with them, calculate on it in them—do not wish to cure it—and by constant practices encourage it. For the means of enjoying themselves the negroes depend much on presents. Their good-natured masters (and their masters are generally very good-natured, though capricious) like to gratify them, and are ashamed to disappoint them—to be thought mean. So it follows that, with the free negroes, habit is upon them; the habits of their associates, slaves, make the custom of society— that strongest of agents upon weak minds. The whites think improvidence a natural defect of character with them, expect it of them; as they grow old, or, as they lose easy means of gaining a livelihood, charitably furnish it to them; expect them to pilfer; do not look upon it as a crime, or at least consider them but slightly to blame; and so every influence and association is unfavorable to providence, forethought, economy.

With such influences upon them, with such a character, with such education, with such associations, it is not surprising that Southerners say that the condition of the slave who is subject to some wholesome restraint, and notwithstanding his improvidence is systematically provided for, is preferable to that of the free black. The free black does not, in general, feel himself superior to the slave; and the slaves of the wealthy and aristocratic families consider themselves in a much better and more honorable position than the free blacks. Their view of the matter is said to be expressed thus: —— *"dirty free niggers!—got nobody to take care of 'em."*

It is for this reason that slaves of gentlemen of high character, who are treated with judicious indulgence, and who can rely with confidence on the permanence of their position, knowing that they will be kindly cared for as they grow old, and feeling their own incapacity to take care of themselves, do often voluntarily remain in slavery when freedom is offered them, whether it be at the South, or North, or in Africa. A great many slaves that have been freed and sent to the North, after remaining there for a time, are said to have returned—longing, like the faithless Israelites, for the fleshpots of Slavery—of their own accord, to Virginia, and their report of the manner in which negroes are treated there, the difficulty of earning enough to provide themselves with the luxuries to which they have been accustomed, the unkindness of the white people to them, and the want of that thoughtless liberality in payments to them which they expect here from their superiors, has not been such as to lead others to pine for the life of an outcast at the North.

A number of Mr. Randolph's slaves, it has been several times mentioned to me, have thus returned. It is well known that Mr. Randolph took a humane and democratic view of Slavery; and his neglect to educate them for the liberty which, after his death, he bequeathed to them, may have added much to that terrible remorse which darkened his death-bed.

It is certainly true that the negroes, either slave or free, are not generally disposed to go to Liberia. It is a distant country, of which they can have but very little reliable information, and they do not like the idea, any more than other people, of emigrating from their native country. But I really think that the best reason for their not being more anxious to go there is, that they are sincerely attached, in a certain way, to the white race. At all events, they do not incline to live in communities entirely separate from the whites, and do not long for entire independence from them. They have been so long accustomed to trusting the government of all weighty matters to the whites, that they would not feel at ease where they did not have them to "take care of 'em." They do not feel inclined to take great responsibilities on themselves, and have no confidence in the talent of their race for self-government. A gentleman told me that he owned a very intelligent negro, who had acquired some property, and that he had more than once offered him his freedom, but he would always reply that he did not feel able to fall entirely upon his own resources, and preferred to have a master. He once offered him his freedom to go to Liberia, and urged him to go there. His reply was to the effect that he would have no objections if the government was in the hands of white folks, but that he had no confidence in the ability of black people to undertake the control of public affairs.

I do not wish to be understood as intimating that the slaves generally would not like to be freed and sent to the North, or that they are ever really contented or satisfied with slavery; only that having been deprived of the use of their limbs from infancy, as it were, they may not wish now suddenly to be set upon their feet, and left to shift for themselves. They may prefer to secure at least plain food and clothing, and comfortable lodging, at their owner's expense, while they will return as little for it as they can, and have only the luxuries of life to work for on their own account. It is not easy to deprive them of the means of securing a share of these.

These luxuries, to be sure, may be of very degrading character, and such as, according to our ideas, they would be better without; but their tastes and habits are formed to enjoy them, and they are not likely to be content without.

But, to live either on their own means, or the charitable assistance of others, at the North, they must dispense with many of these things. It is as much as most of them—more than some of them, with us—can do, by their labor, to obtain the means of subsistence, such as they have been used to being provided with, without a thought of their own, at the South. And if they are known to indulge in practices that are habitual with the race, they will not only lose the charity, but even the custom, of most of their philanthropic friends; and then they must turn to pilfering again, or meet that most pitiful of all extremities—poverty from want of work. Again: suppose them to wish to indulge in their old habits of sensual pleasure, they can only do so by forsaking the better class of even their own color, or by drawing them down to their own level. In this way, Slavery, even now, day by day, is greatly responsible for the degraded and immoral condition of the free blacks of our cities, and especially of Philadelphia. It is, perhaps, necessary that I should explain that licentiousness and almost indiscriminate sexual connection among the young is very general, and is a necessity of the system of Slavery. A Northern family that employs slave-domestics, and insists upon a life of physical chastity in its female servants, is always greatly detested; and they frequently come to their owners and beg to be taken away, or not hired again, though acknowledging themselves to be kindly treated in all other respects. A slave-owner told me this of his own girls hired to Northern people.

That the character and condition of some is improved by coming to the North, it is impossible to deny. From a miserable, half barbarous, half brutal state they have been brought in contact with the highest civilization. From slaves they have, sometimes, come to be men of intelligence, cultivation, and refinement. There are no white men in the United States that display every attribute of a strong and good soul better than some of the freed slaves. What would Frederick Douglass have been had he failed to escape from that service which Bishop Meade dares to say is the service of God; had his spirit been once broken by that man who, Bishop Meade would have taught him, was God's chosen overseer of his body? What has he become since he dared commit the sacrilege of coming out of bondage? All the statesmanship and kind mastership of the South has done less, in fifty years, to elevate and dignify the African race, than he in ten.

In order to be in time for the train of cars in which I was to leave Petersburg for Norfolk, I was called up at an unusual hour in the morning and provided with a very poor breakfast, on the ground that there had not been time to prepare a decent one, (though I was charged full time on the bill), advised by the landlord to hurry when I seated myself at the table, and two minutes afterwards informed that, if I remained longer, I should be too late.

Thanks to these kind precautions, I reached the station twenty minutes before the train left, and was afterwards carried with about fifty other people at the rate of ten miles an hour to City-point, where all were discharged under a dirty shed, from which a wharf projected into James river.

The train was advertised to connect here with a steamboat for Norfolk. Finding no steamboat at the wharf, I feared, at first, that the delay in leaving Petersburg and the slow speed upon the road had detained us so long that the boat had departed without us. But observing no disappointment or concern expressed by the other passengers, I concluded the boat was to call for us, and had yet to arrive. An hour passed, during which I tried to keep warm by walking up and down the wharf; rain then commenced falling, and I returned to the crowded shed and asked a young man, who was engaged in cutting the letters G. W. B., with a dirk-knife, upon the head of a tobacco-cask, what was supposed to have detained the steamboat.

"Detained her? there aint no detention to her as I know on; 'taint hardly time for her to be along yet."

Another half hour, in fact, passed, before the steamboat arrived, nor was any impatience manifested by the passengers. All seemed to take this hurrying and waiting process as the regular thing. The women sat sullenly upon trunks and packing-cases, and watched their baggage and restrained their children; the men chewed tobacco and read newspapers, lounged first on one side and then on the other, some smoked, some walked away to a distant tavern, some reclined on the heaps of freight and went to sleep, and a few conversed quietly and intermittingly with one another.

The shores of the James river are low and level—the scenery uninteresting; but frequent planters' mansions, often of great size and of some elegance, stand upon the bank, and sometimes these have very pretty and well-kept grounds about them—finer than any other I have seen at the South—and the plantations surrounding them are cultivated with neatness and skill. Many men distinguished in law and politics here have their homes.

I was pleased to see the appearance of enthusiasm with which some passengers, who were landed from our boat at one of these places, were received by two or three well-dressed negro servants, who had come from the house to the wharf to meet them. Black and white met with kisses, and the effort of a long-haired sophomore to maintain his supercilious dignity, was quite ineffectual to kill the kindness of a fat mulatto woman, who joyfully and pathetically shouted, as she caught him off the gang-plank, "Oh Massa George, is you come back!" Field negroes, standing by, looked on with their usual besotted expression, and neither offered nor received greetings.

I arrived in Norfolk on the eve of a terrific gale, during which vessels at anchor in the Roads went down, and the city and country were much excited by various disasters, both on shore and at sea.

JAN. 10th. Norfolk is a dirty, low, ill-arranged

town, nearly divided by a morass. It has a single creditable public building, a number of fine private residences, and the polite society is reputed to be agreeable, refined, and cultivated, receiving a character from the families of the resident naval officers. It has all the immoral and disagreeable characteristics of a large seaport, with very few of the advantages that we should expect to find as relief to them. No lyceum or public libraries, no public gardens, no galleries of art, and though there are two "BETHELS," no "home" for its seamen; no public resorts of healthful and refining amusement, no place better than a filthy, tobacco-impregnated bar-room or a licentious dance-cellar, so far as I have been able to learn, for the stranger of high or low degree to pass the hours unoccupied by business.

Lieut. Maury has lately very well shown what advantages were originally possessed for profitable commerce at this point, in a report, the intention of which is to advocate the establishment of a line of steamers hence to Para, the port of the mouth of the Amazon. I have the best wishes for the success of the project in its important features, and the highest respect for the judgment of Lieut. Maury, but it seems to me pertinent to inquire why are the British Government steamers not sent exclusively to Halifax, the nearest port to England, instead of to the more distant and foreign port of New York? If a Government line of steamers should be established between Para and Norfolk, and should be found in the least degree commercially profitable, how long would it be before another line would be established between New York and Para, by private enterprise, and then how much business would be left for the Government steamers while they continued to end their voyage at Norfolk? So, too, with regard to a line from Antwerp to Norfolk, (a proposition to grant State aid for establishing which, was the chief topic of public discussion in Virginia, at the time of my visit). Lieut. Maury says, however:

"Norfolk is in a position to have commanded the business of the Atlantic sea-board: it is midway the coast. It has a back country of great facility and resources; and, as to approaches to the ocean, there is no harbor from the St. Johns to the Rio Grande that has the same facilities of ingress and egress at all times and in all weathers. * * * The back country of Norfolk is all that which is drained by the Chesapeake Bay — embracing a line drawn along the ridge between the Delaware and the Chesapeake, thence northerly, including all of Pennsylvania that is in the valley of the Susquehanna, all of Maryland this side of the mountains, the valleys of the Potomac, Rappahannock, York, and James rivers, with the Valley of the Roanoke, and a great part of the State of North Carolina, whose only outlet to the sea is by the way of Norfolk."

This is a favorite theme with Lieut. Maury, who is a Virginian. In a letter to the *National Intelligencer*, Oct. 31, 1854, after describing similar advantages which the town possesses to those enumerated above, he continues:

"Its climate is delightful. It is of exactly that happy temperature where the frosts of the North bite not, and the pestilence of the South walks not. Its harbor is commodious and safe as safe can be. It is never blocked up by ice. It has the double advantage of an inner and an outer harbor. The inner harbor is as smooth as any mill-pond. In it vessels lie with perfect security, where every imaginable facility is offered for loading and unloading. * * * The back country, which without portage is *naturally* tributary to Norfolk, not only surpasses that which is tributary to New York in mildness of climate, in fertility of soil, and variety of production, but in geographical extent by many square miles. The proportion being as *three to one* in favor of the Virginia port. * * * The *natural* advantages, then, in relation to the sea or the back country, are superior, *beyond comparison*, to those of New York."

There is little, if any exaggeration in this estimate; yet, if a deadly, enervating pestilence had always raged here, this Norfolk could not be a more miserable, sorry little seaport town than it is.[1] It was not possible to

[1] This was written and printed long before the late sad visit of yellow fever to Norfolk. I should hardly let it stand now, if I had not previously thought and said, when in the town, that its undrained and filthy condition was such that it seemed to me incredible that its people could live in health. If the condition of the town, at the time of my visit, was not very extraordinary, this dreadful visitor certainly did not come uninvited.

Since writing this note, my attention has been called to an article in the *Boston Medical and Surgical Journal*, written by a person who had resided for two years in Norfolk, and who says the town is "destitute of sewerage, and its streets are extremely filthy, being often strewed with refuse vegetables and other garbage, which result from the immense quantity of provisions brought into the city for export. These matters become rotten, and emit a most noisome stench. The turkey-buzzard, the natural scavenger of the South, is not found in Norfolk, but his place is supplied by cows, who wander at will through the town, and gather an unhealthy subsistence from the cabbage-stalks and other substances which lie in heaps on the ground. The condition of Portsmouth is much worse than that of Norfolk. It is connected with Gosport by a causeway, nearly a mile in length, if we are not mistaken, across a swamp or flat, from which arises a powerful stench."

prevent the existence of some agency here for the transhipment of goods, and for supplying the needs of vessels, compelled by exterior circumstances to take refuge in the harbor. Beyond this bare supply of a necessitous demand, and what results from the adjoining naval rendezvous of the nation, there is nothing.

Singularly simple, child-like ideas about commercial success, you find among the Virginians—even among the merchants themselves. The agency by which commodities are transferred from the producer to the consumer, they seem to look upon as a kind of swindling operation; they do not see that the merchant acts a useful part in the community, or, that his labor can be other than selfish and malevolent. They speak angrily of New York, as if it fattened on the country without doing the country any good in return. They have no idea that it is *their* business that the New Yorkers are doing, and that whatever tends to facilitate it, and make it simple and secure, is an increase of their wealth by diminishing the costs and lessening the losses upon it.

They gravely demand why the government mail steamers should be sent to New York, when New York has so much business already, and why the nation should build costly custom-houses, and post-offices, and mints, and sea defences, and collect stores and equipments there, and not at Norfolk, and Petersburg, and Richmond, and Danville, and Lynchburg, and Smithtown, and Jones's Cross-Roads? It seems never to have occurred to them that it is because the country needs them there, because the skill, enterprise, and energy of New York merchants, the confidence of capitalists in New York merchants, the various facilities for trade offered by New York merchants, enable them to do the business of the country cheaper and better than it can be done anywhere else, and that thus they can *command* commerce, and need not petition their Legislature, or appeal to mean sectional prejudices to obtain it, but all imagine it is by some shrewd Yankee trickery it is done. By the bones of their noble fathers they will set their faces against it—and their faces are not of dough—so they bully their local merchants into buying in dearer markets, and make the country tote its gold on to Philadelphia to be coined ; and their conventions resolve that the world shall come to Norfolk, or Richmond, or Smithtown, and that no more cotton shall be sent to England until England will pay a price for it that shall let negroes be worth a thousand dollars a head, &c., &c., &c.

Then, if it be asked why Norfolk, with its immense natural advantages for commerce, has not been able to do their business for them as well as New York ; or why Richmond, with its great natural superiority for manufacturing, has not prospered like Glasgow, or Petersburg like Lowell — why Virginia is not like Pennsylvania, or Kentucky like Ohio ?—they will perhaps answer that it is owing to the peculiar tastes they have inherited ; " settled mainly (as was Virginia) by the sons of country gentlemen, who brought the love of country life with them across the Atlantic, and infused it into the mass of the population, they have ever preferred that life, and the title of country gentleman, implying the possession of landed estates, has always been esteemed more honorable than any other."[1] It is simply a matter of taste—an answer which reminds us of Æsop's fox.

Ask any honest stranger who has been brought into intimate intercourse for a short time with the people, why it is that here has been stagnation, and there constant, healthy progress, and he will answer that these people are less enterprising, energetic, and sensible in the conduct of their affairs—that they live less in harmony with the laws that govern the accumulation of wealth than those.

Ask him how this difference of character should have arisen, and he will tell you it is not from the blood, but from the education they have received; from the institutions and circumstances they have inherited. It is the old, fettered, barbarian labor-system, in connection with which they have been brought up, against which all their enterprise must struggle, and with the chains of which all their ambition must be bound.

This conviction I find to be universal in the minds of strangers, and it is forced upon one more strongly than it is possible to make you comprehend by a mere statement of isolated facts. You could as well convey an idea of the effect of mist on a landscape, by enumerating the number of particles of vapor that obscure it. Give Virginia blood fair play, remove it from the atmosphere

[1] Dr. Little's History of Richmond.

of slavery, and it shows no lack of energy and good sense.

It is strange the Virginians dare not look this in the face. Strange how they bluster in their legislative debates, in their newspapers, and in their bar-rooms, about the "Yankees," and the "Yorkers," declaring that they are "swindled out of their legitimate trade," when the simple truth is, that the Northern merchants do that for them that they are unable to do for themselves. As well might the Chinese be angry with us for sending our clipper ships for their tea, because it is a business that would be more "legitimately" (however less profitably) carried on in "junks."

There's a yarn I have heard from the Staaten Island coasters, who run down to the capes of Virginia for oysters, which illustrates admirably how Virginia commerce would be "legitimately" carried on, that is, in the manner naturally resulting from her system.

Among the largest and luckiest of the Virginia merchant-marine, is the fine, fast-sailing, light-draft, putty-bottomed, packet-sloop, the Abstraction. The "old Ab" was formerly owned and commanded by Captain Jerry S., and was manned by one black boy, sixty years old, named Mopus, and commonly called Uncle Mopus. Mopus was a slave, and Captain Jerry had bought him with the sloop.

Mopus was a proper slave, patient, meek, stupid, and stubborn,— a talking donkey. He never had been taught to read or to comprehend figures. He could not understand the dial, and the binnacle-compass was a sort of fetish to him; the mystery of which he was too humble to desire to penetrate. He piously left these great things in the hands of his owner, and resigned himself to the will of that Providence which had given him a master to take care of him, who was responsible for his safety and profits, as well as the sloop's.

This resignation and faith of the good Mopus, however, often gave Captain Jerry a deal of trouble, for it obliged him to be nearly always on deck and wide awake, and he sometimes thought he might better sell Mopus, and buy a nigger that was not so good, (Captain Jerry, as I heard it, used to put in a word between so and good, and bear down on it,) but the danger that such a one would prove entirely reckless of all moral suggestions, as smart niggers are very apt to, and go and steal himself, prevented his doing so, and he tried to make the best of Mopus' muscles, and to supply the necessary brain-power for the sloop from his own private skull.

One night, Captain Jerry having been up all the previous night, and having just worked the sloop out of Hampton Roads, against wind and tide, and being quite overcome with fatigue, thought he might venture to trust Mopus with the helm for a few hours, the sloop's course being now due north, up Chesapeake Bay, wind light and quartering, a clear sky, and nothing in the way for fifty miles.

Mopus knew the North Star very well, as niggers generally do, and telling him to keep the bow-sprit pointing straight at it, and not to disturb him until he saw land to starboard, Captain Jerry put out the binnacle-light to save oil, and turned-in.

Captain Jerry had the habit, which small-craft men are apt to get, of consulting aloud with himself. No sooner had he closed the companion scuttle than Mopus, with head to the stove-pipe, heard—"Moon fulled Thursday—slack water at six—North Star—that 'll do till daylight sartain—due North—Tangier island—not afore meridian—can't go wrong till arter daylight, no how—good snooze this time—go in—off boots."

Mope was a capital helmsman; and for two hours, while the breeze held, he kept on a bee-line to the northward. Then it fell calm; and then there came little catspaws from northwest, and Mope, after giving a pull of the main-sheet, left the helm a minute to flatten the jib. While he was forward, a flaw from the northeast took him all aback. Belaying jib-sheet, he came aft, and put helm up to wear round. Just as he jibed, came another flaw from the southeast, and a pretty smart one. Mope met it, trimmed close, and seeing it was going to be steady, left the helm again, and shoved down the centre board. Then he went to the hatchway and got his coat, after which he took a pull at the scuttle-butt, and struck a light for a smoke.

All this time old Abby, with her head southeast, was shaking like a nail-mill. Mope finally hauled the jib up to port, till the mainsail filled, then took the helm again, and kept her rap full heading south, but running off to the westward, now and then, in search for the North Star, which, as he could not see it anywhere else, he thought for a long time must have got behind the mainsail.

He had smoked out two pipes before he found it, and then it was *right over the stern*, which at first struck him as a singular circumstance. There it was, "pointers and all;" he could not be mistaken. But how did it get *there?*

Mope pondered over it for two pipes more, all the while giving her a good full and nothing off. He was at first inclined to treat it as a mystery; but when, about two o'clock, the moon rose, he grew bold, knotted his eyebrows, clenched his teeth, took off his tarpaulin, and struck his reflective organs with his clenched fist.

At length the problem was solved, and his lips trembled and gathered inward and puckered back with that pleasure which niggers, in common with human beings, enjoy, when they are conscious of having acquitted themselves well of a trying and honorable responsibility. He immediately hauled the boom down close to the taffrail; he went forward, and belayed the jib to windward, lighted his pipe again, and kept a good lookout till, as day broke, he made land to starboard, just as he expected;—land to starboard and —why did n't he see it before?—a light right ahead, and not very far ahead either.

"All right," thought Mopus, "daylight, humph! let an old nigger alone to find the way to the North;" and he let the jib draw away, went aft, took the helm and called the skipper.

The skipper turned out:

"Hallo, uncle, close hauled? Wind's come out o' norrard, has it? Why, Mopus! why! what the devil— what light 's that? Why, Mope! why you——Where you been taking the sloop to now, you black rascal! here 's the North Star over the starn!"

"Oh yes, massa, past de Norf Star an hour ago; all right, sar, here 's de land right off here to luward. Made a fine run, sar. Oh! I knows how to fotch 'em along, I does myself, ha! ha! ha! Takes old Mope arter all, don't it? ha! ha! ha!"

"Ye-es (through his teeth) mighty fine run! Old Point, by the blood of Pocahontas! just where I 'd got her last night at sunset!—you grinnin' catamount! Takes old Mope! You bloody old cuss! I 'll sell you for a chaw of tobacco to the first white man that 'll take you off my hands."

Incidents, trifling in themselves, constantly betray to a stranger the bad economy of using enslaved servants. The catastrophe of one such occurred since I began to write this letter. I ordered a fire to be made in my room, as I was going out this morning. On my return, I found a grand fire—the room door having been closed and locked upon it, and, by the way, I had to obtain assistance to open it, the lock being "out of order." Just now, while I was writing, down tumbled upon the floor, and rolled away close to the valance of the bed, half a hod-full of ignited coal, which had been so piled up on the diminutive grate, and left without a fender or any guard, that this result was almost inevitable. If

I had not returned at the time I did, the house would have been fired, and probably an incendiary charged with it, while some Northern Insurance Company made good the loss to the owner. And such carelessness of servants you have momentarily to notice.

But the constantly-occurring delays, and the waste of time and labor that you encounter everywhere, are most annoying and provoking to a stranger. The utter want of system and order, almost essential, as it would appear, where slaves are your instruments, is amazing—and when you are not in haste, often amusing. At a hotel, for instance, you go to your room and find no conveniences for washing; ring and ring again, and hear the office-keeper ring again and again. At length two servants appear together at your door, get orders, and go away. A quarter of an hour afterwards, perhaps, one returns with a pitcher of water, but no towels; and so on. Yet as the servants are attentive and anxious to please (expecting to be " remembered " when you leave), it only results from the want of system and order.

Until the negro is big enough for his labor to be palpably profitable to his master, he has no training to application or method, but only to idleness and carelessness. Before the children arrive at a working age, they hardly come under the notice of their owner. An inventory of them is taken on the plantation at Christmas; and a planter told me that he had sometimes had them brought in at twelve or thirteen years old, that had escaped the vigilance of the overseer up to that age. The only whipping of slaves that I have seen in Virginia, has been of these wild, lazy children, as they are being broke in to work. It is at this moment going on in the yard beneath my window. They cannot be depended upon a minute out of sight.

You will see how difficult it would be, if it were attempted, to eradicate the indolent, careless, incogitant habits so formed in youth. But it is not systematically attempted, and the influences that continue to act upon a slave in the same direction, cultivating every quality at variance with industry, precision, forethought, and providence, are innumerable.

It is impossible that the habits of the whole community should not be influenced by, and be made to accommodate to these habits of its laborers. It irresistibly affects the whole industrial character of the people. You may see it in the habits and manners of the free white mechanics and trades-people. All of these must have dealings or be in competition with slaves, and so have their standard of excellence made low, and become accustomed to, until they are content with slight, false, unsound workmanship. You notice in all classes, vagueness in ideas of cost and value, and injudicious and unnecessary expenditure of labor by a thoughtless manner of setting about work.[1]

I had an umbrella broken. I noticed it as I was going out from my hotel during a shower, and stepped

---

[1] A ship's officer told me that he had noticed that it took just about three times as long to have the same repairs made in Norfolk that it did in New York.

into an adjoining locksmith's to have it repaired. He asked where he should send it when he had done it. "I intended to wait for it," I answered; "how long is it going to take you, and how much shall you charge?"

"I can't do it in less than half an hour, sir, and it will be worth a quarter."

"I should n't think it need take you so long, it is merely a rivet to be tightened."

"I shall have to take it all to pieces, and it will take me all of half an hour."

"I don't think you need take it to pieces."

"Yes, I shall—there's no other way to do it."

"Then, as I can't well wait so long, I will not trouble you with it;" and I went into the hotel, and with the fire-poker did the job myself, in less than a minute, as well as he could have done it in a week, and went on my way, saving half an hour and quarter of a dollar, like a "Yankee."

Virginians laugh at us for such things: but it is because they are indifferent to these fractions, or, as they say, above regarding them, that they cannot do their own business with the rest of the world, and all their commerce, as they are constantly and most absurdly complaining, only goes to enrich Northern men. A man forced to labor under their system is morally driven to indolence, carelessness, indifference to the results of skill, heedlessness, inconstancy of purpose, improvidence, and extravagance. Precisely the opposite qualities are those which are encouraged, and inevitably developed in a man who has to make his living, and earn all his comfort by his voluntarily-directed labor. These opposite qualities are those which are essentially necessary to the success of an adventurer in commerce. The commercial success of the free states is the offspring of their voluntary labor system. The inability of the Virginians to engage in commerce is the result of their system of involuntary servitude. The condition of the laborers predetermines the condition of all the people.

Several ships were here, under orders, waiting for crews; with the rest, the Powhattan steam-frigate, among whose officers I found some acquaintances. What sort of hands they had to take, and how difficult they found the duty of efficiently commanding them, may be imagined from the disgraceful fact, that, at that time, but twelve dollars a month was allowed by Government to be paid for the best men for the national service, while merchantmen were paying twenty-five dollars for common able seamen; and yet, because, when under these circumstances, the crews obtained were not smart, clean, sober, docile, and contented, I heard officers ascribe their difficulties to the disuse of the cat and the old terrifying system of discipline.

The United States Navy should be a school of the utmost excellence of seamanship, not a refuge for irreclaimable sots, loafers, and ruffians, who cannot, or dare not, take employment elsewhere at the market rate of wages.

I, as a one-twenty-three-millionth proprietor of it, wonder if it would not be better policy to go into exactly the opposite extreme, and, by paying the best wages, get the best men—the highest priced labor in open market is usually believed to be the cheapest.

And I wonder if it would not be possible to obtain men for the labor of ships, as well as for any other labor, who would always perform the services required of them heartily, promptly, and fully, as an honest return for their wages and rations; who would obey orders, not like whipped curs and cowed slaves, but as free men, and brave men, and wise men, with a republican respect for right laws, and a sensible understanding of the fit division of responsibility between them and their officers. I fear not, unless some thorough, comprehensive, and generously-directed educational department shall be adopted as a permanent, and indivisible part of our naval system.

The "Great Dismal Swamp," together with the smaller "Dismals" (for so the term is used here), of the same character, along the North Carolina Coast, have hitherto been of considerable commercial importance as furnishing a large amount of lumber, and especially of shingles for our Northern use as well as for exportation. The district from which this commerce proceeds is all a vast quagmire, the soil being entirely composed of decayed vegetable fibre, saturated and surcharged with water; yielding or *quaking* on the surface to the tread of a man, and a large part of it, during most of the year, half inundated with standing pools. It is divided by creeks and water-veins, and in the cen-

Virginia

tre is a pond six miles long and three broad, the shores of which, strange to say, are at a higher elevation above the sea, than any other part of the swamp, and yet are of the same miry consistency.

The Great Dismal is about thirty miles long and ten miles wide on an average; its area about 200,000 acres. And the little Dismal, Alligator, Catfish, Green, and other smaller swamps, on the shores of Albemarle and Pamlico, contain over 2,000,000 acres. A considerable part of this is the property of the State of North Carolina, and the proceeds of sales from it form the chief income of the department of education of that Commonwealth.

An excellent canal,[1] six feet in depth, passes for more than twenty miles through the swamp, giving passage

---

[1] Of the main products of the country, the annual freightage on the Dismal Swamp Canal is about as follows:

Shingles	24,000,000
Staves	6,000,000
Plank and scantling, cubic feet	125,000
Ship timber	40,000
Cotton bales	4,500
Shad and herring, barrels	50,000
Naval stores, barrels	30,000
Spirits turpentine, barrels	700
Bacon, cwts.	5,000
Lard, kegs	1,300
Maize, bushels.	2,000,000
Wheat, bushels	30,000
Peas, bushels	25,000

The canal was made with the assistance of the National Government and the State of Virginia, who are still the largest owners. It is admirably constructed, repairs are light, and it is a good six per cent. stock.

not only to the lumber collected from it, but to a large fleet of coasting vessels engaged in the trade of the Albemarle and Pamlico Sounds, and making a safe outlet towards New York for all the corn, cotton, tar, turpentine, etc., produced in the greater part of the eastern section of North Carolina, which is thus brought to market without encountering the extremely hazardous passage outside, from Cape Hatteras to Cape Henry. This canal is fed by the water of the pond in the centre of the swamp, its summit-level being many feet below it.

Much of the larger part of the "Great Dismal" was originally covered by a heavy forest growth. All the trees indigenous to the neighboring country I found still extensively growing, and of full size within its borders. But the main production, and that which has been of the greatest value, has been of cypress and juniper; (the latter commonly known as white cedar, at the North). From these two, immense quantities of shingles have been made. The cypress also affords ship timber, now in great demand, and a great many rough poles of the juniper, under the name of "cedar-rails," are sent to New York and other ports, as fencing material, (generally selling at seven cents a rail,) for the farms of districts that have been deprived of their own natural wood by the extension of tillage required by the wants of neighboring towns or manufactories.

The swamp belongs to a great many proprietors. Most of them own only a few acres, but some possess large tracts and use a heavy capital in the business. One, whose acquaintance I made, employed more than a hundred hands in getting out shingles alone. The value of the swamp land varies with the wood upon it, and the facility with which it can be got off, from 12½ cents to $10 an acre. It is made passable in any desired direction in which trees grow, by laying logs, cut in lengths of eight or ten feet, parallel and against each other on the surface of the soil, or "sponge," as it is called. Mules and oxen are used to some extent upon these roads, but transportation is mainly by hand to the creeks, or to ditches communicating with them or the canal.

Except by those log-roads, the swamp is scarcely passable in many parts, owing not only to the softness of the sponge, but to the obstruction caused by innumerable shrubs, vines, creepers and briars, which often take entire possession of the surface, forming a dense brake or jungle. This, however, is sometimes removed by fires, which of late years have been frequent and very destructive to the standing timber. The most common shrubs are various smooth-leafed evergreens, and their dense, bright, glossy foliage, was exceedingly beautiful in the wintry season of my visit. There is a good deal of game in the swamp—bears and wild cats are sometimes shot, raccoons and opossums are plentiful, and deer are found in the drier parts and on the outskirts. The fishing, in the interior waters, is also said to be excellent.

Nearly all the valuable trees have now been cut off

from the swamp. The whole ground has been frequently gone over, the best timber selected and removed at each time, leaving the remainder standing thinly, so that the wind has more effect upon it; and much of it, from the yielding of the soft soil, is uprooted or broken off. The fires have also greatly injured it. The principal stock, now worked into shingles, is obtained *from beneath the surface*—old trunks that have been preserved by the wetness of the soil, and that are found by "sounding" with poles, and raised with hooks or pikes by the negroes.

The quarry is giving out, however, and except that lumber, and especially shingles, have been in great demand at high prices of late, the business would be almost at an end. As it is, the principal men engaged in it are turning their attention to other and more distant supplies. A very large purchase had been made by one company in the Florida everglades, and a schooner, with a gang of hands trained in the "Dismals," was about to sail from Deep-creek, for this new field of operations.

The labor in the swamp is almost entirely done by slaves; and the way in which they are managed is interesting and instructive. They are mostly hired by their employers at a rent, perhaps of one hundred dollars a year for each, paid to their owners. They spend one or two months of the winter—when it is too wet to work in the swamp—at the residence of their master. At this period little or no work is required of them; their time is their own, and if they can get any employment, they will generally keep for themselves what they are paid for it. When it is sufficiently dry—usually early in February—they go into the swamp in gangs, each gang under a white overseer. Before leaving, they are all examined and registered at the Court-house, and "passes," good for a year, are given them, in which their features and the marks upon their persons are minutely described. Each man is furnished with a quantity of provisions and clothing, of which, as well as of all that he afterwards draws from the stock in the hands of the overseer, an exact account is kept.

Arrived at their destination, a rude camp is made, huts of logs, poles, shingles, and boughs being built, usually upon some place where shingles have been worked before, and in which the shavings have accumulated in small hillocks upon the soft surface of the ground.

The slave lumberman then lives measurably as a free man; hunts, fishes, eats, drinks, smokes and sleeps, plays and works, each when and as much as he pleases. It is only required of him that he shall have made, after half a year has passed, such a quantity of shingles as shall be worth to his master so much money as is paid to his owner for his services, and shall refund the value of the clothing and provisions he has required.

No "driving" at his work is attempted or needed. No force is used to overcome the indolence peculiar to the negro. The overseer merely takes a daily account of the number of shingles each man adds to the general stock, and employs another set of hands, with mules, to draw them to a point from which they can be shipped, and where they are, from time to time, called for by a schooner.

At the end of five months the gang returns to dry-land, and a statement of account from the overseer's book is drawn up, something like the following:

Sam Bo to John Doe, Dr.

Feb.	1. To clothing (outfit)	$ 5.00
Mar.	10. To clothing, as per overseer's account	2.25
Feb.	1. To bacon and meal (outfit). . .	19.00
July	1. To stores drawn in swamp, as per overseer's account	4.75
July	1. To half-yearly hire, paid his owner .	50.00
		$81.00

Per Contra, Cr.

July	1. By 10,000 shingles, as per overseer's account, 10c.	100.00
	Balance due Sambo	$19.00

which is immediately paid him, and which, together with the proceeds of sale of peltry which he has got while in the swamp, he is always allowed to make use of as his own. No liquor is sold or served to the negroes in the swamp, and, as their first want when they come out of it is an excitement, most of their money goes to the grog-shops.

After a short vacation, the whole gang is taken in the schooner to spend another five months in the swamp as before. If they are good hands and work steadily, they will commonly be hired again, and so continuing, will spend most of their lives at it. They almost invariably have excellent health, as do also the white men engaged in the business. They all consider the water of "the Dismals" to have a medicinal virtue, and quite probably it is a mild tonic. It is greenish in color, and I thought I detected a slightly resinous taste upon first drinking it. Upon entering the swamp also, an agreeable resinous odor, resembling that of a hemlock forest, was perceptible.

The negroes working in the swamp were more sprightly and straightforward in their manner and conversation than any field-hand plantation-negroes that I saw at the South; two or three of their employers with whom I conversed spoke well of them, as compared with other slaves, and made no complaints of "rascality" or laziness.

One of those gentlemen told me of a remarkable case of providence and good sense in a negro that he had employed in the swamp for many years. He was so trustworthy, that he had once let him go to New York as cook of a lumber-schooner, when he could, if he had chosen to remain there, have easily escaped from slavery.

Knowing that he must have accumulated considerable money, his employer suggested to him that he might *buy* his freedom, and he immediately determined to do so. But when, on applying to his owner, he was asked $500 for himself, a price which, considering he was an elderly man, he thought too much, he declined the bargain; shortly afterwards, however, he came to his employer again, and said that although he thought his owner was mean to set so high a price upon him, he had been thinking that if he was to be an old man he would rather be his own master, and if he did not live long, his money would not be of any use to him at any rate, and so he had concluded he would make the purchase.

He did so, and upon collecting the various sums that he had loaned to white people in the vicinity, he was found to have several hundred dollars more than was necessary. With the surplus, he paid for his passage to Liberia, and bought a handsome outfit. When he was about to leave, my informant had made him a present, and, in thanking him for it, the free man had said that the first thing he should do, on reaching Liberia, would be to learn to write, and, as soon as he could, he would write to him how he liked the country: he had been gone yet scarce a year, and had not been heard from.

When it is no longer found profitable to get lumber out of these swamps, they will be dead property, as little or no large wood is growing to supply the place of that taken off, except in the drier parts, where pines come up, as on " old-fields." It is probable that some extensive scheme of draining and reclaiming them will eventually be adopted. I am aware of but a single attempt, as yet, to cultivate the sponge or true swamp soil. This was made by a Mr. Wallace, on the northeast border of the Great Dismal. He had, with creditable spirit and skill, reclaimed four hundred acres. Having a sufficient outfall, he cuts wide drains parallel to each other, and about one hunded and twenty-five yards apart. These serve, at first, to float away, for market, all the timber of value left on the tract, as well as to draw the water from the surface. The ground is then grubbed, as much as it is thought necessary, and the stumps and worthless logs burnt. After cultivation, the soil is almost an impalpable powder, the foot sinks to the ankle in crossing it, and it rises in clouds of dust, when disturbed in a dry season. It is, of course, easy of cultivation, and is very productive in corn and potatoes—the only crops of which Mr. W. had yet made much trial.

Mr. W. told me that he had sold, during the previous summer, two thousand one hundred barrels of potatoes, which were produced on forty acres, and were taken by contract and delivered at Norfolk, by middlemen for the New York market, at four dollars a barrel. Thus the return from forty acres was over eight thousand dollars, and this without any expenditure for manure and with very light cultivation. In New York, the potatoes sold readily, early in the season, at from five to ten dollars a barrel.

Land of this description, thus managed, can be bought, in its unreclaimed state, at from one to five dollars an acre. The success of Mr. Wallace has somewhat increased the value of it, in his neighborhood. He reckons that the cost of reclaiming and fitting it entirely, in the manner that his experience leads him to think most profitable, would be fifty dollars an acre. From this is to be deducted the value of timber obtained from it.

Persons moving here from the North, will be very subject to bilious fever during the fall months; by prudence it may be partially escaped, but the danger is a permanent one at that season. It is not often fatal, but probably has a ruinous effect upon the general constitution.

The market-gardens at Norfolk—which have been profitably supplying New York markets with poor early vegetables, and half-hardy luxuries for several years past—do not differ at all from market-gardens elsewhere. They are situated in every direction for many miles from the city, offering a striking contrast, in all respects, to the large, old-fashioned Virginian farms, among which they are scattered.

On one of the latter, of over a thousand acres, a friend told me he had seen the negroes moving long-strawy manure with shovels, and upon inquiry found there was not a dung-fork on the place.

The soil is a poor sandy loam, and manure is brought by shipping from Baltimore, as well as from the nearer towns, to enrich it. The proprietors of the market-gardens are nearly all from New Jersey, and brought many of their old white laborers with them. Except at picking-time, when everything possessing fingers is in demand, they do not often employ slaves.

The *Norfolk Argus* says that, from about the 20th June to the 20th July, from 2000 to 2500 barrels of potatoes will be shipped daily from that city to Philadelphia and New York, together with 300 to 500 barrels of cucumbers, musk-melons, etc.

While driving in a chaise from Portsmouth to Deep-river, I picked up on the road a jaded looking negro, who proved to be a very intelligent and good-natured fellow. His account of the lumber business, and of the life of the lumbermen in the swamps, in answer to my questions, was clear and precise, and was afterwards verified by information obtained from his master.

He told me that his name was Joseph, that he belonged to a church in one of the inland counties, and that he was hired out by the trustees of the church to his present master. He expressed entire contentment with his lot, but showed great unwillingness to be sold to go on to a plantation. He liked to " mind himself," as he did in the swamps. Whether he would still more prefer to be entirely his own master, I did not ask.

The Dismal Swamps are noted places of refuge for runaway negroes. They were formerly peopled in this way much more than at present; a systematic hunting of them with dogs and guns having been made by individuals who took it up as a business about ten years ago. Children were born, bred, lived and died here. Joseph Church told me he had seen skeletons, and had helped to bury bodies recently dead. There were people in the swamps still, he thought, that were the children of runaways, and who had been runaways themselves all their lives. What a life it must be; born outlaws; educated self-stealers; trained from infancy to be constantly in dread of the approach of a white man as a thing more fearful than wild-cats or serpents, or even starvation.

There can be but few, however, if any, of these

"natives" left. They cannot obtain the means of supporting life without coming often either to the outskirts to steal from the plantations, or to the neighborhood of the camps of the lumbermen. They depend much upon the charity or the wages given them by the latter. The poorer white men, owning small tracts of the swamps, will sometimes employ them, and the negroes frequently. In the hands of either they are liable to be betrayed to the negro-hunters. Joseph said that they had huts in "back places," hidden by bushes, and difficult of access; he had, apparently, been himself quite intimate with them. When the shingle negroes employed them, he told me, they made them get up logs for them, and would give them enough to eat, and some clothes, and perhaps two dollars a month in money. But some, when they owed them money, would betray them, instead of paying them.

I asked if they were ever shot. "Oh, yes," he said, "when the hunters saw a runaway, if he tried to get from them, they would call out to him, that if he did not stop they would shoot, and if he did not, they would shoot, and sometimes kill him.

"*But some on 'em would rather be shot than be took, sir,*" he added, simply.

A farmer living near the swamp confirmed this account, and said he knew of three or four being shot in one day.

No particular breed of dogs is needed for hunting negroes: blood-hounds, fox-hounds, bull-dogs, and curs were used, and one white man told me how they were trained for it, as if it were a common or notorious practice.[1] They are shut up when puppies, and never allowed to see a negro except while training to catch him. A negro is made to run from them, and they are encouraged to follow him until he gets into a tree, when meat is given them. Afterwards they learn to follow any particular negro by scent, and then a shoe or a piece of clothing is taken off a negro, and they learn to find by scent who it belongs to, and to *tree* him, etc. I don't think they are employed in the ordinary driving in the swamp, but only to overtake some particular slave, as soon as possible after it is discovered that he has fled from a plantation. Joseph said that it was easy for the drivers to tell a fugitive from a regularly employed slave in the swamps.

"How do they know them?"

"Oh, dey looks *strange*."

"How do you mean?"

"*Skeared* like, you know, sir, and kind o' strange, cause dey has n't much to eat, and ain't decent [not decently clothed], like we is."

When the hunters take a negro who has not a pass, or "free papers," and they don't know whose slave he is, they confine him in jail, and advertise him. If no one claims him within a year he is sold to the highest bidder, at a public sale, and this sale gives title in law against any subsequent claimant.

[1] I have since seen a pack of negro-dogs, chained in couples, and probably going to the field. They were all of a breed, and in appearance between a Scotch stag-hound and a fox-hound.

The form of the advertisements used in such cases is shown by the following, which are cut from North Carolina newspapers, published in counties adjoining the Dismals. Such advertisements are quite as common in the papers of many parts of the Slave States as those of horses or cattle "Taken up" in those of the North:

"WAS TAKEN UP and committed to the Jail of Halifax County, on the 26th day of May, a dark colored boy, who says his name is JORDAN ARTIS. Said boy says he was born free, and was bound out to William Beale, near Murfreesboro', Hertford County, N. C., and is now 21 years of age. The owner is requested to come forward, prove property, pay charges, and take the said boy away, within the time prescribed by law; otherwise he will be dealt with as the law directs.

"O. P. SHELL, Jailer.
"Halifax County, N. C., June 8, 1855."

"TAKEN UP,

"AND COMMITTED to the Jail of New Hanover County, on the 5th of March, 1855, a Negro Man, who says his name is EDWARD LLOYD. Said negro is about 35 or 40 years old, light complected, 5 feet 9½ inches high, slim built, upper fore teeth out; says he is a Mason by trade, that he is free, and belongs in Alexandria, Va., that he served his time at the Mason business under Mr. Wm. Stuart, of Alexandria. He was taken up and committed as a runaway. His owner is notified to come forward, prove property, pay charges, and take him away, or he will be dealt with as the law directs.

"E. D. HALL, Sheriff."

In the same paper with the last are four advertisements of Runaways: two of them, as specimens, I transcribe.

"$200 REWARD.

"RAN AWAY from the employ of Messrs. Holmes & Brown, on Sunday night, 20th inst., a negro man named YATNEY or MEDICINE, belonging to the undersigned. Said boy is stout built, about 5 feet 4 inches high, 22 years old, and dark complected, and has the appearance, when walking slow, of one leg being a little shorter than the other. He was brought from Chapel Hill, and is probably lurking either in the neighborhood of that place, or Beatty's Bridge, in Bladen County.

"The above reward will be paid for evidence sufficient to convict any white person of harboring him, or a reward of $25 for his apprehension and confinement in any Jail in the State, so that I can get him, or for his delivery to me in Wilmington.

"J. T. SCHONWALD."

"RUNAWAY

"FROM THE SUBSCRIBER, on the 27th of May, his negro boy ISOME. Said boy is about 21 years of age; rather light complexion; very coarse hair; weight about 150; height about 5 feet 6 or 7 inches; rather pleasing countenance; quick and easy spoken; rather a downcast look. It is thought that he is trying to make his way to Franklin county, N. C., where he was hired in Jan. last, of Thomas J. Blackwell. A liberal Reward will be given for his confinement in any Jail in North or South Carolina, or to any one who will give information where he can be found.

"W. H. PRIVETT,
"Canwayboro', S. C."

Handbills, written or printed, offering rewards for the return of Runaway slaves, are to be constantly seen at nearly every court-house, tavern, and post-office in the Southern States. The frequency with which these losses must occur, however, on large plantations, is most strongly evidenced by the following paragraph from the domestic-news columns of the *Fayetteville Observer*. A man who would pay these prices must anticipate frequent occasion to use his purchase.

"Mr. J. L. Bryan, of Moore county, sold at public auction, on the 20th instant, a pack of ten hounds, trained for hunting runaways, for the sum of $1,540. The highest price paid for any one dog was $301; lowest price, $75; average for the ten, $154. The terms of sale were six months' credit, with approved security, and interest from date."

The newspapers of the Southwestern States frequently contain advertisements similar to the following, which is taken from the *West Tennessee Democrat*:

"BLOOD-HOUNDS.— I have TWO of the FINEST DOGS for CATCHING NEGROES in the Southwest. They can take the trail TWELVE HOURS after the NEGRO HAS PASSED, and catch him with ease. I live just four miles southwest of Boliver, on the road leading from Boliver to Whitesville. I am ready at all times to catch runaway negroes.—March 2, 1853.

"DAVID TURNER."

CHAPTER III

THE ECONOMY OF VIRGINIA—STATISTICS OF THE ELEMENTS OF WEALTH AND THE RESULTS OF LABOR

THE *Richmond Enquirer*, a very strong and influential pro-slavery newspaper of Virginia, in advocating some railroad projects, thus describes the progress of the State relatively to that of some of the free-states, since the Revolution. (Dec. 29, 1852.)

"Virginia, anterior to the Revolution, and up to the adoption of the Federal Constitution, contained more wealth and a larger population than any other State of this Confedracy. * * *

"Virginia, from being first in point of wealth and political power, has come down to the fifth in the former, and the fourth in the latter. New York, Pennsylvania, Massachusetts and Ohio stand above her in wealth, and all, but Massachusetts, in population and political power. Three of these States are literally chequered over with railroads and canals; and the fourth (Massachusetts) with railroads alone. * * *

"But when we find that the population of the single city of New York and its environs exceeds the whole free population of Eastern Virginia, and the valley between the Blue Ridge and Alleghany, we have cause to feel deeply for our situation. Philadelphia herself contains a population far greater than the whole free population of Eastern Virginia. The little State of Massachusetts has an aggregate wealth exceeding that of Virginia by more than one hundred and twenty-six millions of dollars — a State, too, which is incapable of subsisting its inhabitants from the production of its soil. And New York, which was as much below Massachusetts, at the adoption of the Federal Constitution, in wealth and power, as the latter was below Virginia, now exceeds the wealth of both. While the aggregate wealth of New York, in 1850, amounted to $1,080,309,216, that of Virginia was $436,701,082 — a difference in favor of the former of $643,608,134. The unwrought mineral wealth of Virginia exceeds that of New York. The climate and soil are better; the back country, with equal improvements, would contribute as much."

The same journal adds, on another occasion:

"In no State of the Confederacy do the facilities for manufacturing operations exist in greater profusion than in Virginia. Every condition essential to success in these employments is found here in prodigal abundance, and in a peculiarly convenient combination. First, we have a limitless supply of water-power — the cheapest of motors — in localities easy of access. So abundant is this supply of water-power that no value is attached to it distinct from the adjacent lands, except in the vicinity of the larger towns. On the Potomac and its tributaries; on the Rappahannock; on the James and its tributaries; on the Roanoke and its tributaries; on the Holston, the Kanawha, and other streams, numberless sites may now be found where the supply of water-power is sufficient for the purposes of a Lawrence or a Lowell. Nor is there any want of material for building at these localities; timber and granite are abundant; and, to complete the circle of advantages, the climate is genial and healthful, and the soil eminently productive. * * * Another advantage which Virginia possesses, for the manufacture of cotton, is the proximity of its mills to the raw material. At the present prices of the staple, the value of this advantage is estimated at 10 per cent."

The *Lynchburg Virginian*, another newspaper of respectability, having a similar purpose in hand, namely, to induce capitalists to invest their money in enterprises that shall benefit the State, observes that—

"The coal-fields of Virginia are the most extensive in the world, and her coal is of the best and purest quality. Her iron deposits are altogether inexhaustible, and in many instances so pure that it is malleable in its primitive state; and many of these deposits in the immediate vicinity of extensive coalfields. She has, too, very extensive deposits of copper, lead and gypsum. Her rivers are numerous and bold, generally with fall enough for extensive water power.

"A remarkable feature in the mining and manufacturing prospects of Virginia is, the ease and economy with which all her minerals are mined; instead of being, as in England and elsewhere, generally imbedded deep within the bowels of the earth, from which they can be got only with great labor and at great cost, ours are found everywhere on the hills and slopes, with their ledges dipping in the direction of the plains below. Why, then, should not Virginia at once employ at least half of her labor and capital in mining and manufacturing? Richmond could as profitably manufacture all cotton and woollen goods as Lowell, or any other town in New England. Why should not Lynchburg, with all her promised facility of getting coal and pig metal, manufacture all articles of iron and steel just as cheaply, and yet as profitably, as any portion of the northern States? Why should not every town and village on the line of every railroad in the State, erect their shops, in which they may manufacture a thousand articles of daily consumption, just as good and cheap as they may be made anywhere? * * *

"Dependent upon Europe and the North for almost every yard of cloth, and every coat, and boot, and hat we wear; for our axes, scythes, tubs, and buckets — in short, for everything except our bread and meat! It must occur to the South that if our relations with the North should ever be severed— and how soon they may be, none can know (may God avert it long!) — we would, in all the South, not be able to clothe ourselves. We could not fell our forests, plough our fields, nor mow our meadows. In fact, we would be reduced to a state more abject than we are willing to look at, even prospectively. And yet, with all these things staring us in the face, we shut our eyes, and go on blindfold."

At the Convention for the formation of the Virginia State Agricultural Society, in 1852, the draft of an address to the farmers of the State was read, approved, and once adopted by the Convention. The vote by which it was adopted was soon afterwards reconsidered, and it was again approved and adopted. A second time it was reconsidered; and finally it was rejected, on the ground that there were admissions in it that would feed the fanaticism of the abolitionists. No one argued against it on the ground of the falsity or inaccuracy of these admissions. Twenty of the most respectable proprietors in the State, immediately afterwards, believing it to contain "matter of grave import," which should not be suppressed for such a reason, united in requesting a copy of it for publication. In the note of these gentlemen to the author, they express the belief that Virginia now "possesses the richest soil, most genial climate, and cheapest labor on earth." The author of the address, in his reply, says: "Fanaticism is a fool for whose vagaries I am not responsible. I am a pro-slavery man—I believe it, at this time, impossible to abolish it, and not desirable if it were possible."

The address was accordingly published. I make the following extracts from it, not only on account of the incontrovertible facts presented in them, but to show that the ostrich-habit, of burying their heads in the ground before anything they don't like, is not universal with Virginians:

"ADDRESS TO THE FARMERS OF VIRGINIA

"'The Southern States stand foremost in agricultural labor, though they hold but the third rank in population.' At the head of these Southern States, in production, in extent of territory, in climate, in soil, and in population, stands the Commonwealth of Virginia. She is a nation of farmers. Eight-tenths of her industry is expended upon the soil; but less than one-third of her domain is in pasturage, or under the plough."

"Out of somewhat more than thirty-nine millions of acres, she tills but little over ten millions of acres, or about twenty-six and a quarter per cent., whilst New York has subdued about forty-one per cent., or twelve and a quarter out of her twenty-nine and a half millions of acres: and Massachusetts, with her sterile soil and inhospitable climate, has reclaimed from the forest, the quarry, and the marsh, about forty-two and a half per cent., or two and one-eighth out of her little territory of five millions of acres. Yet, according to the census of 1840, only six-tenths of the labor of New York, and four-tenths of that of Massachusetts, or, relatively, one-fifth and two-fifths less than our own, is expended upon agriculture. * * *

"The live stock of Virginia are worth only three dollars and thirty-one cents for every arable acre; but in New York they are worth six dollars and seven cents, and in Massachusetts four dollars and fifty-two cents.

"The proportion of hay for the same quantity of land is, for Virginia, eighty-one pounds; for New York, six hundred and seventy-nine pounds; for Massachusetts, six hundred and eighty-four pounds. * * *

"With access to the same markets, and with hundreds of mechanics of our own, who can vie with the best Northern manufacturers, we find that our implements are inferior, that the New York farmer spends upon his nearly three times as much as we do upon ours, and the Massachusetts farmer more than double. * * *

"Manure is indispensable to good husbandry. Judging from the history of agriculture in all other countries, we may safely say, that farming can never attain to continued perfection where manure is not put on with an unsparing hand. By far the larger part of this can only be made by stock, which should, at the same time, be made the source of profit, at least sufficient to pay the cost of their keep, so that, *other things being equal*, it is a safe rule to estimate the condition of a farming district by the amount of live stock it may possess, and the provision made for their sustenance. Applied in this instance, we see that the New York farmer has invested in live stock two dollars and seventy-six cents, and the Massachusetts farmer one dollar and twenty-one cents per acre more than the Virginia farmer. In pasturage we cannot tell the difference. It is well, perhaps, for the honor of the State, that we cannot. But in hay, New York has five hundred and ninety-eight pounds, and Massachusetts six hundred and three pounds more per acre than we have. This, however, does not present the true state of the case. Land-locked by mountain barriers, as yet impassable for the ordinary agricultural staples, or debarred from their production by distance and prohibitory rates of transportation, most of the wealth and exports of many considerable portions of our State consists of live stock alone. What proportion these parts bear to the whole, we have been unable definitely to ascertain; but it is, no doubt, so great as to warrant us in assuming a much more considerable disparity than the statistics show in the live stock of the whole Atlantic slope, as compared with New York and Massachusetts. And we shall appreciate, still more highly, the skill of the Northern farmer, if we reflect that a readier market for every, the most trivial, product of his farm, operates a constant temptation to break up his rotation and diminish his stock.

"In the above figures, carefully calculated from the data of authentic documents,[1] we find no cause for self-gratulation, but some food for meditation. They are not without use to those who would improve the future by the past. They show that we have not done our part in the bringing of land into cultivation; that, notwithstanding natural advantages which greatly exceed those of the two States drawn into parallel with Virginia, we are yet behind them both—that with forty and sixty per cent. respectively of their industry devoted to other pursuits, into which it has been lured by prospects of greater gain, they have done more than we have done. * * *

"Whilst our population has increased for the last ten years, in a ratio of 11.66, that of New York has increased in a ratio of 27.52, and that of Massachusetts at the still heavier and more startling rate of 34.81. With a territorial area thirty per cent.

---

[1] Abstract of the Seventh Census, and the able work of Professor Tucker, on the "Progress of the United States in Population and Wealth."

larger than New York, we have but little more than one-third of her Congressional representation; and Massachusetts, only one-eighth our size, comes within two of our number of representatives, we being cut down to thirteen, while she rises to eleven. And thus we, who once swayed the councils of the Union, find our power gone, and our influence on the wane, at a time when both are of vital importance to our prosperity, if not to our safety. As other States accumulate the means of material greatness, and glide past us on the road to wealth and empire, we slight the warnings of dull statistics, and drive lazily along the field of ancient customs, or stop the *plough* to speed the *politician*—should we not, in too many cases, say with more propriety, the *demagogue!*

"State pride is a good thing, it is one mode in which patriotism is manifested. But it is not always a wise one. Certainly not, when it makes us content on small grounds. And when it smothers up improvement in self-satisfaction, it is a most pernicious thing. We have much to be proud of in Virginia. In intellect and fitness to command, in personal and social qualities, in high tone and noble bearing, in loyalty, in generosity, and magnanimity, and disinterestedness, above all, in moral purity, we once stood—let us hope, still stand—pre-eminent among our sister States. But the possession and practice of these virtues do not comprise our whole duty as men or as citizens. The great decree which has gone forth ordaining that we shall 'increase, and multiply, and replenish the earth,' enjoins upon us quite other duties, which cannot be neglected with impunity; so we have found out by experience — for we *have* neglected these duties. And when we contemplate our field of labor, and the work we have done in it, we cannot but observe the sad contrast between capacity and achievement. With a wide-spread domain, with a kindly soil, with a climate whose sun radiates fertility, and whose very dews distill abundance, we find our inheritance so wasted that the eye aches to behold the prospect."

The Census of 1850 gives the following values to agricultural land in the adjoining States of Virginia and Pennsylvania:

	In Virginia	In Pennsylvania
No. of acres improved land in farms,	10,360,135	8,626,619
" unimproved,	15,792,176	6,294,728
Cash value of farms,	$216,401,543—$8 an acre.	$407,876,099—$25 an acre

Considering that, at the Revolution, Virginia had nearly twice the population of Pennsylvania, was in possession of much more wealth or disposable capital, and had much the best natural facilities for external commerce and internal communication, if her political and social constitution had been and had continued equally good, and her people equally industrious and enterprising with those of Pennsylvania, there is no reason why the value of her farms should not have been, at this time, at least equal to those of Pennsylvania. Were it so, it appears that Virginia, in that particular alone, would now be richer than she is by four hundred and thirty millions of dollars.

If it should be thought that this difference between the value of land in Virginia and Pennsylvania is in some degree due to more fertile soils in the latter, a similar comparison may be made with the other adjoining free State, and old State of New Jersey, the climate of which, owing to its vicinity to the ocean, differs imperceptibly from that of Virginia, while its soil is decidedly less fertile, taking both States on an average. The average value of farming-land in New Jersey is recorded at $44.

Give this value to the Virginia farms, and the difference between it and their present value would buy, at a large valuation, all the slaves now in the State, send them to Africa, provide each family of them five hundred dollars to start with when they reached there, and leave still a surplus which, divided among the present white population of the State, would give between two and three thousand dollars to each family.

Some Southern writers have lately objected to comparisons of density of population, as indications of the prosperity of communities. Between two adjoining communities, however, where there are no restrictions upon the movements of the populations, and when the people are so ready to move as both those of Pennsylvania and New Jersey, and of Virginia have shown themselves to be, the price of land must indicate with considerable exactness the comparative value or desirableness of it, all things considered, to live upon. The Virginians do not admit, and have no occasion to do so, that Pennsylvania and New Jersey have any advantage over Virginia, in soil, in climate, or in any natural quality.

Why, then, these differences?

In intellectual productions, the same general comparative barrenness is noticeable. One or two of the richest men in material wealth in the United States, live in Virginia; but there are, also, more excessively poor men than anywhere else. The best examples of the application of science, economically to agriculture, can, I suspect, be found in Virginia; but the generally-followed system of agriculture is the worst, under the circumstances, that the ingenuity of penny-wise simpletons has yet contrived in this country. So it is with intellectual wealth : there are a few minds learned and highly cultivated, but says the *Richmond Whig* — the leading Know-nothing newspaper in the Southern States—with a provincial simplicity, the sincerity of which will hardly be credible to men of the world:

"We receive nearly all our books from Northern or foreign authors—gotten up, printed by Northern or foreign publishers —while we have among us numberless men of ripe scholarship, profound acquirements, elegant and forcible writers—men willing to devote themselves to such labor, *only a Southern book is not patronized*. The North usually scowls at it, ridicules it, or damns it with faint praise; and the South takes on a like hue and complexion and neglects it. We have printers and publishers able, willing, and competent to publish, but, such is the *apathy* on the part of Southern people, that it involves hazard to Southern publishers to put them out. Indeed, until recently, almost all the publications, even of Southern books, issued (and that was their only hope of success) from Northern houses. The last chance now of getting a Southern book sold, is to manage to secure the favorable notice of the Northern press, and then the South buys it. Our magazines and periodicals languish for support."

Mr. Howison, " the Virginia Historian," observes :

"The question might be asked, where is the literature of Virginia, and it would not be easily answered. It is a melancholy fact, that her people have never been a reading people. In the mass they have shown an indifference to polite literature and education in general, depressing to the mind that wishes to see them respectable and happy."

" It is with pain," says the same authority, " that we are compelled to speak of the horrible cloud of ignorance that rests on Virginia," and he computes that (1848) there are in the State 166,000 youth, between seven and sixteen years of age, and of these

126,000 attend no school at all, and receive no education except what can be imparted by poor and ignorant parents. Besides these, he reckons 449,087 slaves and 48,852 free negroes, with few exceptions, wholly uneducated.

"The policy which discourages further extension of knowledge among them is necessary: but the fact remains unchanged, that they exist among us, *a huge mass of mind, almost entirely unenlightened*. We fear that the most favorable estimates will leave, in our State, 683,000 rational beings who are destitute of the merest rudiments of knowledge."

What is the cause of the comparative poverty of Virginia thus asserted and described?

This is a question often asked, and is one of direct personal interest to many at the North; to capitalists, for instance, who are urged to invest their funds in Virginia lands, mines, and other stocks, and to creditors of the State, and of corporations and individuals in the State. It is especially interesting to a large class of persons who would prefer to live in a milder climate than that of any of the free States, but who are withheld from immigrating to Virginia by the potent fact, that wealth has not accumulated to the people at large in that State, with anything like the ease and rapidity that it has to those of the adjoining Northern States.

I am myself one of this class, and it certainly was a great temptation to me, while I was enjoying the delightful January climate of Virginia, to be offered any amount of land which I was certain could be easily made to produce, under good tillage, twenty-five or thirty bushels of wheat to the acre, within twenty-four hours of New York by rail, and forty-eight by water-carriage, at exactly one fortieth of the price, by the acre, at which I could sell my New York farm. And, since my return from the South, I have been several times consulted by persons, some of them of considerable estate, who had determined, more or less definitely, to remove to Virginia, induced thereto by such letters as the following, which are constantly addressed to Northern capitalists, farmers, and skilled laborers, or manufacturers, by Virginia land-owners. This particular one I take from the *American Agriculturist*, to the editor of which it was directed, and by whom it was published, gratis and without comment, as such advertisements usually are, in our agricultural newspapers:

"VIRGINIA—INDUCEMENTS FOR NORTHERN MEN TO INVEST CAPITAL. Why is it that capitalists do not seek for a home in Western Virginia? Why is it that manufacturers do not explore this delightful country? Is it not worth their notice? Are there no inducements offered here for the honest, industrious laborer? I will offer some reasons why men of the North should look to the South for a home for themselves and offspring. Western Virginia is, in the first place, one of the most desirable portions of the Southern States. Every facility is here offered for the investment of capital. Our mountains teem with rich ores of every kind; our lands blossom with golden harvests. The rippling streams that gurgle down our mountain-slopes furnish every variety of water-power, easily adapted to the propelling of machinery. The States west and south furnish a ready market for the sale of manufactured articles, or agricultural products. The farmers here are dependent, notwithstanding the facilities of manufacturing, to a very great extent, upon the North for all their implements of husbandry and household articles. Suppose, then, that we had some fifty or a hundred different manufacturing establishments in Western Virginia, it would supersede the necessity of importing such things from abroad as wagons, buggies, clocks, brooms, rakes, shoes, boots, coats, pants, etc., etc. Every merchant in the Southern and Western States supplies his customers with these articles from the North. Now, suppose for one moment, that our merchants can buy from the Northern manufacturers, and pay the carriage upon articles gotten up there, and sold to the Southern States at fine profit, is it not reasonable to suppose, if the article was manufactured here, the amount now consumed in transportation would be saved to the manufacturer located here upon the spot, and make him a handsome profit?

"No man can form an adequate idea of the extent of this trade, unless he travel through the Southern States. Scarcely a broom, a clock, a boot, or shoe, or anything of the kind is used in the South that is not manufactured by Northern industry; and yet all articles used can be readily manufactured here as well as there, and, if taken hold of by some enterprising men, would be found more profitable. In fact, several Northern men have already settled in Northern Virginia, and are now pushing forward a happy and prosperous trade. The Virginia and Tennessee Railroad will soon be completed, along the line of which an immense traffic must be conducted. Then have you no thorough-going business men, who cannot find employment at the North, and who cannot earn more than a mere livelihood? If so, I advise them to turn their faces at once toward Western Virginia, where the smiles of Providence and the rays of a Southern sun will cheer and animate them in their rapid strides to happiness and wealth."

Here is another one, ingeniously contrived for wide-awake people who read the *Tribune*, and are supposed to have prejudices :

"The effects of Slavery in this region have only been such as to render it a more profitable locality for the new settler, provided, always, he does not suffer himself to be engrafted with its spirit. This suggests to my mind another observation, taken from the experience of settlers from the North. A single family, of New England habits and tastes, settling among neighbors of the slave-holding, work-hating class, becomes, in a short time, tired of the isolation from all the friends and the habits to which they have been accustomed, and disgusted with the condition of things they find around them. The wife misses her relations and neighbors, and her Sunday-meeting, and, after a year or two of trial, declares she will stay no longer; the children want the ready companionship of more thickly populated districts; and the experiment is given up, not because it will not pay in a pecuniary sense, but for the reasons I have mentioned. Now, to obviate this difficulty, let families come and settle in groups, or let a new settler, in selecting a location, choose one in a neighborhood already occupied with small farmers or mechanics of his own class, with whom he can associate, and whose example will back him in continuing his system of working with his own hand. This plan has been adopted, as you are aware, in some of the northeastern counties of Virginia, which now contain a population of active, intelligent and prosperous farmers and mechanics, from non-slaveholding States, while single settlements in other equally favorable localities have been abandoned. The price of land in the lower counties of this State varies from three to fifty dollars an acre. In many situations, land of good quality can now be bought, covered with timber, valuable either for fuel or for ship-building, in close proximity to water-carriage, or to a line of railroad, at eight or ten dollars an acre. The clearing of the land will often pay most or all the cost, leaving a soil of good quality, and easily cultivated, and which, from the nature of things, must rapidly enhance in value."

I have read at least a hundred such advertisements in different Northern newspapers; a dozen were printed in the *Daily Times*, contemporaneously with my own letters from the South; and in the more pro-slavery journals they may be seen, in one form or another, almost weekly.

When Virginia gentlemen thus carefully argue the advantages which their State offers to an immigration from the free States; and when they publicly urge that Slavery is no obstacle, but the contrary, to the success of such immigrants, it seems to me they have no business to stigmatize as impertinent, Northern curiosity to learn all about the matter.

Even the condition of the slaves, moral and material, the Internal Slave Trade, the effects of Slavery on the character of the people, I consider to be as distinctly a part of the general rural economy of the country, as legitimately connected with the value of public stocks, and as pertinent a subject of inquiry, as any of those points with regard to which every farmer in the United States was required to give information, under the head of crops and live-stock, in the census of 1850. Nor do I believe, that justice or kindness to the Slave States, or regard to the stability of the Union, can be opposed to a thorough—so it be honest—investigation of the condition of those States, and study of the causes of that condition.

Let me frankly, and with the most respectful and friendly disposition towards those who disagree with me, state my convictions on this subject.

Very little candid, truthful, and unprejudiced public discussion has yet been had on this vexed subject of Slavery. The extremists of the South esteem their opponents as madmen, or robbers; and invariably misrepresent, misunderstand, and, consequently, entirely fail to meet their arguments. The extremists of the North esteem the slave-holders as robbers and tyrants, wilfully and malevolently oppressive and cruel. But

I suppose more has been done, to prevent reasonable views and judicious action, by those, both North and South, who have held moderate and more reasonable opinions, than by those of either of the extreme parties. I mean that, in the endeavor to suppress agitation, they have produced an unhealthy distrust, and an unsound and dangerous condition of the public mind. In the feverish effort to secure peace, they have forgotten, as is now apparent, the easiest lessons of history and disregarded the simplest demands of prudence. "Men," says Macaulay, "are never so likely to settle a question rightly, as when they discuss it freely." The principle is at the basis of free institutions. Its reverse is the apex of despotism. The attempt to suppress discussion has given every advantage to the unterrified partisans on both sides, who assume to fight for truth and rights.

Since the repeal of the Missouri Compromise, I presume no one doubts, whatever he may desire, that Slavery must continue to be an important, if not an engrossing element in our politics. It is impossible that it should not, while slaves are an important article of commerce, and while their value can be materially affected by the national legislation. Speculation on such legislation will occur, and will be guarded against, and there will be more or less consideration of the constitutional rights of each side of the Union, according as the people are rightly informed and honestly dealt with by politicians.

Northern men have, at present, too little information about the South that has not come to them in a very inexact, or in a very suspicious form, as in novels and narratives of fugitive slaves. Northerners travelling in the South, are generally merchants, looking after their personal business; invalids sauntering through the winter in sunny places; or wealthy people, looking for pleasure to the society of the hospitable wealthy. There is but little Southern literature; and what there is is mainly imaginative or controversial. Of the masses of the South, black and white, it is more difficult for one to obtain information, than of those of any country in Europe. I saw much more of what I had not anticipated and less of what I had, in the Slave States, than, with a somewhat extended travelling experience, in any other country I ever visited.

To return to the question of the condition of Virginia and of its causes.

The leading agriculturists of the State who are least afraid of "abolitionism," declare the conviction that not only has Virginia at this time richer soils and cheaper than the wealthier States, but also the cheapest labor in the world; the organ of the State Agricultural Society sustains the same opinion; and Mr. Ruffin, the most eminent rural economist in the State, is allowed to advocate the same opinion in a Report of the United States Patent Office.

If it is true that here are richer soils, cheaper soils, and less expensive means of developing their wealth than in Pennsylvania, New York, and Massachusetts, why is it that the immensely more abundant capital of those States is not attracted to Virginia?

Of course a question so important to the property-holders of the State cannot fail to be gravely considered, and answered according to every reflective man's sagacity. In fact, no new project of legal or social change is ever advocated, that its friends do not contend that the measure will remove either the sole cause or one of the chief causes of the decadence of Virginia. Thus seldom a day passes in the session of the Legislature, that some one does not give his judgment upon the subject. At every gathering of the people, for political purposes or for the advancement of schemes for the general benefit, some orator is almost sure to take up the topic of the poverty and slow progress of the State; and, after denouncing the fanaticism and licentiousness of any one who dares suspect that slavery has anything to do with it, to explain what, in the orator's opinion, is the real cause, and what is the right way to remove it.

Among the causes thus presented, the following are the only ones having any breadth of application, of which I can recollect to have heard.

1. The want of better education of the mass of the people (for it is maintained that the wealthier class are better educated than any in the free States).

2. The want of more agricultural science and skill.

3. The want of more and better roads, canals, etc.

4. The want of direct commerce with Europe and elsewhere.

5. The want of manufactures.

All these alleged causes, and all others, that I have

ever heard assigned for the decrepitude of the State, are reduced to the following two, by simply asking, why Virginia has these wants more than the free States:

1. The more debilitating effects of the climate upon white people; and

2. The gentle blood and the corresponding character, averse to commercial speculation, inherited by the people.

These are the only reasons that I know of, except those pointing to slavery and social aristocracy, that appear on the face worthy of a moment's consideration.

In regard to the first, the authority of those who sustain the opinion, that slavery is a blessing to the State, might be cited for the averment, that the climate of the greater part of Virginia is no less favorable to the activity of the white man than that of the more northern States. North of the country bordering upon a slave population, no similar connection between climate and prosperity is to be found; the wealth of Massachusetts is greater than that of the States lying north of her; land is of higher value in New Jersey than in Maine; the agriculture of parts of Eastern Pennsylvania is more commendable and more profitable than that of any part of New York; the manufacturing industry of New York is far greater than that of Virginia, but not so great as that of the States between her and Virginia, and between which and herself there is as great a difference of climate, and of the same nature, as that between them and Virginia. The most active, enterprising, successful and prosperous States of antiquity, were those of a climate warmer than that of States in commercial subjection to them, and warmer than that of Virginia. Any slight additional enervating effect that the climate of Virginia may possibly have upon those born and bred under it, must be more than compensated for, to the agricultural interest of the State, by the greater length of the season in which the ground is in a condition to be worked, and the greater cheapness with which cattle can be wintered; to manufacturing, mining, and commercial interests, by the smaller liability of their operations being interrupted by ice, etc.

With regard to the second reason, which is that held by the *Richmond Enquirer*, as will be inferred from the polite and modest passage extracted below,[1] it must be considered that since the earlier settlements of the American colonies, the climate and the institutions of

[1] " The relations between the North and the South are very analogous to those which subsisted between Greece and the Roman Empire after the subjugation of Achaia by the Consul Mummius. The dignity and energy of the Roman character, conspicuous in war and in politics, were not easily tamed and adjusted to the arts of industry and literature. The degenerate and pliant Greeks, on the contrary, excelled in the handicraft and polite professions. We learn from the vigorous invective of Juvenal, that they were the most useful and capable of servants, whether as pimps or professors of rhetoric. Obsequious, dexterous and ready, the versatile Greeks monopolized the business of teaching, publishing, and manufacturing in the Roman Empire—allowing their masters ample leisure for the service of the State, in the Senate or in the field. The people of the northern States of this Confederacy exhibit the same aptitude for the arts of industry. They excel as clerks, mechanics, and tradesmen, and they have monopolized the business of teaching, publishing, and peddling."

the New World have effected important modifications in the character as well as the physique of the descendants of the settlers, why, then, with a climate so unessentially dissimilar, if it be not for the institutions which are fundamentally dissimilar, has this change been so much less favorable to material prosperity in Virginia than in the adjoining States? The people of the free States, with as great differences of origin between themselves as between the majority of them and the majority of Virginians, are now comparatively homogeneous in the elements of character which lead to prosperity. Is the difference of blood between them and those of Virginia, sufficient to account for the differences in character assumed to be found on crossing the line of freedom and slavery? But not one-tenth certainly, probably not one-thousandth, of the fathers of Virginia were of gentle blood, as those who take this ground seem to assume. The majority of them were sold and bought as laborers. There is no evidence that those who were gentle born, were less endowed with the disposition to gain wealth than their fellow-countrymen who settled New England, or the Dutch of New York, or the Swedes and Germans that contributed so largely to the settlement of New Jersey and Pennsylvania—the contrary is, in fact, very obvious. That the few people of gentle blood had a paramount influence upon the character of the province, through their legislative and social power, I do not deny; indeed, I believe that through their exercise of this power and through a similar undemocratic, uneconomical and unjust, though not unpardonable, exercise of power at the present time, by a part of the people over the remainder, the character of the whole has been unfavorably affected; and to this despotism and this submission to injustice, it may not be unreasonable to attribute whatever want of prosperity there is in Virginia, when compared with the States where such causes have been wanting or have been less.

By any man whose own mind is not fettered by the system, or who is not very greatly affected by prejudice or by self-interest, in sustaining the system, it is difficult for me to believe that this cause must not be considered far more satisfactory than any other that I have ever heard suggested.

There are many gentlemen who believe, I doubt not, with perfect sincerity, Slavery to have been, and to be, a blessing to both the white and to the black people of the State; but the great reasons of their devotion to the system are, so far as I have learned them, rather prospective than otherwise, after all. They believe there are seeds, at present almost inert, of disaster at the North, against which Slavery will be their protection; indications that these are already beginning to be felt or anticipated by prophetic minds, they think they see in the demands for "Land Limitation," in the anti-rent troubles, in strikes of workmen, in the distress of emigrants at the eddies of their current, in diseased philanthropy, in radical democracy, and in the progress of socialistic ideas in general. The North, say they, has progressed under the high pressure of unlimited competition; as the population grows denser, there will be terrific explosions, disaster, and ruin, while they will ride quietly and safely at the anchor of Slavery. What they suppose to be the cause of the sad waste of natural wealth, what the necessity of the ignorance and poverty of the poor white people, what the reason that capital is not attracted by the superior soundness of their form of government and society, except it may be the stupidity of capitalists, I may very probably have failed to ascertain, because of the general disinclination they have to converse with a Northerner on this topic. The only distinct answer that I have received has been, that it is not Slavery, for nothing is more evident to them, although it may not be so to a stranger, than that Slavery is a blessing everywhere, and always (I quote, as far as convenient, the words that have been addressed to me) to the slave, in Christianizing and civilizing him; to the master, in cultivating those habits of charitable feeling which the presence of the weak, the poor, and the dependent is always suggesting, and in cherishing in him that commanding elevation of character and administrative power which is claimed to have always distinguished the owners of slaves, and the value of which they deem to have always been apparent in our national statesmanship. An institution which they know has such good influences, and which is so favorable to political success, they cannot believe to be destructive to industrial energy and effective of commercial dependence. There is nothing essentially productive in competition; on the contrary, it is evident that the work of many laborers must be more profitable when directed by one controlling mind, than when independent and uncombined; therefore, say they, slave-labor must be cheaper than free-labor. In every way, they are convinced that Slavery is, or should be, and can be made a great advantage and blessing to them, and, therefore, by God's grace, they are determined to maintain and defend it as their fathers did, and to bequeath it, as their fathers did to them, to their children, unimpaired and unmitigated, an inheritance forever.

Having confidence myself that all the fatal dangers, apprehended for Northern society, may be and will be anticipated and provided against by measures already under consideration; and doubting if Slavery, while it prevents popular education, offers sufficient precaution against them, I think it is to be established convincingly, that Slavery alone is a sufficient cause, at this time, to account for any difference there may be between the value of property and all commercial and industrial prosperity, in Virginia and the neighboring free States.

Several thousand slaves were hired in Eastern Virginia, during the time of my visit there. The wages paid for able workingmen, sound, healthy, in good condition, and with no especial vices, from twenty to thirty years old, were from $110 to $140; the average, as nearly as I could ascertain, from very extended inquiry, being $120 per year, with board and lodging, and certain other expenses. These wages must represent exactly the cost of slave-labor, because any considerations which would prevent the owner of a slave disposing of his labor for those wages, when the labor for his own purposes would not be worth as much, are so many hindrances upon the free disposal of his property, and thereby deduct from its actual value, as measured with money.

As the large majority of slaves are employed in agricultural labor, and many of those, hired at the prices I have mentioned, are taken directly from the labor of the farm, and are skilled in no other, their wages represent the cost of agricultural labor in Eastern Virginia.

In New York, the usual wages for similar men, if Americans, white or black, are exactly the same in the money part; for Irish or German laborers the most common wages are $10 per month, for summer, and $8 per month, for winter, or from $96 to $120 a year, the average being about $108.

The hirer has, in addition to paying wages for the slave, to feed and to clothe him; the free laborer requires also to be boarded, but not to be clothed by his employer. The opinion is universal in Virginia that the slaves are better fed than the Northern laborers. This is, however, a mistake, and we must consider that the board of the Northern laborer would cost at least as much more as the additional cost of clothing to the slave. Comparing man with man, with reference simply to equality of muscular power and endurance, I think, all these things considered, the wages for common laborers are *twenty-five per cent.* higher in Virginia than in New York. But let it be supposed they are equal.

Loss of profit to the employer of free laborers, from the illness or disability, real or counterfeited, of the laborer to work, need be nothing. To the slave-master it is of varying consequence: sometimes small, often excessively embarrassing, and always a subject of anxiety and suspicion. I have never made the inquiry on any plantation where as many as twenty negroes were employed together, that I have not ascertained that one or more of the field-hands was not at work on account of some illness, strain, bruise or wound, of which he or she was complaining; and in such cases I have hardly ever heard the proprietor or overseer fail to express his suspicion that the invalid was really as well able to work as any one else on the plantation. It is said to be nearly as difficult to form a satisfactory diagnosis of negroes' disorders, as it is of infants', because their imagination of symptoms is so vivid, and because not the smallest reliance is to be placed on their accounts of what they have felt or done. If a man is really ill, he fears lest he should be thought to be simulating, and therefore exaggerates all his pains, and locates them in whatever he supposes to be the most vital parts of his system.

Frequently the invalid slaves will neglect or refuse to use the remedies prescribed for their recovery. They will conceal pills, for instance, under their tongue, and declare they have swallowed them, when, from their producing no effect, it will be afterwards evident that they have not. This general custom I heard ascribed to habit, acquired when they were not very disagreeably ill, and were loth to be made quite well enough to have to go to work again.

Amusing incidents, illustrating this difficulty, I have heard narrated, showing that the slave rather enjoys getting a severe wound that lays him up :— he has his hand crushed by the fall of a piece of timber, and after the pain is alleviated, is heard to exclaim, "Bress der Lord—der haan b'long to masser—don't reckon dis chile got no more corn to hoe dis yaar, no how."[1]

Mr. H., of North Carolina, observed to me, in relation to this difficulty, that a man who had had much experience with negroes could generally tell, with a good deal of certainty, by their tongue, and their pulse, and their general aspect, whether they were really ill or not.

"Last year," said he, "I hired out one of my negroes to a railroad contractor. I suppose he found that he had to work harder than he would on the plan-

[1] It is, perhaps, well I should say that this soliloquy was repeated to me by a Virginia planter, as if it had occurred within his own hearing. A similar illustration of the pleasure with which a slave finds himself exempted from labor, having been mentioned in the "Key to Uncle Tom's Cabin," the Reverend E. J. Stearns, of St. John's College, Maryland, in a rejoinder to that work, thinks it unnecessary to deny the truth of it, but, with the usual happy keenness of clerical controversialists, settles the matter without being personally disrespectful to Mrs. Stowe's authority, by quoting the *final* authority :—"'No man ever hated his own flesh, but nourisheth it, and cherisheth it ;' *and again*, 'So ought men to love their wives as their own bodies.'"

tation, and became discontented, and one night he left the camp without asking leave. The next day he stopped at a public-house, and told the people he had fallen sick working on the railroad, and was going home to his master. They suspected he had run away, and, as he had no pass, they arrested him and sent him to the jail. In the night the sheriff sent me word that there was a boy, who said he belonged to me, in the jail, and he was very sick indeed, and I had better come and take care of him. I immediately suspected how it was, and, as I was particularly engaged, I did not go near him till towards night, the next day. When I came to look at him, and heard his story, I felt quite sure in my own mind that he was not sick; but, as he pretended to be suffering very much, I told the sheriff to give him plenty of salts and senna, and to be careful that he did not get much of anything to eat. The next day I got a letter from the contractor, telling me that my nigger had run away, without any cause. So I rode over to the jail again, and told them to continue the same treatment until the boy got a good deal worse or a good deal better. Well, the rascal kept it up for a week, all the time groaning so you 'd think he could n't live many hours longer; but, after he had been in seven days, he all of a sudden said he 'd got well, and he wanted something to eat. As soon as I heard of it, I sent them word to give him a good paddling,[1] and handcuff him, and send him back to the

[1] Not something to eat, but punishment with an instrument like a ferule.

railroad. I had to pay them for taking up a runaway, besides the sheriff's fees, and a week's board of the boy to the county."

But the same gentleman admitted that he had sometimes been mistaken, and had made men go to work when they afterwards proved to be really ill; therefore, when one of his people told him he was not able to work, he usually thought, "very likely he'll be all the better for a day's rest, whether he's really ill or not," and would let him off without being very particular in his examination. Lately he had been getting a new overseer, and when he was engaging him, he told him that this was his way. The overseer replied, "It's my way, too, now; it did n't use to be, but I had a lesson. There was a nigger one day at Mr. ——'s who was sulky, and complaining; he said he could n't work. I looked at his tongue, and it was right clean, and I thought it was nothing but damned sulkiness so I paddled him, and made him go to work; but, two days after, he was under ground. He was a good eight hundred dollar nigger, and it was a lesson to me about taming possums, that I ain't agoing to forget in a hurry."

The liability of women, especially, to disorders and irregularities which cannot be detected by exterior symptoms, but which may be easily aggravated into serious complaints, renders many of them nearly valueless for work, because of the ease with which they can impose upon their owners. "The women on a plantation," said one extensive Virginian slave-owner to me, "will hardly earn their salt, after they come to the breeding age : they don't come to the field, and you go to the quarters and ask the old nurse what's the matter, and she says, 'Oh, she's not well, master ; she's not fit to work, sir ;' and what can you do ? You have to take her word for it that something or other is the matter with her, and you dare not set her to work; and so she lays up till she feels like taking the air again, and plays the lady at your expense."

I was on one plantation where a woman had been excused from any sort of labor for more than two years, on the supposition that she was dying of phthisis. At last the overseer discovered that she was employed as a milliner and dressmaker by all the other colored ladies of the vicinity ; and upon taking her to the house, it was found that she had acquired a remarkable skill in these vocations. She was hired out the next year to a fashionable dressmaker in town, at handsome wages; and as, after that, she did not again "raise blood," it was supposed that when she had done so before it had been by artificial means. Such tricks every army and navy surgeon is familiar with.

The interruption and disarrangement of operations of labor, occasioned by slaves "running away," frequently causes great inconvenience and loss to those who employ them. It is said to often occur when no immediate motive can be guessed at for it—when the slave has been well-treated, well-fed, and not over-worked ; and when he will be sure to suffer hardship from it, and be subject to severe punishment on his return, or if he is caught.

This is often mentioned to illustrate the ingratitude and especial depravity of the African race. I should suspect it to be, if it cannot be otherwise accounted for, the natural instinct of freedom in a man, working out capriciously, as the wild instincts of domesticated beasts and birds sometimes do.

But the learned Dr. Cartwright, of the University of Louisiana, believes that slaves are subject to a peculiar form of mental disease, termed by him *Drapetomania*, which, like a malady that cats are liable to, manifests itself by an irrestrainable propensity to *run away;* and in a work on the diseases of negroes, highly esteemed at the South for its patriotism and erudition, he advises planters of the proper preventive and curative measures to be taken for it.

He asserts that, "with the advantage of proper medical advice, strictly followed, this troublesome practice of running away, that many negroes have, can be almost entirely prevented." Its symptoms and the usual empirical practice on the plantations are described: "Before negroes run away, unless they are frightened or panic-struck, they become sulky and dissatisfied. The cause of this sulkiness and dissatisfaction should be inquired into and removed, or they are apt to run away or fall into the negro consumption." When sulky or dissatisfied without cause, the experience of those having most practice with *drapetomania*, the Doctor thinks, has been in favor of "whipping them *out of it*." It is vulgarly called, "whipping the devil *out of them*," he afterwards informs us.

Another droll sort of "indisposition," thought to be peculiar to the slaves, and which must greatly affect their value, as compared with free laborers, is described by Dr. Cartwright, as follows:

"DYSÆSTHESIA ÆTHIOPICA, or Hebetude of Mind and Obtuse Sensibility of Body. * * * From the careless movements of the individuals affected with this complaint, they are apt to do much mischief, which appears as if intentional, but is mostly owing to the stupidness of mind and insensibility of the nerves induced by the disease. Thus they break, waste, and destroy everything they handle—abuse horses and cattle—tear, burn, or rend their own clothing, and, paying no attention to the rights of property, steal others to replace what they have destroyed. They wander about at night, and keep in a half nodding state by day. They slight their work—cut up corn, cane, cotton, and tobacco, when hoeing it, as if for pure mischief. They raise disturbances with their overseers, and among their fellow-servants, without cause or motive, and seem to be insensible to pain when subjected to punishment. * * *

"When left to himself, the negro indulges in his natural disposition to idleness and sloth, and does not take exercise enough to expand his lungs and vitalize his blood, but dozes out a miserable existence in the midst of filth and uncleanliness, being too indolent, and having too little energy of mind, to provide for himself proper food and comfortable clothing and lodging. The consequence is, that the blood becomes so highly carbonized and deprived of oxygen that it not only becomes unfit to stimulate the brain to energy, but unfit to stimulate the nerves of sensation distributed to the body. * * *

"This is the disease called *Dysæsthesia* (a Greek term expressing the dull or obtuse sensation that always attends the complaint). When roused from sloth by the stimulus of hunger, he takes anything he can lay his hands on, and tramples on the rights as well as on the property of others, with perfect indifference. When driven to labor by the compulsive power of the white man, he performs the task assigned to him in a headlong, careless manner, treading down with his feet or cutting with his hoe the plants he is put to cultivate — breaking the tools he works with, and spoiling everything he touches that can be injured by careless handling. Hence the overseers call it 'rascality,' supposing that the mischief is intentionally done. * * *

"The term, 'rascality,' given to this disease by overseers, is founded on an erroneous hypothesis, and leads to an incorrect empirical treatment, which seldom or never cures it."

There are many complaints described in Dr. Cartwright's treatise, to which the negroes, in Slavery, seem to be peculiarly subject.

" More fatal than any other is congestion of the lungs, *peripneumonia notha*, often called cold plague, etc. * * *

"The *Frambœsia*, Piam, or Yaws, is a *contagious* disease, communicable by contact among those who greatly neglect cleanliness. It is supposed to be communicable, in a modified form, to the white race, among whom it resembles pseudo syphilis, or some disease of the nose, throat, or larynx. * * *

"Negro-consumption, a disease almost unknown to medical men of the Northern States and of Europe, is also sometimes fearfully prevalent among the slaves. 'It is of importance,' says the Doctor, 'to know the pathognomic signs in its early stages, not only in regard to its treatment, but to detect impositions, as negroes, afflicted with this complaint are often for sale; the acceleration of the pulse, on exercise, incapacitates them for labor, as they quickly give out, and have to leave their work. This induces their owners to sell them, although they may not know the cause of their inability to labor. Many of the negroes brought South, for sale, are in the incipient stages of this disease; they are found to be inefficient laborers, and are sold in consequence thereof. The effect of superstition — a firm belief that he is poisoned or conjured — upon the patient's mind, already in a morbid state (dyæsthesia), and his health affected from hard usage, overtasking or exposure, want of wholesome food, good clothing, warm, comfortable lodging, with the distressing idea (sometimes) that he is an object of hatred or dislike, both to his master or fellow-servants, and has no one to befriend him, tends directly to generate that erythism of mind which is the essential cause of negro-consumption.' * * * 'Remedies should be assisted by removing the *original cause* of the dissatisfaction or trouble of mind, and by using every means to make the patient comfortable, satisfied and happy.'"

Longing for home generates a distinct malady, known to physicians as *Nostalgia*, and there is an analogy between the treatment commonly employed to cure it and that recommended in this last advice of Dr. Cartwright, which is very suggestive.

Under the slave system of labor, discipline must always be maintained by physical power. A lady of New York, spending a winter in a Southern city, had a hired slave-servant, who, one day, refused outright to perform some ordinary light domestic duty required of her. On the lady's gently remonstrating with her, she immediately replied: " You can't make me do it, and I won't do it: I ain't afeard of you whippin' me." The servant was right; the lady could not whip her, and was too tender-hearted to call in a man, or to send her to the guard-house to be whipped, as is the custom with Southern ladies, when their patience is exhausted, under such circumstances. She endeavored, by kindness and by appeals to the girl's good sense, to obtain a moral control over her; but, after suffering continual annoyance and inconvenience, and after an intense trial of her feelings, for some time, she was at length obliged to go to her owner, and beg him to come and take her away from the house, on any terms. It was no better than having a lunatic or a mischievous and pilfering monomaniac quartered upon her.[1]

But often when courage and physical power, with the strength of the militia force and the army of the United States, if required, at the back of the master, are not wanting, there are a great variety of circumstances that make a resort to punishment inconvenient, if not impossible.

Really well-trained, accomplished, and docile house-servants are seldom to be purchased or hired at the South, though they are found in old weathy families rather oftener than first-rate English or French servants are at the North. It is, doubtless, a convenience to have even moderately good servants who cannot, at any time of their improved value or your necessity, demand to have their pay increased, or who cannot be drawn away from you by prospect of smaller demands and kinder treatment at your neighbor's; but I believe few of those who are incessantly murmuring against this healthy operation of God's good law of supply and demand would be willing to purchase exemption from it, at the price with which the masters and mistresses of the South do. They would pay, to get a certain amount of work done, three or four times as much, to the owner of the best sort of hired slaves, as they do to

[1] The *Richmond American* has a letter from Raleigh, N. C., dated Sept. 18, which says: "On yesterday morning, a beautiful young lady, Miss Virginia Frost, daughter of Austin Frost, an engineer on the Petersburg and Weldom Railroad, and residing in this city, was shot by a negro girl, and killed instantly. Cause—reproving her for insolent language."

the commonest, stupidest Irish domestic drudges at the North, though the nominal wages by the week or year, in Virginia, are but little more than in New York.

The number of servants usually found in a Southern family, of any pretension, always amazes a Northern lady. In one that I visited, there were exactly three negroes to each white, and this in a town, the negroes being employed solely in the house.

A Southern lady, of an old and wealthy family, who had been for some time visiting a friend of mine in New York, said to her, as she was preparing to return home: "I cannot tell you how much, after being in your house so long, I dread to go home, and to have to take care of our servants again. We have a much smaller family of whites than you, but we have twelve servants, and your two accomplish a great deal more, and do their work a great deal better than our twelve. You think your girls are very stupid, and that they give you much trouble: but it is as nothing. There is hardly one of our servants that can be trusted to do the simplest work without being stood over. If I order a room to be cleaned, or a fire to be made in a distant chamber, I never can be sure I am obeyed unless I go there and see for myself. If I send a girl out to get anything I want for preparing the dinner, she is as likely as not to forget what is wanted, and not to come back till after the time at which dinner should be ready. A hand-organ in the street will draw all my girls out of the house; and while it remains near us I have no more command over them than over so many monkeys.

The parade of a military company has sometimes entirely prevented me from having any dinner cooked; and when the servants, standing in the square looking at the soldiers, see my husband coming after them, they only laugh, and run away to the other side, like playful children.[1] And when I reprimand them, they only say they don't mean to do anything wrong, or they won't do it again, all the time laughing as though it was all a joke. They don't mind it at all. They are just as playful and careless as any wilful child; and they never will do any work if you don't compel them."

The slave employer, if he finds he has been so unfortunate as to hire a sulky servant, that cannot be made to work to his advantage, has no remedy but to solicit from his owner a deduction from the price he has agreed to pay for his labor, on the same ground that one would from a livery-stable keeper, if he had engaged a horse to go a journey, but found that he was not strong or skilful enough to keep him upon the road. But, if the slave is the property of his employer, and becomes "rascally," the usual remedy is that which the veterinary surgeon recommended when he was called upon for advice how to cure a balky horse: "*Sell* him, my lord." "Rascals" are "sent South" from Virginia, for the cure or alleviation of their

[1] In the city of Columbia, S. C., the police are required to prevent the negroes from running in this way after the military. Any negro neglecting to leave the vicinity of a parade, when ordered by a policeman or any military officer, is required, by the ordinance, to be whipped at the guard-house.

complaint, in much greater numbers than consumptives are from the more Northern States.

"How do you manage, then, when a man misbehaves, or is sick?" I have been often asked by Southerners, in discussing this question.

If he is sick, I simply charge against him every half day of the time he is off work, and deduct it from his wages. If he is careless, or refuses to do what in reason I demand of him, I discharge him, paying him wages to the time he leaves. With new men in whom I have not confidence, I make a written agreement, before witnesses, on engaging them, that will permit me to do this. As for "rascality," I never had but one case of anything approaching to what you call so. A man insolently contradicted me in the field: I told him to leave his job and go to the house, took hold and finished it myself, then went to the house, made out a written statement of account, counted out the balance in money due him, gave him the statement and the money, and told him he must go. He knew that he had failed of his duty, and that the law would sustain me, and we parted in a friendly manner, he expressing regret that his temper had driven him from a situation which had been agreeable and satisfactory to him. The probability is, that this single experience educated him so far that his next employer would have no occasion to complain of his "rascality;" and I very much doubt if any amount of corporal punishment would have improved his temper in the least.

That slaves have to be "humored" a great deal, and

that they very frequently cannot be made to do their master's will, I have seen much evidence. Not that they often directly refuse to obey an order, but, when they are directed to do anything for which they have a disinclination, they undertake it in such a way, that the desired result is sure not to be accomplished. In small particulars for which a laborer's discretion must be trusted to in every-day work, but more especially when emergencies require some extraordinary duties to be performed, they are much less reliable than the ordinary run of laborers employed on our farms in New York. They cannot be driven by fear of punishment to do that which the laborers in free communities do cheerfully from their sense of duty, self-respect, or regard for their reputation and standing with their employer. A gentleman who had some free men in his employment in Virginia, that he had procured in New York, told me that he had been astonished, when a dam that he had been building began to give way in a freshet, to see how much more readily than negroes they would obey his orders, and do their best without orders, running into the water waist deep, in mid-winter, without any hesitation or grumbling.

The manager of a large candle-factory in London, in which the laborers are treated with an unusual degree of confidence and generosity, writes thus in a report to his directors:

"The present year promises to be a very good one as regards profit, in consequence of the enormous increase in the demand for candles. No mere driving of the men and boys, by ourselves and those in authority under us, would have produced the sudden and very great increase of manufacture, necessary for keeping pace with this demand. It has been effected only by the hearty good-will with which the factory has worked, the men and boys making the great extra exertion, which they saw to be necessary to prevent our getting hopelessly in arrears with the orders, as heartily as if the question had been, how to avert some difficulty threatening themselves personally. One of the foremen remarked with truth, a few days back; 'To look on them, one would think each was engaged in a little business of his own, so as to have only himself affected by the results of his work.'"

A farmer in Lincolnshire, England, told me that once, during an extraordinary harvest season, he had had a number of laborers at work without leaving the field or taking any repose for sixty hours—he himself working with them, and eating and drinking only with them during all the time. Such services men may give voluntarily, from their own regard to the value of property to be saved by it, or for the purpose of establishing their credit as worth good wages; but to require it of slaves would be intensely cruel, if not actually impossible. A man can work excessively on his own impulse as much easier than he can be driven to by another, as a horse travels easier in going towards his accustomed stable than in going from it. I mean—and every man who has ever served as a sailor or a soldier will know that it is no imaginary effect—that the actual fatigue, the waste of bodily energy, the expenditure of the physical capacity, is greater in one case than the other.

Sailors and soldiers both, are led by certain inducements to place themselves within certain limits, and for a certain time, both defined by contract, in a condition resembling, in many particulars, that of slaves; and, although they are bound by their voluntary contract and by legal and moral considerations to obey orders, the fact that force is also used to secure their obedience to their officers, scarcely ever fails to produce in them the identical vices which are complained of in slaves. They obey the letter, but defeat the intention of orders that do not please them, they are improvident, wasteful, reckless: they sham illness, and as Dr. Cartwright gives specific medical appellations to discontent, laziness, and rascality, so among sailors and soldiers, when men suddenly find themselves ill and unable to do their duty in times of peculiar danger, or when unusual labor is required, they are humorously said to be suffering under an attack of the powder-fever, the cape-fever, the ice-fever, the coast-fever, or the reefing-fever. The counteracting influences to these vices, which it is the first effort of every good officer to foster, are, first, regard to duty; second, patriotism; third, *esprit du corps*, or professional pride; fourth, self-respect, or personal pride; fifth, self-interest, hope of promotion, or of bounty, or of privileges in mitigation of their hard service, as reward for excellence. Things are never quickly done at sea, unless they are done with a will, or "cheerly," as the sailor's word is—that is, cheerfully. An army is never effective in the field when depressed in its *morale*.

None of these promptings to excellence can be operative, except in a very low degree, to counteract the indolent and vicious tendencies of the Slavery, much more pure than the slavery of the army or the ship, by which the exertions of the Virginia laborer are obtained for his employer.

It is very common, among the Virginians, to think that the relation of field-laborers to their employers is, by the effect of circumstances, rendered very little less slavish than that of their own slaves to them. It is true that in many respects the position of agricultural laborers, in some parts of England and other countries (where the land is owned and rented only in excessively large quantities, and the principle of competition has, therefore, very little influence to counteract the power of the capitalists to prevent a man's getting his living by labor, except on their conditions), approaches, in the degree of their moral subjection, to that of slaves.

But this is true only in a very few districts, nowhere in the United States, unless it be in the Slave States, where sometimes similar causes produce somewhat similar effects upon the poor whites. And, everywhere, the services rendered by the free-laborers are rendered not from fear of punishment, are claimed not by right of force, but are rendered in obedience to, and claimed by express right of, a contract voluntarily made : consequently, compared with that of the slave, their labor is actively, cheerfully, and discreetly given. Circumstances may have made it necessary for the laborer to accept the terms offered by the employer ; but those circumstances no more constitute slavery than do the circumstances which induce merchants and manufacturers in towns to pay what they deem extravagant prices for flour, render them the slaves of the farmers, who say to them, "Pay these prices, or go without."

It is a very low mind that cannot appreciate the difference between services rendered from such motives and under such obligations, honorable, manly, and just obligations, voluntarily entered into, and the services of a slave, rendered from fear that he shall be whipped if he does not render them.

The employer of a free-laborer no more dare whip him than the laborer dare whip the employer. Their rights are equal, in all respects, before the law, and the claim of the laborer to his stipulated wages, his tacitly stipulated diet and lodging, is just as good, and renders him just as truly the owner of his employer, as the claim of the employer upon the free-laborer for his stipulated measure, by days or months, of muscular labor, and his tacitly stipulated exercise of skill and discretion, render him the owner of his employé. The man who would work cheerfully and to the best of his discretion, for the employer, in one case is a fool; the man who would not work cheerfully and to the best of his discretion, for his employer, in the other is dishonest and imprudent.

The following is from the organ of the New York city Know Nothings, of Feb. 21, 1855: "If to rise with the lark and labor the live-long day, saddled with care, loaded down with anxiety, until we sink under the burden, is freedom, then we are not slaves. If to do half this work, without any of its cares, or troubles, with the full quota of pleasure, is the want of it, then who would be free?"

Such a view of life is not only disgraceful to a man, but the prevalence of such ideas, however patriotic may be the foundation on which they have been cultivated, is most pernicious to the character of our own laboring-class, and to all industry into which competition can enter. There are some badly-educated American women who choose to die as seamstresses, rather than to live as cooks or chamber-maids, because they are taught by such writers that the position of a servant, or of those who sell their labor and skill by measure of time and not by measure of amount, is worse than that of slaves. Even prostitution is felt to be less a disgrace than this false parallel to Slavery, and so, unconsciously deluded by this false analogy, they answer this writer's question, actually preferring death to this imaginary degradation.

"It is with dogs," says the best authority on the subject, "as it is with horses; no work is so well done as that which is done cheerfully."[1] And it is with men, both black and white, as it is with horses and with dogs; it is even more so, because the strength and cunning of a man is less adapted to being "broken" to the will of another than that of either dogs or horses.

The writer, whose opinion, that Slavery is a better system for the laborer than the system of Northern

[1] Lieut. Col. W. N. HUTCHINSON, on Dog Breaking.

States, I have just quoted, estimates that the labor of a slave is only half that, in a day, of a man actuated by anxiety for his own advantage at his work. If it were not that Slavery, present at the South and past in our own land and the lands where most of our laborers have been educated, had an influence still to make labor a less respected commodity than most others in our market, in consequence of which the mutual obligations of capitalist and laborer are sometimes less definitely felt than they should be, I think no one would be surprised to learn that this estimate of the difference in the amount of work accomplished in a day, by voluntary laborers and slave laborers, was not in the slightest degree extravagantly expressed. But upon this point I shall now give some exact information.

Mr. T. R. Griscom, of Petersburg, Virginia, stated to me, that he once took accurate account of the labor expended in harvesting a large field of wheat; and the result was that one quarter of an acre a day was secured for each able hand engaged in cradling, raking, and binding. The crop was light, yielding not over six bushels to the acre. In New York a gang of fair cradlers and binders would be expected, under ordinary circumstances, to secure a crop of wheat, yielding from twenty to thirty bushels to the acre, at the rate of about two acres a day for each man.

Mr. Griscom formerly resided in New Jersey; and since living in Virginia has had the superintendence of very large agricultural operations, conducted with slave-labor. After I had, in a letter, intended for publication, made use of this testimony, I called upon him to ask if he would object to my giving his name with it. He was so good as to permit me to do so, and said that I might add that the ordinary waste in harvesting wheat in Virginia, through the carelessness of the negroes, beyond that which occurs in the hands of ordinary Northern laborers, is equal in value to what a Northern farmer would often consider a satisfactory profit on his crop. He also wished me to say that it was his deliberate opinion, formed not without much and accurate observation, that four Virginia slaves do not, when engaged in ordinary agricultural operations, accomplish as much, on an average, as one ordinary free farm laborer in New Jersey.

Mr. Griscom is well known at Petersburg as a man remarkable for reliability, accuracy, and preciseness; and no man's judgment on this subject could be entitled to more respect.

Another man, who had superintended labor of the same character at the North and in Virginia, whom I questioned closely, agreed entirely with Mr. Griscom, believing that four negroes had to be supported on every farm in the State to accomplish the same work which was ordinarily done by one free laborer in New York.

A clergyman from Connecticut, who had resided for many years in Virginia, told me that what a slave expected to spend a day upon, a Northern laborer would, he was confident, usually accomplish by eleven o'clock in the morning.

The Economy of Virginia

In a letter on this subject, most of the facts given in which have been already narrated in this volume, written from Virginia to the *New York Daily Times*, I expressed the conviction that, at the most, not more than one-half as much labor was ordinarily accomplished in Virginia by a certain number of slaves, in a given time, as by an equal number of free laborers in New York. The publication of this letter induced a number of persons to make public the conclusions of their own experience or observations on this subject. So far as I know, these, in every case, sustained my conclusions, or, if any doubt was expressed, it was that I had underestimated the superior economy of free-labor. As affording evidence more valuable than my own on this important point, from the better opportunities of forming sound judgment, which a residence at different times, in both Virginia and a free State had given the writers, I have reprinted, in an appendix, two of these letters, together with a quantity of other testimony from Southern witnesses on this subject, which I beg the reader, who has any doubt of the correctness of my information, not to neglect.

On mentioning to a gentleman in Virginia, who believed that slave-labor was better and cheaper than free-labor, Mr. Griscom's observation, he replied: that without doubting the correctness of the statement of that particular instance, he was sure that if four men did not harvest more than an acre of wheat a day, they could not have been well *driven*. He knew that, if properly driven, threatened with punishment, and punished if necessary, negroes would do as much work as it was possible for any white man to do. The same gentleman, however, at another time, told me that negroes were very seldom punished, not oftener, he presumed, than apprentices were, at the North; that the driving of them was generally left to overseers, who were the laziest and most worthless dogs in the world, frequently not demanding higher wages for their services than one of the negroes, they were given to manage, might be hired out for. Another gentleman told me that he would rather, if the law would permit it, have some of his negroes for overseers, than any white man he had ever been able to obtain in that capacity.

Another planter, whom I requested to examine a letter on the subject, that I had prepared for the *Daily Times*, that he might, if he could, refute my calculations, or give me any facts of an opposite character, after reading it said: "The truth is, that in general, a slave does not do half the work he easily might; and which, by being harsh enough with him, he can be made to do. When I came into possession of my plantation, I soon found the overseer then upon it was good for nothing, and told him I had no further occasion for his services: I then went to driving the negroes myself. In the morning, when I went out, one of them came up to me and asked what work he should go about. I told him to go into the swamp and cut some wood. 'Well, massa,' said he, 's'pose you wants me to do kordins we's been use to doin'; ebery niggar cut a cord a day.'

'A cord! that's what you have been used to doing, is it?' said I. 'Yes, massa, dat's wot dey always makes a niggar do roun' heah—a cord a day, dat's allers de task.' 'Well, now, old man,'[1] said I, 'you go and cut me two cords to-day.' 'Oh, massa! two cords! Nobody couldn do dat. Oh! massa, dat's too hard! Nebber heard o' nobody's cuttin' more 'n a cord o' wood in a day, roun' heah. No nigger could n' do it.' 'Well, old man, you have two cords of wood cut to-night, or to-morrow morning you shall get two hundred lashes—that's all there is about it. So, look sharp!' And he did it, and ever since no negro has ever cut less than two cords a day for me, though my neighbors never get but one cord. It was just so with a great many other things—mauling rails—I always have two hundred rails mauled in a day; just twice what it is the custom of the country to expect of a negro, and just twice as many as my negroes had been made to do before I managed them myself."

This only makes it more probable that the amount of labor ordinarily and generally performed by slaves in Virginia is very small, compared with that done by the laborers of the free States, and confirms the correctness of the estimates that I have given.

These estimates, let it be recollected, in conclusion, are all deliberately and carefully made by gentlemen

[1] "Old Man," is a common title of address to any middle-aged negro in Virginia, whose name is not known. "Boy" and "Old Man" may be applied to the same person. Of course, in this case, the slave is not to be supposed to be beyond his prime of strength.

of liberal education, who have had unusual facilities of observing both at the North and at the South—gentlemen who own or employ slaves themselves, and who sustain Southern designs on the political questions connected with slavery. I have not given them because they were extreme, but because I could obtain no others equally exact. The conclusion to which they directly point is, that the cost of any certain amount of labor, by measure, of tasks and not of time, is *between three and four hundred per cent.* higher in Virginia than in the free States. To this is to be added the cost of clothing the slaves, of the time they lose in sickness, or otherwise, and of all they pilfer, damage, and destroy through carelessness, improvidence, recklessness, and " rascality."

Labor is the creator of wealth. There can be no honest wealth, no true prosperity without it; and in exact proportion to the economy of labor is the cost of production and the accumulation of profit upon the capital used in its employment.

Let any one allow as much as he can, in view of the testimony, for exaggeration in these estimates, and reduce them accordingly. It seems to me hardly possible that he should be able still to doubt, that in the additional cost of labor alone, a grand, if not all-sufficient cause may be found for the acknowledged slow progress and the poverty of Virginia, compared with the free States.

Considering that the wages of a week's labor would pay for the transportation of a laborer from the free

States to a community where slave-labor predominates, it might, at the first thought upon the matter, appear impossible that there could be, for any length of time, any essential difference in the cost of labor between the two districts. The law of supply and demand is not, indeed, inoperative against slavery; it is a constant counteracting influence to its evils, and, if it were not for the internal slave-trade, which makes slaves valuable property, otherwise than for labor, it would probably, before this, unless the competition of free-labor had been excluded by know-nothing measures, have forced the adoption of *some* method of relieving the State of its heavy burden; but this great first law of Commerce acts very slowly.

The laborer who, in New York, gave a certain amount of labor for his wages in a day, soon finds, in Virginia, that the ordinary measure of labor is smaller than in New York: a " day's work " or a month's does not mean the same that it did in New York. He naturally adapts his wares to the market. Just as in New York a knavish custom having been some time ago established, of selling a measure of three quarters of a bushel of certain articles under the name of a bushel, no man now finds it to his advantage to offer them by the full bushel, at a correspondingly higher price. Though every one cries out against the custom, and demands a bushel for a bushel, few are willing to pay proportionately for it; few are willing to sell it without being paid more than proportionately on account of their deviation from custom; and the custom must be reformed very slowly. So the laborer, finding that the capitalists of Virginia are accustomed to pay for a poor article at a high price, prefers to furnish them the poor article at their usual price, rather than a better article, unless at a more than correspondingly better price.

But there are other laws, also, that come in play in this case, to qualify the action of the laws of demand and supply.

"Man is a social animal." The largest part of the labor required in Virginia is, and long has been, performed by negroes. The negroes are a degraded people; degraded not merely by position, but actually immoral, low-lived; without healthy ambition; but little influenced by high moral considerations, and, in regard to labor, not all affected by regard for duty. This is universally recognized, and debasing fear, not cheering hope, is in general allowed to be their only stimulant to exertion. A capitalist was having a building erected in Petersburg, and his slaves were employed in carrying up the brick and mortar for the masons on their heads; a Northern man, standing near, remarked to him that they moved so indolently it seemed as if they were trying to see how long they could be in mounting the ladder without actually stopping. The builder started to reprove them, but after moving a step turned back and said: "It would only make them move more slowly still when I am not looking at them, if I should hurry them now. *And what motive have they to do better?* It's no concern of theirs how long the masons wait. I am sure, if I was in their place, I should n't move as fast as they do."

Now, let the white laborer come here from the North or from Europe—his nature demands a social life—shall he associate with the poor, slavish, degraded, low-lived, despised, unambitious negro, with whom labor and punishment are almost synonymous? or shall he be the friend and companion of the white man, in whose mind labor is habitually associated with no ideas of duty, responsibility, comfort, luxury, cultivation, or elevation and expansion either of mind or estate, as it is where the ordinary laborer is a free man—free to use his labor as a means of obtaining all these and all else that is to be respected, honored or envied in the world?

Associating with either or both, is it not inevitable that he will be rapidly demoralized—that he will soon learn to hate labor, give as little of it for his hire as he can, become base, cowardly, faithless—" worse than a nigger "?

Such, I am sure, is the fact, with regard to the majority of laborers who have come here, and I cannot doubt that such is the cause. And, when we reflect how little the great body of our working-men are consciously much affected by moral considerations, in their movements, one is tempted to suspect that the Almighty has endowed the great transatlantic migration with a new instinct, by which it is unconsciously repelled from the demoralizing and debilitating influence of slavery, as migrating birds have sometimes been thought to be from pestilential regions. I know not how else to account for the remarkable indisposition to be sent to Virginia, which I have seen manifested by poor Irishmen and Germans, who could have known, I think, no more of the evils of slavery to the whites, in the Slave States, than the slaves themselves know of the effect of conscription in France, and who certainly could have been governed by no considerations of self-respect. This experience I have had, in consequence of having been requested by several persons, in Virginia, to send them white laborers. I can understand better what induced two men of the same sort, who had previously lived a short time on farms in the Free States, to return North, after completing a short engagement to work upon a slave plantation, though they had obtained high wages, and were well treated by their employer, and could give no better reason to me, for their course, than that they "did n't like to work with them niggers."

That the native white population is thoroughly demoralized, in respect to those qualities essential to a good laborer, and that this demoralization is the direct result of slavery, I have given some evidence, which I received from a slave-holder, in one of my earlier letters (p. 100); but I will add the recorded testimony of others.

From the Patent Office Report, for 1847.

"As to the price of labor, our mechanics charge from one to two dollars a day. As to agricultural labor, we have none. Our poor are poor because *they will not work*, therefore are seldom employed.
"CHAS. YANCEY,
"Buckingham Co., Virginia."

The sentence, "as to agricultural labor, we have none," must mean no free-labor: the number of slaves in this county being, according to the census, 8,161, or nearly 3,000 more than the whole white population! There are, also, 250 free negroes in the county.

From a Correspondent of the American Agriculturist, Feb. 14, 1855.

"As to laborers, we work, chiefly, slaves, not because they are cheaper, but rather, because they are the only *reliable* labor we can get. The whites here engage to work *for less price than the blacks* can be got for; yet, they will not work well, and *rarely work out the time specified*. If any of your friends come here, and wish to work whites, I would advise them, by all means, to bring them with them; for, our white laborers are far inferior to our blacks, and our black labor is far inferior to what we read and hear of your laborers.

"G. G. G.,
"Albermarle Co., Virginia."

In Albemarle, there are over thirteen thousand slaves, to less than twelve thousand whites.

In the northwestern counties, Cabell, Mason, Brooke, and Tyler, in or adjoining which there are no large towns, but a free laboring population, with slaves in ratio to the freemen, as one to fifteen, only, the value of land is over seven dollars and three quarters an acre.

In Southampton, Surrey, James-Town, and New-Kent, in which the slave population is as 1 to 2.2, the value of land is but little more than half as much—$4.50 an acre.

In Surrey, Prince George, Charles City, and James, adjoining counties on James River, and originally having some of the most productive soil in the State, and now supplied with the public conveniences which have accrued in two hundred years of occupation, by a civilized and Christian community, the number of slaves being, at present, to that of whites, as 1 to 1.9, the value of land is but $6 an acre.

In Fairfax, another of the first-settled counties, and one in which, twenty years ago, land was even less in value than in the James River counties, it is now worth twice as much. The slave population, once greater than that of whites, has been reduced, by emigration and sale, till there are now less than half as many slaves as whites. In the place of slaves, has come another sort of people. The change which has taken place, and the cause of it, is thus simply described in the Agricultural Report of the County to the Commissioner of Patents. (*See Patent Office Report*, 1852.)

"In appearance, the county is so changed, in many parts, that a traveler, who passed over it ten years ago, would not now recognize it. Thousands and thousands of acres had been cultivated in tobacco, by the former proprietors, would not pay the cost, and were abandoned as worthless, and became covered with a wilderness of pines. These lands have been purchased by northern emigrants; the large tracts divided and subdivided, and cleared of pines; and neat farm-houses and barns, with smiling fields of grain and grass, in the season, salute the delighted gaze of the beholder. Ten years ago, it was a mooted question, whether Fairfax lands could be made productive; and, if so, would they pay the cost? This problem has been satisfactorily solved by many, and, in consequence of the above altered state of things, *school-houses and churches have doubled in number.*"

There is much more evidence in my hands, but I think I may, as the lawyers say, rest on this. I see not how any one can still doubt that Slavery is the present cause of the comparative adversity or poverty of Virginia, or that Freedom would be found an immediate, certain, and, to all but the few slave-holders (they are not, I suppose, one to a hundred of the people), entirely satisfactory remedy.

But I cannot pass from Virginia without considering her condition from another and broader point of view.

It is very customary to speak of our Confederacy of States as The Great Experiment. The great experiment of what? Of the effect, I suppose is meant, of a form of government in which all men are declared to be equal; in which there are no privileged orders; no ruling class; in which the laboring class is dignified by being made, equally with the capitalist and the professional scholar, the recipient of governmental power.

Yet, the United States, in the aggregate, cannot rightly be considered as more than approximating such an experiment. It affords, however, thirty distinct experiments in governmental and social science, which might be studied and examined, one comparatively with another, most usefully. And I am convinced that the average progress in happiness and wealth, which has been made by the people of each State, is in almost exact ratio to the degree in which the democratic principle has been radically carried out in their constitution, laws, and customs.

In studying the question of the causes of the poverty of Virginia, I have been obliged to examine the past as well as the present character of her labor, and I have been astonished to see the important bearing which certain facts in her history have upon the great problem of statesmanship.

Men of literary taste or clerical habits are always apt to overlook the working-classes, and to confine the records they make of their own times, in a great degree, to the habits and fortunes of their own associates, or to those of people of superior rank to themselves, of whose sayings and doings their vanity, as well as their curiosity, leads them to most carefully inform themselves. The dumb masses have often been so lost in this shadow of egotism, that, in later days, it has been impossible to discern the very real influence their character and condition has had on the fortune and fate of nations.

Of the laborers in the colony of Virginia, although, after *a self-sustaining community* had been once firmly established, they undoubtedly formed a very large majority of all the people, very little notice is ever taken by any chronicler or historian, further than in simple memoranda of their arrival by the cargo or hundred. Information with regard to them is only to be obtained by a labored investigation of evidence incidentally recorded.

As very little of the knowledge thus attainable has been made readily accessible to the mass of the reading public, or to those who might most profit by it, I have thought it best to offer here a somewhat desultory review of the more significant facts relative to the industrial development of Virginia.

CHAPTER IV

THE EXPERIENCE OF VIRGINIA — SOME DATA AND PHENOMENA OF THE VIRGINIA EXPERIMENTS IN POLITICAL ECONOMY

IN the shipping-lists and other records of the first settlement of Virginia, a large proportion of the colonists are carefully designated "gentlemen." The circumstance, that the clergyman and surgeon-general have the honor to be mentioned in this company, but the untitled physician and surgeon are reckoned among the common people, will indicate pretty clearly the meaning of the distinction.

In the first ship, there are fifty "gentlemen," with one hair-dresser, one tailor, one drummer, one mason, one blacksmith, four carpenters, and but eight professed laborers.

Speaking of the immigrants by the first three ships, Captain John Smith, in his autobiography, says there were not two dozen that had ever done a real day's work in their lives, before they left England. Of these, eight were Dutchmen and Poles. The rest of the nominal laborers had previously been gentlemen's lackeys and house-servants, or were bankrupt tradesmen and desperate loafers. "Ten good workmen would have done more substantial work than ten (of the best of them) in a week."

To keep them all from perishing, Smith was obliged to drive them to work almost at the sword's point; and when he had the whole responsibility of government to occupy his mind, and its various duties of superintendence to take up his time, he himself did more hard and irksome manual labor, with his own hands, than any other man in the colony.

Smith, of course, was unpopular, was conspired against, and denounced as a shrewd, ambitious, self-seeking demagogue. His enemies never dared try to tar and feather him; but they finally obtained his dismissal from the governorship. No sooner, however, did he leave the miserable rabble of snobs and flunkies to take care of themselves, than their absolute helplessness was made manifest. Presently they were reduced to such extremity as is described in the following passage from the "Observations of William Symmons, Doctor of Divinitie."

"—So great was our Famine, that a Saluage we slew, and buried, the poorer Sort tooke him up againe, and eat him and so did diuers others one another, boyled and stewed with Roots and Herbs! And one amongst the rest did kill his Wife, powdered her, and had eaten part of her before it was knowne, for which he was executed as he well deserued; now whether she was better roasted, boyled or carbonado'd, I know not, but of such a Dish as powdered Wife I neuer heard of. This was that Time which still to this Day we call the staruing Time; it were too vile to say and scarce to be belieued, what we endured: but the Occasion was our owne, for want of Prouidence, Industrie, and Gouernment, and not the barrennesse and defects of the Country, as is generally supposed."

At length, in a fit of desperation, the surviving adventurers packed what provisions their recklessness had not yet destroyed, in boats, abandoned their enterprise, and actually embarked with the intention of coasting to the northward until they should fall in with the honest laboring fishermen on the banks of Newfoundland, of whom they could ask charity. Before they got out of the river, however, they were met by Sir Thomas Dale, just arriving from England, with a Governor's commission. He obliged them to return, and, after a short experience of their laziness and imprudence, proclaimed martial law, ordered them all, gentle and simple, to work in gangs under overseers, and threatened to shoot the first man who refused to labor, or was disobedient.[1] Yet but six hours' work was all that it was deemed prudent or necessary to require. Smith says that one day's labor of each man was amply sufficient to provide him with food for a week; but most of the Colonists would actually starve rather than do this much.

William Box writes home an account of the dreadful

[1] One reads, not without admiration of the candor of the writer, the following observation of Mr. Howison: "If it be admitted that the Southern States of the American Union have acted wisely in enacting, for the slaves unhappily existing within their borders, laws different from those applied to the whites, then we presume that none who approve this distinction can object to the principle upon which the martial law of Sir Thomas Dale was introduced."—Dale found it necessary to apply to the Cavaliers the same motive to labor which their descendants now consider only requisite for the African race. Is it blood or education that is the essential evil?

amount of hard work that it is necessary to have done, but is careful to add—

"Neuertheleſs it must not be conceiued that this Buſineſs of planting a Colony excludes Gentlemen whose Breeding never knew what a Day's Labor was, for though they cannot dig, use the Spade or practise the Ax, there is abundant Occasion for such to imploy the force of Knowledge, the Excuse of Counsel, the Operation and Power of their best Breeding and Qualities."

Smith, however, wrote to the Treasurer in London—

"When you send again I entreat you send rather but Thirty Carpenters, Husbandmen, Gardeners, Fishermen, Blacksmiths, Masons, and Diggers Up of Trees' Roots, well prouided, than a Thousand of such as we have, for except we be able to both lodge and feed them, the most will consume for want of Neceſsaries before they can be made good for any thing."

He says elsewhere—

"They desired but to pack over so many as they could, saying Necefsity would make them get Victuals for themselves, as for good laborers they were more usefull here in England; but they found it otherwayes, the Charge was all one to send a Workman as a Roarer, whose Clamors to appease we had much adoe to get Fish and Corne to maintaine them from one Supply till another came, with more Loyterers without Victuals still, to make us worse and worse: for the most of them would rather starve than worke."

The Colony, still languishing, though things much improved under Sir Thomas Dale, in 1618 the company petitioned the Crown to make them a present of "vagabonds and condemned men," to be sent out as slaves; and the King, thankful, probably, to get rid of the burden of taking care of these men, who had been too lazy heretofore to take care of themselves in any other way than by pilfering and knavery, was graciously pleased to grant their request. The following year a hundred head of this valuable stock was driven out of Bridewell and other London knave-pens, on board ship, and exported to Virginia.

The next year, twenty head of black men, direct from Africa, were landed from a Dutch ship, in James River, and were immediately bought by the gentlemen of the Colony.

These were the first negro slaves in the country at present included in the United States. The same year the first cheerful labor by the voluntary immigrants to New England, by the May-Flower, was applied to the sterile soil of Massachusetts Bay.

Notwithstanding the gentlemen of Virginia were thus relieved from the necessity of personal labor, the Colony continued to demand from England such large supplies of provisions, and other stores, which it seemed well fitted to produce within itself, that the King ordered a commission to ascertain what was the secret of its remarkable adversity and continued helplessness and poverty.

An examination of the chartered Companies' books showed that more than one hundred and fifty thousand dollars had been then already sunk in the endeavor to establish and sustain the Colony.

Smith was examined at length.[1] Being asked what

[1] Smith had once been a slave himself, and had been driven to agricultural labor by his Tartar master, exactly as the African slaves now are in America. He knew very well, therefore,

charge he thought, at the time he left, would have defrayed the necessary expenses of establishing the Colony on a safe footing, he answered, that twenty thousand pounds, if it could have been expended in *wages to good laborers and mechanics*, would have been amply sufficient, and added that one hundred *good hired hands* would have been worth more than a thousand of such as had been sent out, and that though Lord Delaware, Sir Thomas Dale, and Sir Thomas Gates, who had been Governors in Virginia since he was there, had been previously persuaded otherwise, they had now come to be of his mind about it.

In reply to the inquiry, what he thought were the defects of the government, he said it was generally complained that the supplies intended for the benefit of the Colony at large, were appropriated by a few individuals to their private advantage, and that even *the laborers sent out to work for the Company were sold to the highest bidders* among the private adventurers. God forbid, he continued, that those who transport these servants thither, and provide them with necessaries, should not be repaid, or that masters should not there have the same privileges over their servants that they had in England; but it was an odious thing, and a source of corresponding evil, that when the cost of their shipment was not more than eight, or at the most, ten

---

the different value of a slave, obliged to work for another's benefit, and a free man, working for himself. It is a curious thing, also, that finally he killed his owner, and fled to the North. See his *Life*, by himself.

pounds each, they should be sold, as they were, to the planters, from the ships, at forty, fifty, and threescore pounds, and this *without any stipulation as to how they should be treated or maintained.* He would have these merchants made such merchandise of themselves, rather than suffer such a bad trade to continue longer, for it was enough to bring a well-settled commonwealth to misery, much more such a one as Virginia.

It was not discontinued until the revolution of 1776.

According to a letter of John Rolfe's, in 1619, there had been many complaints that the Governors, Captains and officers bought and sold men and boys, or set them over, from one to another, for a yearly rent; also that tenants and servants were frequently misused, and covenants were not kept with them, and the Council in England, in order to amend these abuses, ordered that a hundred men should be provided at the Company's charge, to serve and attend the Governor; fifty, the Deputy Governor; fifty, the Treasurer, and smaller numbers for the other officers, and likewise to each officer a competency sufficient to enable him to live well in his office, without resorting to those scandalous means. These servants they were required to deliver up in good order to their successors; but complaint is afterwards made that they generally failed to do so, and that many of them were sold to the planters, and the proceeds pocketed by the chivalrous cavaliers.

Being next asked how he would remedy the evils under which the Colony suffered, Smith recommended, first, that the officers should be held to a more strict accountability for the funds placed in their hands; second, that less should be expended from the common stock in maintaining the officers' and deputies' servants, and thirdly, that sufficient workmen, and means to maintain them, should be provided, and that the practice of sending out delinquents who could not be ruled by the laws of England should be stopped forthwith. To improve a commonwealth with debauched people, he maintained, was out of the question; no wise man would choose to seek his fortune in such company. There was more ado, he repeated, in conclusion, about the administration of their paltry government, than was necessary for that of the kingdoms of Ireland and Scotland; *the number of officers in Virginia, with their attendants, was greater than that of all the workers.*

The report of the investigating commission was never made public, but it resulted in an abrogation of the charter of the Company, and a bar upon their property, if not a formal confiscation of it, which has never been defended on any other grounds than such as are held to justify the forcible suppression of a public nuisance. The chief cause of the failure of the Colony had evidently been the indolence and imbecility of the people; nevertheless, the practice of sending out malefactors was not discontinued, nor were any pains taken to encourage the emigration of industrious poor men, eager to improve their circumstances.[1]

[1] In 1614, shortly after Lord Delaware's return from Virginia, being in the House of Commons on the reception of a petition from Virginia, he made the capital observation: "All Virginia requires is but *a few honest laborers, burdened with children.*"

The Experience of Virginia

The king, however, had the sense to make the *gentlemen* of the Colony dependent neither on wages, nor partnership in profits, but wholly on their own individual good management. Patents of land, to any extent, were given to all applicants, except non-conformists, on the payment of a quit-rent to the Crown, of two shillings an acre. This led to a large immigration of speculators, who immediately commenced planting tobacco, with all the laborers, of any sort, that they could command.

Four years later, Smith says, the Colony has increased wonderfully beyond expectation, and that tobacco is raised in such excessive quantities, that the market is already quite overstocked with it. He looks for a good effect to follow—that the small profit of raising tobacco "will cause the people to come together to work upon soap-ashes, iron, rape-oil, madder, pitch and tar, flax and hemp." We shall see that even he had not sufficiently appreciated the irreparable mischief which the degradation of labor must entail upon a community.

The more the people of the Colony increase in numbers, the more distinctly do they continue to be classed under the two grand divisions—gentlemen and laborers. Under the head of gentlemen are to be included the colonial officers, the clergy, and the large land-proprietors, sometimes still styled adventurers (a term equivalent to speculators,) but generally called planters. Lawyers and physicians are seldom mentioned. The laborers are sub-divided, under the three heads of heathen slaves, convict slaves or servants, and bond-servants: no doubt there were some freemen laboring for wages also, and a few mechanics and others, living by job-work, but there is never any mention of such.

Christian slaves, or servants, were criminals and State prisoners, who were often given as property, by the English kings, to those they wished to reward among their courtiers and favorite officers, and by them sold to the colonists. The majority of them were not resolute ruffians, but idle and dissolute fellows, vagrants, and pickpockets. I have found no clear indication of their number, but, even before the confiscation of the Company's charter, it had been so great, and had occasioned Virginia so bad a reputation, that Smith wrote: "Some did choose to be hanged ere they would go thither, *and were.*"

Shortly before the Revolution, the usual annual importation of felons into the adjoining smaller province of Maryland was three hundred and fifty in number; that to Virginia was probably larger.[1]

"The Fortunes and Misfortunes of the celebrated Moll Flanders, who was born in Newgate," a novel, by De Foe, written in 1683, first published in London, 1722, gives much evidence of the notorious character of the Virginia emigration, some of which I subjoin, in extracts.

"She often told me how the greateſt part of the Inhabitants of that Colony came thither in very indifferent Circumſtances from England; that, generally ſpeaking, they were of two Sorts;

[1] Grahame.

either, firſt, ſuch as were brought over by Maſters of Ships, to be ſold as Servants; or, ſecond, ſuch as are tranſported, after having been found guilty of Crimes puniſhable with Death."

—"Depend upon it," ſays ſhe, "there are more Thieves and Rogues made by that one Priſon of Newgate, than by all the Clubs and Societies of Villains in the Nation. ''T is that curſed Place,' ſays my Mother, 'that half peoples this Colony,' (Virginia).

"'Hence, Child,' ſays ſhe, 'many a Newgate-Bird becomes a great Man, and we have,' continued ſhe, 'ſeveral Juſtices of the Peace, Officers of the trained Bands, and Magiſtrates of the Towns they live in, that have been burned in the Hand.'"

—"That he had ſome intimation, that if he would ſubmit to tranſport himſelf, he might be admitted to it without a Trial, but that he could not think of it with any Temper, and thought he could much eaſier ſubmit to be hanged."

Transportation to Virginia was the choice, as appears by the context, and thus Smith's amusing assertion is confirmed.

"Some of them [convict paſsengers to Virginia] had neither Shirt nor Shift, Linen or Woolen, but what was on their Backs."

—"The Mortification of being brought on board, like a Priſoner, piqued him very much, ſince it was firſt told him that he ſhould tranſport himſelf, ſo that he might go as a Gentleman at Liberty. It is true he was not ordered to be ſold when he came there."

—"Ordered to be tranſported (to Virginia) in reſpite from the Gallows,

"A VIRGINIA GENTLEMAN.—The Caſe was plain, he was born a Gentleman, and was not only unacquainted, but indolent, and when we did ſettle, would rather go into the Woods with his Gun—which they call, there, Hunting—than attend the natural Buſineſs of the Plantation."

The greater energy and industry of his wife, who had been a prostitute and a convict, only made him content to remain in Virginia.

—"An Englifh Woman-fervant and a Negro Man-fervant, things abfolutely necefsary for all People that pretended to fettle in that Country."

It was not criminals alone that were sent into this bondage, but captives of war, of all nations, and State prisoners, victims of the Star Chamber and of the Ecclesiastical Courts; persons suspected of traitorous designs upon the monarchy, and infidels to the Court theology; all were herded together with petty pilferers, convicted murderers, and heathen blackamoors, and driven by overseers to work in the tobacco fields of their cavalier purchasers.

Charles II. ordered a shipment of Quakers to Virginia, where they were sold as slaves, for dissenting from *his* true church. Their non-resistance principles must have added much to their value. The common rascals, though always money's worth, were usually considered extra-hazardous. In 1720, Beverly says: "as for malefactors condemned to transportation, *though the greedy planter will always buy them*, yet, it is to be feared they will be very injurious to the country, which has always suffered many murthers and robberies."

Medical science had not then been pushed to that profundity of analysis, which now distinguishes it, at the South; but, in the unprofessional records of the times, the distinguishing symptoms may be clearly recognized, of both *drapetomania* and *dysæsthesia*, and it is clear, I think, that these maladies prevailed among this class of laborers, to an exceedingly interesting extent. *Drapetomania* would, indeed, seem, though Professor Cartwright does not mention it, to have then been more prevalent among the whites than the negroes. Dr. Little, in his History of Richmond, has not failed to notice this singular pathological fact. He says that, in the earliest colonial newspapers, "Runaway servants are advertised; *generally white men*, convicts sold for their crimes; the nation, as well as the description of the person is given, and sometimes the manner of carrying himself, when in liquor. *We find Englishmen, Irish, Welsh, and Scotch, all in print, as runaway convict slaves.*"

Owing, probably, to the neglect of sufficient quarantine precautions, *Dysæsthesia Ethiopica* must have been introduced by the African traders, at an early period; and its contagion was not confined to the Ethiopian stock, but, perhaps, from their then more close association in the labors of the plantation, it too frequently, also, attacked the white slaves. A case is mentioned by Beverly, where violent remedies were obliged to be used, to check it.

"The rigorous circumfcription of their Trade, the Perfecution of the Sectaries, and the little Demand for Tobacco, had like to have had very fatal Confequences. For the poor People (chiefly Servants who had ferved out their Bond, probably,) becoming thereby very uneafie, their Murmerings were watch'd and fed, by feveral mutinous and rebellious OLIVERIAN Soldiers, fent thither as Servants. Thefe depending upon the difcontented People of all Sorts, formed a villainous Plot to deftroy their Mafters, and afterwards to fet up for themfelves. This Plot was brought fo near to Perfection, that it was the very Night before the defigned Execution, e'er it was difcover'd; and then it came out by the relenting of one of their Accomplices, whofe name was Birkenhead. This Man was Servant to Mr. Smith of Purton, in Gloucester County, near which Place, viz., at Poplar Spring, the Mifcreants were to meet the Night following, and put in Execution their horrid Confpiracy." * * * "Four of thefe Rogues were hanged; but Birkenhead was gratified with his Freedom, and a Reward of Two Hundred Pounds Sterling. For the Discovery and happy Diffapointment of this Plot, an anniverfary Thankfgiving was appointed on the 13th of September, the Day it was to have been put in Execution. And it is great Pity fome other Days are not commemorated as well as that."

The term *servant* was, I believe, always applied, in the provincial days of Virginia, to white men and women, who were bound to service for a limited time, and the term slaves, to those held for life. Well-bred people now designate their slaves, both field hands and house servants, by that title. I presume the fashion of doing so arose after the Revolution, and was due to the same feeling which prevented the word slave from being permitted in the Constitution of the United States.

Poor people of all sorts, in England, were induced, by well-worked puffs of the delightful climate, and abundant, spontaneous productions of Virginia, to indenture themselves as servants for terms of years, for the sake of being transported thither. There was a profession of men, called *Spirits*, who made it their business to cajole weak young men and women, in this way, and then send them to the colony, and sell them to the planters, as servants or laborers. They were in such demand, that they were often disposed of on board ship, to the highest bidders, at profits of thirty or forty pounds to the spirited speculators.

The following advertisement is taken from the *Virginia Gazette*, March 3d, 1768:

"JUST arrived, the Neptune, Captain Arbuckle, with one hundred and ten HEALTHY SERVANTS, Men, Women and Boys, among whom are MANY VALUABLE TRADESMEN, viz.: Tailors, Weavers, Barbers, Blackſmiths, Carpenters and Joiners, Shoemakers, a Stay Maker, Cooper, Cabinet Maker, Bakers, Silverſmiths, a Gold and Silver Refiner, and many others.

"The Sale will commence at Leedſtown, on the Rappahannoc, on Wedneſday, the 9th of this inſtant (March). A reaſonable Credit will be allowed on giving approved Security to

"THOMAS HODGE." [1]

These servants stood in the relation of debtors to their masters, bound to discharge the cost of their immigration "by the entire employment of their powers to the benefit of their creditors." [2] It was illegal for any man to deal with them, except their masters. Having no property of their own, by the penal laws, they were to be whipped at the rate of one stroke for each sixty cents of the fines imposed in like cases on freemen. Masters were forbidden to whip their servants naked, nor were they given permission to kill them, under any circumstances, but they were allowed by law to *dismember irreclaimable runaways*, if they thought best.[3] Any resistance or offer of violence, on the part of a servant to his master, subjected him to one year's additional servitude, and maid-servants, having illegitimate children, also forfeited to their masters one year's additional service; if, however, their master was the father, it was to be paid to the church-

[1] Howison.   [2] Bancroft.   [3] Hildreth.

wardens. By a subsequent law, any unmarried white woman having a child, was to be fined fifteen pounds, or to be sold for five years; if she was already a servant, the time to commence at the end of the service for which she was bound: the child was to be bound out till thirty years of age.

The white servants, at an early period, were reported to be treated with great cruelty, and to be employed at unusual labors. Beverly denies that it was so in his time (1720). Probably, from the danger, which cruel treatment occasioned, of their revolt, as well as from the check which the reports of it produced upon the importation of servants, laws were passed to prevent cruelty, and to insure that wholesome diet and clothing should be provided for them.

"If a Mafter fhould be fo cruel as to ufe his Servant ill, who is faln fick, or lame in his Service and thereby rendered unfit for Labour, he muft be removed by the Church Wardens out of the Way of fuch Cruelty." "All Servants whatever, have their Complaints heard, without Fee or Reward; but if the Mafter be found faulty, the Charge of the Complaint is caft upon him, otherwife the bufinefs is done ex Officio." Mafters "are always to appear on the firft Complaint of their Servants, otherwife to forfeit the Service of them until they do appear." "All Servants' Complaints are to be received at any Time in Court without Procefs, and fhall not be delayed for want of Form; but the Merits of the fame fhall be immediately inquired into by the Juftices."[1]

None of these laws applied to negro slaves (or to any born out of Christendom); nor has there been any equally humane legislation in their behalf to this day.

[1] Beverly.

Whenever there shall be a sincere and earnest desire on the part of the controlling power of any slave State to legislate on Slavery *for the negro's sake*, the Virginia enactments of two centuries ago, with regard to the protection of white bond-servants, will serve as a model.

"An inexperienced examiner," says Mr. Howison, "of the present time, in reading the criminal code of Virginia as to slaves, would declare that it was stained with blood; and in truth it is appalling to note the number and the character of the offences for which death is denounced against them. But it affords the purest consolation to reflect that these laws seldom operate *in practice*. The executive is clothed with the merciful power of selling slaves condemned to die, and transporting them beyond the limits of the State. The owner then receives value; but if the slave so transported returns, he is liable to execution, without reprieve, and the owner loses his value." Either these laws are barbarous or the transportation is unjust and unmerciful to those living out of the State. How would Virginia act, if Pennsylvania should pass a law, permitting the governor to set all criminals, deserving death, over the border, with a threat to kill them if they were ever seen within her limits again?

When the time for which these servants were covenanted to labor had expired, they, of course, were entitled to be at liberty. It was not customary to pay them anything as wages; but the law required that they should always be provided with two suits of clothes, ten bushels of corn, and a gun of twenty shillings value, when at length they became self-dependent. They could be made freeman of the province on application to the Governor, and after certain formalities. Chiefly recruited, originally, among the most miserable rabble of London, educated to agricultural labor as the yoke-mates of slaves and criminals, and then suddenly turned adrift with a Brummagem fire-lock and ten bushels of maize, to shift for themselves, their social elevation was not likely to be very rapid. Regard to family descent is a notoriously weak point among the wealthy people of Virginia, even at this day, "Poverty and the want of education on the part of the mass of the freedmen," says Hildreth, "kept them, too often, in a subservient position, and created in the Middle as well as the Southern Colonies an inferior order of poor whites, a distinction of classes and an inequality almost unknown in republican New England."

It was early enacted that all persons brought into the Colony, who had not been Christians in their own country, and even though they afterwards were converted, should be made and held slaves for life. One of the avowed objects of the Virginia speculation being to convert the native savages, a provision of the royal charter inculcated kindness to the Indians, and forbade their being made slaves. This was afterwards disregarded, and multitudes of them were brought into subjection, and held as slaves for life, on the ground that they were prisoners of war, and rightful subjects of oppression, in the name of Christ.

In 1662, forty-two years after the first importation of

negroes, there being already many mulatto children, the paternity of which it would be disagreeable to inquire about, owing to the laws against libertinism, it was enacted, in direct contradiction to the supreme English law, that the children of slaves should follow the condition of the mother, and not ever of the father. This law, which has been maintained to the present time, of course offers a direct encouragement to the most mischievous licentiousness. In the French, Dutch, Danish, German, Spanish, and Portuguese colonies, the white fathers of colored children have always been accustomed to educate and emancipate them, and endow them with property. In Virginia, and the English colonies generally, the white fathers of mulatto children have always been accustomed to use them in a way that most completely destroys the oft complacently-asserted claim, that the Anglo-Saxon race is possessed of deeper natural affection than the more demonstrative sort of mankind.

In 1669, that the cupidity of planters might not prevent them from permitting the christening of their slaves' children, from a doubt of their right to hold Christians in slavery, it was formally enacted that the Christian offspring of all slaves might be used as property, by the owners of the mothers of it.

Both these laws being, as is evident from repeated decisions of English Courts, "*unconstitutional*," or enacted in defiance of the common and fundamental law, at the time they were passed, no person can be legally defined a slave, in Virginia, except by his heathenism or infidelity, to this day. The law made no account of color, but only of creed, in distinguishing a man entitled to freedom from a man subject to be enslaved. The slavery of negroes, in Virginia, at this time, rests only on custom.[1]

Laws were afterwards passed, at various times, to discourage the emancipation of slaves by grateful or conscientious owners, and free negro-women were taxed in distinction from white.

Slaves were, by special exception, denied trial by jury. When charged with a capital crime, a special commission was appointed to judge them, and, if they were condemned to death, their owners were remunerated for their loss from the public treasury.

In 1692, an act was passed for suppressing " outlying slaves." After setting forth that negroes, mulattoes, and other slaves, ofttimes absent themselves from their masters, and lurk in obscure places, killing hogs, and committing other injuries to the plantations, it authorizes forces to be raised by the sheriffs, for hunting them, which, if they run away or resist being taken, may kill them with guns, or in " any other way whatsoever." For each slave so destroyed, the owner was entitled to obtain from the public treasury four thousand pounds of tobacco. In 1701, a proclamation was recorded, offering a reward of two thousand pounds of tobacco to any one who should *kill* a certain runaway-slave Billy.

---

[1] In England, Massachusetts, and Connecticut, Slavery ceased by decisions based on the Common Law, not by special legislative acts of abolition.

Planters, by special enactment, were not to be judged guilty of felony if they killed their own slaves.[1]

In 1687, when there was an insurrection of the slaves, the whole number of them in the colony fell little short of one third the whole number of inhabitants.[2] In 1724, the importation of Africans amounted to one thousand annually.[3] At the Revolution, Jefferson estimated the number of slaves in the State to be 270,000; that of whites, of all classes, 296,000. The number of the slaves in the Eastern counties was so great as to occasion continual uneasiness.

No one can fail to notice that, among all three of these varieties of laborers provided to the land-proprietors of Virginia, there could have been but very few accustomed to steady labor, before their arrival there. None of them, while they remained servants, had any direct interest in the result of their labors; there was nothing, in the nature of the relation between them and their masters, to make them interested in their master's wealth or welfare: between the large majority

---

[1] Contemporaneously with these laws, it is not surprising to find that all persons who doubt the authority of the Bible, or who question the dogma of the Trinity, of whatever race or nation, are ineligible to office, and are subject to imprisonment for three years if they express their opinions; that Quakers are denied admission to the country, and, if they persist in coming, are ordered to be treated as felons; that strict measures are taken to prevent "the infection of Puritanism" from reaching the people, and to secure the formal observance of public worship; that fines, of from one to fifty pounds of tobacco, are laid on non-attendance at church on Sunday, Sunday travelling, profane swearing, "profanely getting drunk," etc.   [2] Burke.   [3] Hildreth.

of them and their masters, there must have been the reverse of confidence and gratitude. They were worked, white and black slaves, criminal and bonded servants, all ganged together, under overseers whose own habits of labor had been formed in Virginia: whether they accomplished much or little, whether they labored skilfully or awkwardly, carefully or carelessly, it was all the same, so they but managed to escape chastisement.

The proprietary planters, who always were the commanding body in the province, received their character from certain emigrating offshoots of aristocratic English families. They endeavored to sustain, so far as it was possible in the wilderness, the manners, morals, politics, forms of religion, and other habits and fashions of the gentry and court of Charles the First. On this account, and because of their brave adherence to the king's party against the people's parliament, they are called Cavaliers. They did not leave their English homes from a desire of greater freedom, politically or morally, for they all belonged to the dominant party and the oppressing church. Pure agriculture promised but little profit in the province, and the market was always glutted with its sole exporting staple: trade they held in contempt. Their chief motive in coming to America seems to have been the hope to obtain the position, assume the airs, and enjoy the consequence in the New World which it was impossible for any but born noblemen and great landlords to possess in the old. The anxiety of each to be master of his own people, upon his own estate, over which and over whom he could exercise the authority and support an imitation of the habits of a lord, induced them first to plant themselves at unsafe distances from each other, upon large properties of wild land, of no value except speculatively, and thus frequently to endangèr the destruction of the colony by the Indians, and always to confine its industry to the bare support of its population and the profitless production of one poor herb.

Even before the seizure of the country by the king, and the general granting of patents to individuals, some of these gentlemen, ambitious to be lords of land, had obtained grants by special arrangement with the charter holders. One of these, Captain Newport, who brought with him fifty servants and tenants, over whom he exercised a magistrate's authority, built a fortress for the defence of his settlement, and being a man of bravery, good judgment, and benevolent disposition, was an extremely valuable acquisition to the country. But the others were of different character, and added to the disorder of the Colony. "Among the rest," says Beverly, " one Captain Martin, having made considerable preparations towards a settlement, obtained a suitable grant of land, and was made of the council there. But he, grasping still at more, *hanker'd after dominion*, as well as possession, and caused so many differences, that at last he put all things in distraction," etc.

In a letter of John Rolfe to the king, 1617, he says of the Virginia gentlemen : "All would be Keisars [kings], none inferior to the others."

Beverly again (writing about eighty years after the

country was thrown open to private adventurers, and having still the advantage of personal intercourse with the gentry who were thus attracted to the country, himself a Virginian), speaks thus of the effect of the measure:

"This Liberty of taking up Land, and the ambition every Man had of being Lord of a vast, tho' unimprov'd Territory, . . . has made the country fall into such an unhappy Settlement and Course of Trade, that to this Day, there is not one place of Cohabitation among them, that may reasonably bear the name of a Town."

The light, rich mould, resting on the sandy soils of Eastern Virginia, was exactly suited to the cultivation of tobacco, and no better climate for this plant was to be found on the globe. This had just been sufficiently proved, and a suitable method of culture learned experimentally, when the land was offered to individual proprietors by the king. Very little else was to be obtained from the soil which would be of value to send to Europe, without an application to it of a higher degree of art than the slaves, or stupid, careless servants of the proprietors could readily be forced to use. Although tobacco had then been introduced into England but a few years, an enormous number of persons had initiated themselves in the appreciation of its mysterious value. The king, having taken a violent prejudice against it, though he saw no harm in the distillation of grain, had forbidden that it should be cultivated in England. Virginia, therefore, had every advantage to supply the demand.

Merchants and the supercargoes of ships, arriving with slaves from Africa, or manufactured goods, spirits, or other luxuries from England, very gladly bartered them with the planters for tobacco, but for nothing else. Tobacco, therefore, stood for money, and the passion for raising it, to the exclusion of everything else, became a mania, like the "California fever" of 1849.

The culture being once established, there were many reasons growing out of the social structure of the colony which, for more than a century, kept the industry of the Virginians confined to this one staple. These reasons were chiefly the difficulty of breaking the slaves, or training the bond-servants to new methods of labor, the want of enterprise or ingenuity in the proprietors to contrive other profitable occupations for them, and the difficulty or expense of distributing the guard or oversight, without which it was impossible to get any work done at all, if the laborers were separated, or worked in any other way than side by side, in gangs, as in the tobacco-fields. Owing to these causes, the planters kept on raising tobacco with hardly sufficient intermission to provide themselves with the grossest animal sustenance, though often, by reason of the excessive quantity raised, scarcely anything could be got for it.

Tobacco is not now considered peculiarly and excessively exhaustive: in a judicious rotation, especially as a preparation for wheat, it is an admirable fallow-crop, and, under a scientific system of agriculture, it is grown with no continued detriment to the soil. But in Virginia it was grown without interruption or alternation, and the fields rapidly deteriorated in fertility. As they did so, the crops grew smaller, in proportion to the labor expended upon them. Yet, from the continual importation of laborers, the total crops of the colony increased annually, and the market value fell proportionately to the better supply. With smaller return for labor, and lower prices, the planters soon found themselves becoming bankrupts instead of nabobs.

How could they help themselves? Only by forcing the merchants to pay them higher prices. But how to do that, when every planter had his crop pledged in advance, and was obliged to hurry it off at any price he could get for it, in order to pay for his food, and drink, and clothing, and to keep his head above water, at credit for the following year?[1] The crop supplied more tobacco than was needed, but no one man would cease to plant it, or lessen his crop for the general good. Then, it was agreed, all men must be made to do so, and the colonial legislature was called upon to make them. Acts were accordingly passed, to prevent any planter from cultivating more than a certain number of plants to each hand he employed in labor, and prescribing the number of leaves which might be permitted to ripen upon each plant permitted to be grown. An in-

[1] "The merchants will trust them with tools and necessaries upon the credit of their crop, before it is grown. So they again plant every year a little more than the year before, and so buy everything they want, with the crop that is before them."—MOLL FLANDERS, 1683.

spection of all tobacco, after it had been prepared for market, was decreed, and the inspectors were bound by oath, after having rejected all of inferior quality, to divide the good into two equal parts, and then to *burn and destroy* one of them. Thus, it was expected the quantity of tobacco offered for sale would be so small, that merchants would be glad to pay better prices for it, and the planters would be relieved of their embarrassment.

Simpler methods were sometimes employed, however. It was once ordered, that all creditors should be satisfied to take forty pounds for every hundred due them from the people of the province, at the time of the passage of the act, and that no man should be legally held to perform above one half of any covenants about freighting tobacco, into which he had previously had the good fortune to enter. It is quite probable that, at this time, higher-law opinions began to prevail among the creditors of the Virginia planters.

Attempts, even, were several times made, to stop the culture of tobacco altogether for a year, by legislative acts, with the intention of forcing the merchants to buy what was on hand, at higher prices, and with the hope that the people, if they were forbidden to spend their labor upon it, would direct it to some other industry. These schemes were always given up when it was found that the adjoining colonies were preparing to take advantage of them, by planting more extensively than usual.

Similar schemes have been proposed in good faith,

and deliberately advocated before Southern Conventions, and in Southern newspapers, to remedy a similar evil, with which, in our own day, cotton-planters have afflicted themselves.

If the fathers of Virginia had had the courage and manliness to enact for every person in their land, whose incompetency to exercise his natural rights should not have been specially, individually, and legally ascertained and declared, an equality of position before the law, and in the control of their government; if they had taken care that all children, of ordinary capacity, should be made by education intellectually competent to exercise their natural rights and perform their natural duties to society and to their posterity; if they had placed a reasonable limit upon the area of land which any one individual might control, to the exclusion of others from cultivating it; and if they had established that neither tobacco nor any other crop might be twice drawn in successive years, from the same soil, it may be thought that they would still have been exceeding the proper limits of governmental action —a point upon which it is natural their descendants should be nervously apprehensive; but, had they done so, there can be no doubt, I think, that the people, who would have occupied the territory of Virginia at this day, would have been in a far happier condition than those who now remain upon it; and I, myself, verily believe that Virginia would now have been even the richest, the best populated, and the happiest commonwealth in America.

But, for our benefit, they made an experiment of another sort of legislation, and, inconsistent as are the laws I have mentioned with our modern "democratic" notions, in one respect, the *laissez faire* principle reigned in their politics, as completely as it has since ever done in Virginia. No governmental interference was ever allowed to prevent the planters from defrauding their posterity of the natural wealth of the land. They were, therefore, able to live sumptuously, but ever discontentedly, as spendthrifts do, and always staggering with debt, though spending, with all their might, their capital stock, their land's fertility.

As their exhausted fields failed to meet the prodigal drafts of their luxury, they only made further clearings in the forest, and "threw out," to use their own phrase, so much of the land as they had ruined. Year after year the process continued; the richer districts were all, at length, gone over; the poorer soils of the slopes began to be attacked; the old-fields, recuperating in the prudent economy of nature, after many years, were again cleared, and, now with some aid of manure, again, for a short time, found capable of producing tobacco.

What this enormous, constant, and ruinous production of tobacco was needed to pay for, we are thus informed.

"The families being altogether in country-seats, they have their graziers, seedsmen, gardiners, brewers, bakers, butchers, and cooks, within themselves. They have plenty and variety of provision for their table; and, as for spicery, and other things that the country don't produce, they have constant supplies of them from *England*. The gentry pretend to have their victuals drest, and served up, as nicely as if they were in *London*. Their small drink is either wine and water, beer, milk and water, or water alone. Their richer sort generally brew their small beer with malt which they have from *England*, though barley grows there very well. Their strong drink is *Madeira* wine, cider, mobby punch, made either of rum from the *Caribbee* islands, or brandy distilled from their apples and peaches, besides *brandy*, wine, and strong beer, which they have constantly from *England*. They have their clothing of all sorts from *England*. The very furs that their hats are made of, perhaps, go first from thence; and most of their hides lie and rot, or are made use of only for covering dry goods in a leaky house. Indeed, some few hides, with much ado, are tanned and made into servants' shoes; but at so careless a rate, that the planters don't care to buy them if they can get others; and sometimes, perhaps, a better manager than ordinary will vouchsafe to make a pair of breeches of a deer-skin. Nay, they are such abominable ill-husbands, that though their country be over-run with wood, yet they have all their wooden ware from *England;* their cabinets, chairs, tables, stools, chests, boxes, cart-wheels, and all other things, even so much as their bowls and birchen brooms, to the eternal reproach of their laziness."—*Beverly*, 1620.

And "Moll Flanders" says, with a detail characteristic of the author of Robinson Crusoe:

"Here we had (by an arrival from England) a supply of all sorts of clothes, as well for my husband as myself; and I took especial care to buy for him all those things that I knew he delighted to have; as two good long wigs, two silver-hilted swords, three or four fine fowling-pieces, a fine saddle, with holsters and pistols, very handsome, with a scarlet cloak. . . . And all this cargo arrived safe, and in good condition, with three women-servants, lusty wenches, suitable enough for the place and to the work we had for them to do, one of which happened to come double, having been got with child by one of the seamen."

They had also to support the little dignity of their little Court with perhaps—by favor of the King—as much rank as that of a real Knight, from England, at its head; and their little church, with its thorough-bred imported clergy, and its little imitation of the great Church of England's persecution of sectaries. A bishop could not be afforded them, and if a young Virginian wished to preach the Gospel of the Carpenter's Son, he crossed the ocean for a qualifying ceremony.[1]

The masses of the people continued to gain in nothing but that animal manliness and hatred of restraint which a life in a wild or thinly-inhabited country always has a strong tendency to encourage. But the

[1] The province was divided into parishes, each of which was required to support a minister, at a salary of 16,000 pounds of tobacco, and handsome perquisites, such as two hundred pounds of tobacco for a marriage, and four hundred pounds for a funeral sermon. The church-wardens were required to collect the minister's tobacco, and bring it to him in hogsheads, convenient for shipping, "that they might have more time for the Exercises of their Holy Office, and live in Decency becoming their Order." Beverly observes that "the labor of a dozen negroes does but answer this salary, and seldom yields a greater crop of sweet-scented tobacco than is allowed to each of the ministers." Besides their salary, a house and glebe was required to be provided the ministers; and it is mentioned that, sometimes, "stocks of cattle and negroes" were added by donation, for which they were only required to surrender an equal value on leaving the parish. All ministers were required to be ordained in England, and to be endorsed by the Governor, and there were laws to prevent dissenting preachers from entering the province. In 1720, a meeting of the Friends, in Nasemond County, was the only congregation of Dissenters; others had existed, Beverly mentions, but were now extinct; and, "it was observed, *by letting them alone, they decreased daily*."

planters, paying but a trifle for their labor and monopolizing its profits, and enjoying the advantage of any rise in the value of the land which might result from the constant immigration the country had to sustain, notwithstanding they were always embarrassed with debt, and always complaining of the low prices at which their creditors would have their tobacco, really grew richer and more lordly; and, had there not been so many, all jealous of each other's preferment, they probably would have become nobles indeed. They were, as a body, the nearest approach to the English aristocracy which America has ever possessed, not only in their follies and vices, but in their virtues and excellences. Of their habits, and the way these always continued, even until after the Revolution, to eat away the natural agricultural capital of the country, the following is given, by one of their descendants, in the pages of the *Southern Planter:*

"The more wealthy proprietors, having no occupation of industry, spent their time mostly in seeking pleasure. Visits to each other were frequent and protracted. It was rare that any one of this class was without some company, either at home or abroad. Besides such exercise of reciprocal hospitality, every idle or homeless 'gentleman' of the whole country found in every mansion a comfortable sojourning-place, and, at least, the outward show, if not the reality of welcome, so long as he might choose to stay. Of course, visits from such persons were ordinary occurrences—and were sometimes protracted for weeks or months. That this particular neighborhood was not 'eaten out' by this class of genteel and honorable vagrants and spongers, was not because of their deficiency of numbers, or of active use of their facilities, but because they had like privileges in every part of the country. This race, fortunately, is now extinct; but many such individuals are still remembered, who, for many years of their adult life, and some for their whole life, pursued no other business, and had no other means of support, except visiting their friends; of course they counted their friends by hundreds.

"The wealthier proprietors were not only hospitable and kind hosts, but also refined and pleasing companions. Their fathers' wealth had served to give to them the education and manners of good society. With many excellent social and moral qualities, their habits of idleness and pleasure-seeking naturally led to the attendant and consequent vices. Social drinking was often carried to excess; and card-playing was sure to be introduced whenever as many neighbors dined together as served to make up a game of loo. Horse-racing was a favorite amusement of all classes; some of the farmers owned and ran race-horses, and nearly all reared horses of the high blood, and at the high cost required for the turf."

How like this is to the "true Irish gentleman," of ten or twenty years ago. But let it not be forgotten that, when the time of retribution came, the slaves suffered no physical want—the peasant starved.

No man of wealth, or with a moderate estate, thought of attending personally to his farming. Every detail of management was intrusted to the overseers, who were rarely stimulated by even the general superintendence and control of their employers. Overseers' wages were generally paid in a certain share or proportion of the crops they made. Thus, they had a direct interest in drawing from the land and labor as much as possible, during the current year of their engagement; and none whatever in preserving or increasing the productive power of the land for later times. It came to be recognized, as a maxim of agricultural morals, that "it was not *just* for a proprietor to interfere with, and change, his overseer's designed direction of the labors of the farm, inasmuch as any abstraction from immediate product, for the sake of future improvement, operated to lessen the overseer's profits for the present year." This doctrine accorded so well with the disposition of every indolent, careless, and wasteful proprietor, that it is no wonder that it came to be generally received, and conformed to in practice.

A carefully-drawn picture of the social condition and habits of the people of Virginia, at a period not long before the Revolution, is given by a writer for *Putnam's Monthly*, who, from the close topographical knowledge, of some parts of the State, he displays, and other internal evidence, is evidently also a Virginian. I quote what is most pertinent.

—"Newspapers, and literature at large, were a proscribed commodity, thanks to Sir William Berkeley and his successors.[1]

---

[1] Sir William Berkeley had said, being then Governor of Virginia: "I thank God there are no free schools nor printing, and I hope we shall not have them these hundred years." At this time, when Boston contained five printing offices, and as many booksellers' shops, there was not one of either in all the rich and populous Southern colonies of Virginia, Maryland, and Carolina. Progress, since, in this particular, has closely corresponded with that of all other industrial progress in the slave countries. The publication of a book, at Richmond — an event occurring not oftener, on an average, than once a year — is as much a subject of universal congratulation, by all the public press of the South, as the birth of a royal heir is in England. No book, I presume, ever paid for the cost of its publication, by its Southern circulation alone, unless it was a strongly sectional, or a religious book. There is a constant complaint that the circulation of Northern magazines

He [the Virginia gentleman] knew not what was going on in the next county, and the man who had made a journey to the little metropolis of Middle Plantation, or Williamsburg, was listened to, by his neighbors, as a miniature Herodotus. At intervals a vessel arrived from London or the West Indies, which brought, with a new Order in Council, or a fresh instalment of negroes, some confused items of foreign news; or, perhaps, some young Virginian, fresh from Oxford or Cambridge, astonished the country gentlemen of his native county, with the last intelligence from the mother-country — the newest Parisian *mode* — or, better still, brought, in his travelling-trunk, the best productions of English or European writers, or the earlier numbers of the *Gentleman's Magazine*, or a file of London papers, which would afford pleasant reading, for the next month, to the neighbors for miles around."

"There were no cities in Virginia, even no towns, at the time of which we speak. The country gentleman had a peculiar and most genuine dislike to centralization in every form. He had an aversion, too, to much government, and gladly encountered the alternative of too little, if he was but left to lord it in peace and quiet over his 'large and well-conditioned household,' [a household, be it remembered, which might be numbered by hundreds]. Here he was supreme lord — a species of feudal baron, living in a sort of noble

---

at the South prevents Southern magazines from being supported; and frequent efforts are made to hinder people from taking them, by accusations of their hostility to Southern interests, or their indifference to Southern prejudices. It is a ridiculous mistake. The old *Southern Literary Messenger* probably sold more at the North, in proportion to its whole circulation, although it never flunkied to the North at all, than any Northern periodical sells at the South, in proportion to its Northern circulation. No Northern magazine would live a month, at least in its present excellence, on its Southern circulation alone; and none, I believe, not prepared expressly for the Southern market, has a tithe of its whole circulation in the Slave States. No Northern editor fears especially to offend the South, as is generally supposed; but many fear that, if they do offend the South, they will be calumniated and injured at the North.

profusion and ease, which gave room for all his peculiarities and idiosyncrasies to spread themselves at will, and gratified at once his hobby of paramount rule, and his virtue of liberal and indiscriminate hospitality. In vain did Government, whether in London or Williamsburg, fulminate act after act at this instinct; decreeing, even, that tobacco, the staple of Virginia, should not be shipped, except at certain spots upon the rivers; in vain were towns laid and incorporated. The cities did not appear, the towns were not built up; and these localities remain to this day, with their dilapidated wharves, and old crumbled warehouses — an eloquent memento of the vain attempt to force this stubborn race from what they clung to with the pertinacity of martyrs — their isolated country life.

"But this life was not in another sense isolated. At every court-day, the country was brought together; visits were courteously exchanged between neighbors; and the owner was proud of his fine-blooded horse, his trotting-mares, or his *six well-conditioned grays*, which thunder along with the old family chariot. This vehicle, which has come all the way from London, was, on all occasions of ceremony, of indispensable importance, and, in journeys of any length, it ever came prominently into play: that was no trifle to travel, in state, the twenty or thirty miles a day which it accomplished. The coachman must time his posts by the road-side taverns, or private residences competent to recruit the energies of himself, his animals, and the half-dozen persons, who temporarily existed in this moving mansion. The appearance of the coach was ever greeted, by the artisan or humble farmer, with great respect, but ill-concealed distaste. The pedestrian was covered with a cloud of dust, as it rolled grandly onward; and the humble carter must carefully keep from the middle of the road, otherwise a splintered wheel and a roll in the dirt would warn him to make way the next time for the 'gentry.' Honorable, hospitable, and, at the bottom of their hearts, kind and charitable, they yet nursed a high and overweening sense of their own importance and dignity. Long supremacy among their negroes and indented servants had taught them to expect implicit obedience from all inferiors; and, if any one, so unfortunate as to belong to the commons, and thus to be inferior to them in blood, refinement, or possessions, did not yield to their arrogance, every means was put in requisition to reduce him to his proper level. Such a man was always welcome to the best the 'gentleman Proprietor's' table afforded; he was treated kindly, assisted, if need be; but, with the profuse hospitality lavished on him, all connection between them ended. To do more would be to forget what, in the nature of things, he could never lose sight of — the fact that he was one of the gentry — his guest, a commoner."

That hospitality was ever so general a virtue among the *common people* in Old Virginia, as to entitle them to the reputation they have acquired for it, there is some reason to doubt. "There being no inns in the country, strangers were entertained at the houses of the inhabitants, and were *frequently involved in law-suits by the exorbitant claims of their hosts for indemnification of the expenses of their entertainment.*"[1] This refers to the latter days of the colony more especially.

Beverly gives a detailed account of the industrial condition of the Province early in the eighteenth century.

"In extreme fruitfulnefs," he says, "it is exceeded by no Other." "No Seed is fown there but it thrives, and moft of the Northern Plants are improved by being tranfplanted thither." "And yet there's very little Improvement made among them, feldom Anything us'd in Traffick but Tobacco." "Fruit trees are wonderfully quick of Growth. Yet they are very few that take any Care at all for an Orchard; nay, many that have good Orchards are fo negligent of them, as to let them go to Ruin, and expofe the Trees to be torn and bark'd by Cattle." "A Garden is nowhere fooner form'd than here, and yet they ha'nt many Gardens in the Country fit to bear the Name of Gardens." "All Sorts of Englifh Grain thrive, yet they don't make a Trade of any of them." "The Sheep

---

[1] Grahame's Hist. of N. A.

increafe well, and bear good Fleeces; but they are generally fuffered to be torn off their Backs by Briars and Bufhes, or elfe are left rotting on the Dunghill with their Skins." "The Woods produce great variety of Incense and fweet Gums, Honey and Sugar. Yet there's no ufe made of any of them, either for Profit or Refrefhment." " All Sorts of Naval Stores may be produced there, as Pitch, Tar, Turpentine, Plank, Timber, and all Sorts of Mafts and Yards, befides Sails, Cordage and Iron; and all thefe may be tranfported by an easy Water-carriage."

"Thefe and a thoufand other Advantages that Country produces, which its Inhabitants make no manner of ufe of. They can fee their Naval Stores daily Benefit other People, who fend thither to build Ships. They receive no Benefit nor Refrefhment from the sweet and precious Things they have growing amongft them; but make ufe of the Induftry of England for all fuch Things.

"What Advantage do they fee the neighboring Plantations make of their Grain and Provifions, while they, who can produce them infinitely better, not only neglect the making a Trade thereof, but even a necefsary Provifion againft an accidental Scarcity, contenting themfelves with a Supply of Food from Hand to Mouth; fo, that if it fhould pleafe God to send them an unfeafonable Year, there would not be found in the Country Provifions fufficient to fupport the People for three Months extraordinary !

"They depend upon the Liberality of Nature, without endeavoring to improve its Gifts by Art or Induftry. They fponge upon the Bleffings of a warm Sun and a fruitful Soil, and almoft grutch the Pains of gathering in the Bounties of the Earth. I fhould be afhamed to publifh this flothful Indolence of my Countrymen, but, that I hope it will fome time or other roufe them out of their Lethargy, and excite them to make the moft of all thefe happy Advantages which Nature has given them; and if it does this, I am fure they will have the Goodnefs to forgive me."—Beverly, p. 284.

We Americans have now a habit of congratulating each other on the material prosperity and independence of our country, and of glorifying our wise government and our "free institutions," as the cause of it. But we should not forget that we have lately, by the dignified and deliberate act of the Republic's servants, given free range, over millions of fertile acres, to essentially the same institutions of society which produced, and which, spite of every advantageous surrounding, are still maintaining, in Virginia, that paralysis of enterprise and imbecility of industry, thus pathetically deplored a hundred and fifty years ago.

When Beverly speaks of the adjoining colonies, as taking the trade of Virginia, he can refer only to the more democratic and free-laboring Northern colonies. In the Carolinas, an exactly similar state of things existed to that in Virginia.

So early as 1676, it is recorded that "New England traders, penetrating into the interior of the province of Albemarle, and bringing their goods to every man's door, had obtained a monopoly of the produce of the province. The proprietors in England endeavored, in vain, to substitute a direct intercourse with Britain, for this disadvantageous commerce."[1]

In 1677, the chief magistrate of this province was deposed and imprisoned by an insurrection of the people, consequent upon an attempt to interrupt the New England trade. The Assembly having once complained that the English proprietors did not give sufficient encouragement to immigration, and that the country consequently suffered from a deficiency of tradesmen and mechanics, they (the English pro-

[1] Grahame's Hist. of North America, p. 120.

prietors) made answer that the inconvenience complained of was promoted by the complainants—

"By the lazy rapacity with which each desired to surround himself with a large expanse of property, over which he could exercise no other act of ownership than that of excluding the occupants by whom it might be most advantageously cultivated."

The Assembly, however, followed its own counsel, and decreed that none should be sued for debt, within the limits of its jurisdiction, for five years after his arrival; that no inhabitant should accept a power of attorney to collect debts contracted abroad, etc. This had the desired effect of attracting immigration; but not of a very respectable or valuable character. Virginia and Maryland both had laws of similar import.

That Beverly did not exaggerate the danger of famine, at a time when the annual export of tobacco, to pay for clothing, slaves, and other imported necessities and luxuries, was between thirty and forty millions of pounds annually,[1] is evident from the legislative precautions taken to prevent it. The prices of every other product except corn were, at one time, fixed by law, with the avowed purpose of inducing farmers to plant it; three officers were appointed in every county, for the express purpose of obliging every settler to plant and tend sufficient corn-ground to insure an adequate supply to maintain his own family! Public granaries were established, to which every planter was ordered

[1] De Bow's Resources, iii., p. 347.

to contribute one bushel of corn, annually, to be disposed of as the Commonwealth should require. I am told, and the Southern agricultural journals confirm it, that such laws are needed now, in some parts of the cotton States, and would be advocated, but for the shame of publishing to the North the irreformable improvidence of the people.

Some of my readers may require yet to have it explained how it was that land monopoly, slavery, and servile or degraded and ignorant labor led to that state of things which Beverly bewailed, and which, indeed, to this day constitutes, strangely enough, both the glory and the shame, which is the basis alike of the weak vanity and the impotent anger of the sons of the Virginia cavaliers.

Manufactories and mechanic arts of all sorts thrive best in towns or dense communities, because different branches assist each other, not only morally, by stimulating mental activity, but materially. The carriage-maker calls upon the blacksmith, the currier, and the worker in leather; the blacksmith may, at any time, be glad of the services of the currier, the cobbler, or the wheel-wright, to mend his bellows. The spinners and weavers need to have near them, masons, machinists, and mill-wrights. All need farmers (not planters) to supply their daily needs. In a country, therefore, where all men "mind nothing but to be masters of a great estate, and to plant themselves separately on their several plantations," trades and manufactures are not likely to thrive. But, suppose one of these plantation lords to own a large number of boys whose labor he desires to appropriate most advantageously to himself. The employment to which they must be trained cannot be of such a character as to require the use of much discretion; because there can be no sufficient motive to induce them to exercise it, which does not involve personal interest in the object of that employment, and therefore, a partnership in its possession, or a receipt of wages in some proportion to skill. In proportion, also, to the amount of discretion required of a slave, the reins of authority must be slackened. If he uses his own skill, he must go his own way. If he goes his own way, he will go negligently and with all possible indolence, unless he has some advantage for himself to gain, by care and dispatch. This he hardly can have, if the result of his labor is to inure wholly to the advantage of another. The selfishness, therefore, of the owner of a slave-boy, will lead him to undertake to make the boy labor at such simple work and under such circumstances as will keep him most easily and certainly under his control.

It is a fact that slave-mechanics, manufacturers' hands, stevedores, servants, and those engaged in almost all employments superior to that of field-hands, in the Southern States, are, nearly always, "gratified" with some sort of wages, or perquisites, or stimulants, to skill and industry, in some form; and are more intelligent, more privileged, and more insubordinate than the general mass. This will be sufficiently apparent from observations I shall hereafter record.

"The struggle for equality in all the relations of life, for the liberty of man against the dominion of man, is necessarily founded on the consciousness of the importance of the individual.

"Their motto is, All by the People: their practice, Nothing for the People."—*Introduction to a History of the Nineteenth Century.*

GERVINUS.

Ignorance is weakness; and the ignorant man instinctively merges his ambition and his claims of justice with those of an aggregate—makes that aggregate an object of partiality and bigotry, and finds satisfaction for his enthusiasm in the success of those who guide and represent it, though that success in no wise affect his own interest.

The peculiar political aspiration of the people of Virginia, as a whole, was, on this account, less to maintain due consideration for individual rights, than to obtain and preserve communal independence and notoriety.

The wealthy and educated class, however, while they were entirely *en rapport* with the general communal spirit, were also remarkably characterized by personal assumption and dignity. And this, because the smallness of their number, proportionately to the whole people, and their widely separated residences, gave to each a high local consideration and power, and led to inordinate self-respect.

The unusual and unexpected exactions of the exterior, royal government aroused, therefore, among the influential class of Virginians, a more passionate discontent than elsewhere; while the poor people were more ready, than those of other colonies, perhaps, to encourage a disposition in their leaders to communal independence.

Virginia, therefore, was early and determined, in the expression of her dissatisfaction with the royal impositions which led to the Revolution.

Yet great agitation, much, and rapid, and excited progress of thought, was necessary, before the aristocratic or the yeoman class could come to the point of actual treason, or bring to it the poor, and ignorant, and the superstitiously loyal.

If it was right for them to resist these demands of their king, the conscientious would ask, how should they define what demands it was not right to resist? If their royal master's authority was exercised by right divine, it was wrong for them to resist it at all—nay, even to feel discontent. If it was not by right divine, then by what right? On what right rests any governmental authority? Is there no alternative between despotism and anarchy? What is the basis of civil government?

There could be no hearty, united, and determined resistance, while these questions were left without some logically satisfactory answer. The people at large could not be called upon, and stirred up to a spirited defence, without knowing, more clearly, what it was that was to be defended—what they were to gain. Stamp-acts and tea-taxes did not really trouble the great majority of Virginians, in the slightest degree, personally, only the people of some property—for the mass were still illiterate vagabonds; but, even among the better sort, no man could trust another, till each knew what all wanted, and to what limit all were prepared to stand out.

The best men in the Province—those in whose goodness, wisdom, and bravery, their neighbors had most confidence—were, therefore, appointed to make a declaration of the principles and purposes by and for which the government of Virginia should thereafter be guided, and which should constitute a platform broad enough for all to stand upon, without jealousies and distrusts, and so just and reasonable as to command the respect and fealty of every individual, and of all classes.

The instrument of this declaration is still preserved, as a curious historical relic, in Virginia, and is interesting, if, for nothing else, as an evidence to what lengths men will go, when they have set their hearts upon an object and find it desperate business to accomplish it. For it announces principles which the intelligent classes in Virginia, always before and generally since, have held to be absurd, preposterous, and dangerous.

For instance, it asserts the equality of men, in freedom and independence—a " self-evident absurdity," as they now say; for a strong and wise man can, at any time, prevent or destroy the freedom and independence of a weak man, of which, proof is not wanting. That every man has certain " inherent rights "— one of which is named liberty; another absurdity, for the same reason. Another, the right of labor (" *of obtaining property* ")—not only absurd, but very horrible: another, the right of enjoying the fruits of his labor, to the fullest degree compatible with security to all other men to equally enjoy the results of their labor—a dangerous and impracticable doctrine: another, the right of private judgment, in matters of religion and morality, so far as it can be exercised compatibly with the preservation to all of this and all other rights; of which, very little is now said.

On this original platform, reasonable or not reasonable—and I do not want any one to doubt a moment that I consider it reasonable, and suppose that I see a meaning quite reconcilable with the facts considered to render it absurd, only I wish to be respectful to those who cannot—on this platform, they impliedly promised, if they should succeed in maintaining their independence of the power then deemed wickedly oppressive, to reorganize society; and they called upon all the people of Virginia, of all classes, of all degrees of muscular strength and intellectual capacity and acquirements, poor and rich, cavalier and base-blooded, to fraternize, and rise, and fight.

And they did it, fraternizing at the same time with others making similar professions, and having similar purposes; and they all fought together, and succeeded, all equally, in obtaining—not the security of these so-called natural rights, but—communal independence of their old king.

By the time they came to the work of forming the instruments of order for their to-be-reorganized society, there had evidently occurred a violent reaction from the fervency and highly stimulated judgment under which the Bill of Rights had been drawn up, among the influential people of Virginia—for the constitution of the new State was widely inconsistent with the principles of liberty, equality, and fraternity, previous distinctly proclaimed, and promised to be used as its supports and barriers.

The people, imposed upon and deprived of their acknowledged rights, be it observed, were, by chance, the weakest, most ignorant, and poorest—consequently, the least likely to regard the imposition, and the least able to resist it.

There were a few men, among those whose natural rights were respected, who did not like this, and who strongly protested against it. Among them, Thomas Jefferson was foremost.

To the new Constitution of Virginia he strongly objected, in several particulars, not only on the score of consistency, but of justice and good judgment. For instance, that the majority of the tax-paying and fighting men of the State were unrepresented in its government; and, again, that things had been so managed that, even among those who were permitted to vote, there were nineteen thousand in the rich plantation-counties of the east, who could elect more members of the legislature than thirty thousand in the more free counties of the west; accordingly, the State would be virtually ruled, not by the people through their elected representatives, but by an oligarchy of slave-holders.[1]

A large majority of the people of the country were

[1] See Jefferson's Notes on Virginia, pages 172, 173.

Dissenters from the Established Church of the English Colony; yet, a proposal to realize the declared right of entire religious freedom was met by an opposition which occasioned, as Jefferson afterwards declared, the most severe political struggle in which he was ever engaged. The most that could be obtained at that time, after all, was an abrogation of the laws which denounced punishment for maintaining unorthodox opinions, and for not attending the Episcopal Church; and acts exempting Dissenters from contributing to the support of the Episcopal clergy, and permitting them to build houses of worship of their own. It was not till several years later that any one else than the Episcopal clergymen were permitted to solemnize or legalize marriages, except by the purchase of a special license. The Episcopal Church still continued to be the "Established Church," and other religious societies were merely "tolerated." [1]

Next to religious freedom, the most important change demanded by the avowed principles of the Revolution, was an alteration of the laws with regard to the descent of property. The laws of primogeniture and descent in tail, were felt to be unnatural, discouraging to industry, and, by their effect in aggravating the evils to society of the excessive possession and control of land, opposed to the declared right of all to the "means of obtaining wealth."

Mr. Howison thus clearly and truly describes these laws and their influence:

[1] Howison, ii., 192.

"Nothing can convey a more vivid idea of the strong aristocratic feeling pervading Virginia, than her course as to this scheme. In England, the courts had set their faces against entails, and permitted them to be *docked* by a fine and recovery; but the law-makers of the Old Dominion held all such innovations in high contempt, and, by a statute enacted in 1705, forbade their use. To complete their work in 1727, they enacted that slaves might be attached to lands, and might be entailed with them, subject to all the incidents proper to the system. Over the whole Eastern region, fine lands were held by families, who guarded their privileges with more than English jealousy.

"An aristocracy neither of talent, nor of learning, nor of moral worth, but of landed and slave interest, was [thus] fostered. The members of the Council of State were always chosen from this class; and in many respects they were regarded as the peerage of the land.

"Where lands could neither be sold nor mortgaged, debts must often have been contracted which were never paid; yet, the tenants in tail, lived in luxurious ease, to which others were strangers. The rich people of Virginia were then richer than at present, and the poor were poorer. There was no prospect for that equal distribution of property which is the legitimate reward of industry. Coaches, drawn by four horses, rolled from the doors of the aristocracy; and plate of gold and silver, in the utmost profusion, glittered on their boards, while the poor artisan and laborer worked for the necessaries of life, without any hope of ever gaining any portion of the property guarded by entail."

A bill, proposed by Jefferson, providing that thereafter all estates in tail should be converted into fee simple, so that the owner might sell, devise, mortgage, or otherwise dispose of them as he thought proper, was at length carried, after another very warm and protracted struggle.

Next, the law of primogeniture was attacked; a strong defence was made for it by the aristocratic party; and when they found it must be repealed, they urged, "in the spirit of compromise," that the Jewish rule of inheritance should be substituted: this gives the eldest son a double portion. Mr. Jefferson answered the proposal, with the remark, that unless the eldest son required a double portion of food, or would do double the work of any other, there was no justice in giving him double the property.

The law was repealed. Mr. Featherstonhaugh, an English Tory who visited the United States in 1836, dates from this repeal all the adversity under which Virginia has since suffered. The seeds of much of the adversity which he witnessed were produced by the law: cutting it away did not destroy at once their vitality; but it removed a pernicious shade from labor, and, but for this timely relief, industry would not, I am convinced, be now known to have ever existed at all in Eastern Virginia, except by the evidence of the desert it had been forced to create.

The argument against all these changes was, not that they were not demanded by justice and sound principles of government, but, that it was not safe to move so rapidly. They were old institutions under which Virginia had existed for a century or more. They were unjust, it might, in some sense, be admitted, and their effects, it could not be denied, were sometimes rather unhappy; but destroy them, replace them with laws more abstractly just, and—who knew that there would not follow worse consequences? It was fanatical to push forward the experiment so rapidly. Besides, people had been born into the world under these laws, and had taken duties and responsibilities upon themselves, in the expectation that they would be sustained. They had a right to demand, it was urged, therefore, that they should be sustained: but now, when the right principles of law have been enunciated, leave it for posterity to enact them. It will then be every man's own fault, if he is not prepared for them.

Jefferson well understood the danger of this course. He urged that justice should be done, and right should be maintained then and there, and at all hazards. And with the prophetic mind of true statesmanship, such as we have had no approach to since, he uttered in 1787 this remarkable warning and prediction: men who pretend to be his disciples, should not pass it lightly—

"The spirit of the times may alter—will alter. Our rulers will become corrupt, our people careless. It can never be too often repeated, that the time for fixing every essential right on a legal basis is while our rulers are honest, and ourselves united. From the conclusion of this war, we shall be going down hill. It will not then be necessary to resort every moment to the people for support. They will be forgotten, therefore, and their rights disregarded. *They will forget themselves, but in the sole faculty of making money,* and will never think of omitting to effect a due respect for their rights. The shackles, therefore, which shall not be knocked off at the conclusion of this war, will remain on us long — *will be made heavier and heavier, till our rights shall revive,* or expire in a convulsion." [1]

Impelled by these convictions, while the country was yet excited with all the turmoil and terror of invasion and war, while a price was yet set upon his head, as there was last year on the heads of men who were laboring to have his principles of government carried

[1] Jefferson's Notes on Virginia, 239.

out in our young states, Mr. Jefferson, besides the radical improvements already noted, earnestly and confidently desired to have permanent enactments introduced into the laws for *the emancipation of the slaves.*[1]

The scheme of emancipation which Jefferson advocated would have provided that all negroes born after it had passed should be entitled to freedom; that they should remain with their parents until of a certain age, " then be brought up, at the public expense, to tillage, arts, or sciences, according to their geniuses, till the females should be eighteen, the males twenty-one years of age, when they should be colonized to such place as the circumstances of the time should render most proper, sending them out with implements of household and the handicraft arts, etc., etc.; that they should then be declared to be a free and independent people; that protection and assistance should be afforded them until they had acquired strength; and that, at the same time, an equal number of white people, *from other parts of the world, should be sent for, and induced, by proper encouragements, to migrate into Virginia.*"[2] He apologizes at length for proposing to expatriate the negroes, on the ground of the impracticability of their amalgamation or comfortable association with the whites.

To the great grief of its author, this project was not carried: he never afterwards ceased to bewail the neglect, or to deplore the consequences. But it is the grand characteristic of Jefferson, that he is not merely a philanthropist, a philosopher, and a patriot; he is

[1] Jefferson's Notes on Virginia, 203.   [2] Ib., 204.

also a strong practical statesman: he knows when to strike and when to hold. With the boldness, generosity, and clear moral vision, reached by the planters in the first struggle for their own liberty, the day for justice and liberality to those beneath them was past. Virginia, during his life-time, was in no condition to be asked to make sacrifices of property; and, after the seven years' exhausting war, to secure temporary peace and harmony, much was properly postponed; but he never ceased to hope that the spirit of the age, "the advancement of the human mind," as the country grew stronger and richer, would yet be able to grapple with the difficulty, and to solve it in accordance with republican principles. Alas! the human mind advances slowly when it has to drag slavery.

The following extracts are taken from the correspondence of Jefferson, published by Congress, 1854:

"TO M. WARVILLE.

"PARIS, February 12, 1788.

"SIR :—I am very sensible of the honor you propose to me of becoming a member of the society for the abolition of the Slave Trade. You know that nobody wishes more ardently to see an abolition, not only of the trade, but of the *condition* of Slavery."

"TO BENJAMIN BANNEKER.

"PHILADELPHIA, August 30, 1791.

"SIR :—I thank you sincerely for your letter of the 19th instant, and for the Almanac it contained. Nobody wishes more than I do to see such proofs as you exhibit, that nature has given to our black brethren talents equal to those of the other colors of men, and that appearance of a want of them is owing mainly to the degraded condition of their existence, both in Africa and America. I can add, with truth, that nobody wishes more ardently to see a good system commenced for raising the condition both of their body and mind to what it ought to be, as fast as the imbecility of their present existence and other circumstances, which cannot be neglected, will permit."

"TO ST. GEORGE TUCKER.

"MONTICELLO, August 28, 1797.

* * * "As to the mode of Emancipation, I am satisfied that must be a matter of compromise between the *passions and prejudices* and the *real* difficulties, which will each have their weight in that operation. But if something is not done, and soon done, we shall be the murderers of our own children. The sooner we put *some* plan under way, the greater hope there is that it *may* be permitted to proceed peaceably to its ultimate effect."

"TO MR. BARROW.

"MONTICELLO, May 1, 1815.

* * * "Some progress is sensibly made in it, yet not so much as I hoped and expected. But it will yield in time to temperate and steady pursuit, to the enlargement of the human mind, and its advancement in science. We are not in a world ungoverned by the laws and the power of a superior agent. Our efforts are in His hand, and directed by Him, and He will give them their effect in His own time. Where the disease is most deeply seated, there it will be slowest in eradication. In the Northern States, it was merely superficial and easily corrected; in the Southern, it is incorporated with the whole system, and requires time, patience, and perseverance in the curative process. That it may finally be effected and its progress hastened, will be the last and fondest prayer of

"THOMAS JEFFERSON."

I extract the following passages from a letter to Edward Coles, first published in the *National Intelligencer*, dated

"MONTICELLO, August 25, 1814.

"DEAR SIR:—Your favor of July 31 was duly received, and was read with peculiar pleasure. The sentiments, breathed through the whole, do honor to both the head and heart of the writer. Mine on the subject of the Slavery of negroes have long since been in the possession of the public, and time has only served to give them stronger root.

"The love of justice and the love of country plead equally the cause of these people, and it is a mortal reproach to us that they should have pleaded it so long in vain, and should have produced not a single effort—nay, I fear, not much serious willingness—to relieve them and ourselves from our present condition of moral and political reprobation. From those of the former generation who were in the fullness of age when I came into public life—which was while our controversy with England was on paper only—I soon saw that nothing was to be hoped. Nursed and educated in the daily habit of seeing the degraded condition, both bodily and mental, of those unfortunate beings, not reflecting that that degradation was very much the work of themselves and their fathers, few minds had yet doubted but that they were as legitimate subjects of property as their horses or cattle. The quiet and monotonous course of colonial life had been disturbed by no alarm and little reflection on the value of liberty; and when alarm was taken at an enterprise of their own, it was not easy to carry them the whole length of the principles which they invoked for themselves. In the first or second session of the Legislature after I became a member, I drew to this subject the attention of Col. Bland, one of the oldest, ablest, and most respected members, and he undertook to move for certain moderate extensions of the protection of the laws to these people. I seconded his motion, and, as a younger member, was more spared in the debate; but he was denounced as an enemy to his country, and was treated with the greatest indecorum.

"From an early stage of our Revolution, other and more distant duties were assigned me, so that from that time till my return from Europe in 1789, and, I may say, till I returned to reside at home in 1809, I had little opportunity of knowing the progress of public sentiment here on this subject. I had always hoped that the younger generation, receiving their early impressions after the flame of liberty had been kindled in every breast, and had become, as it were, the vital spirit of every American, that the generous temperament of youth, analogous to the motion of their blood, and above the suggestions of avarice, would have sympathized with oppression wherever found, and proved their love of liberty beyond their own share of it. But my intercourse with them since my return has not been sufficient to ascertain that they had made toward this point the progress I had hoped. Your solitary but welcome voice is the first which has brought this sound to my ear, and I have considered the general silence which prevails on this subject as indicating an apathy unfavorable to our hopes. Yet the hour of emancipation is advancing in the march of time. It will come; and, whether brought on by the generous energy of our own minds, or by the bloody process of St. Domingo, excited and conducted by the power of our present enemy, if once stationed permanently within our country, offering asylum and arms to the oppressed, is a leaf of our own history, and not yet turned over."

Although the planters were not then willing to surrender the property they had in slaves, and desired to postpone emancipation until they could better afford to do so, it was universally known, felt, and acknowledged, that Slavery had been, and still continued to be, a great injury to the country, pernicious to morals, destructive to industry, and a dead weight upon enterprise. In the Convention of 1774, it was *unanimously* resolved, that:

"*The abolition of domestic slavery is the greatest object of desire in those colonies where it was unhappily introduced in their infant state. But, previous to the enfranchisement of the slaves we have, it is necessary to exclude all further importations from Africa.* Yet our repeated attempts to effect this by prohibitions, and by imposing duties which might amount to a prohibition, have been hitherto defeated by his Majesty's negative; thus preferring the immediate advantages of a few African corsairs to the lasting interests of the American States, and to the rights of human nature, deeply wounded by this infamous practice. Nay, the single interposition of an interested individual against a law, was scarcely ever known to fail of success, though in the opposite scale were placed the interests of a whole country. That this is so shameful an abuse of a power trusted with his Majesty for other purposes, as, if not reformed, would call for some legal restrictions." [1]

At a general meeting of the freeholders of Prince George's county, in 1775, it was unanimously resolved: "That the African trade is injurious to this colony, obstructs the population of it by freemen, prevents manufacturers and other useful emigrants from settling among us, and occasions an increase of the balance of trade against this colony." [2]

In Princess Ann, Fairfax, (*Geo. Washington presiding*), Culpeper, Nansemond, Caroline, Hanover, and Surrey counties, resolutions of similar import were also passed at formal meetings of the freeholders, and generally by unanimous vote. Subsequently, in the discussion of the power of the general government with regard to Slavery, Mr. Mason said, in the Virginia Legislature:

"The present question concerns not the importing States alone, but the whole Union. The evil of having slaves was experienced during the late war. Had slaves been treated as they might have been by the enemy, they would have proved dangerous instruments in their hands. But their folly dealt by the slaves as it did by the Tories. Slavery discourages arts and manufactures. The poor despise labor when performed by slaves. They prevent the immigration of whites, who really enrich and strengthen a country. They produce the most pernicious effects on manners. Every master of slaves is born a

---

[1] American Archives, 4th series, i., 636.   [2] *Ibid.*, 494.

petty tyrant. They bring the judgment of heaven on a country. By an inevitable chain of causes and effects Providence punishes national sins by national calamities. He lamented that some of our eastern brethren, from a lust of gain, have embarked in this nefarious traffic. As to the State being in the possession of the right to import, that was the case with many other rights now to be given up. He held it essential, in every point of view, that the General Government should have power to prevent the increase of slavery."

The importation of slaves from the West Indies and Africa was forbidden: the emancipation of those already living in the land was merely postponed, as it was distinctly understood, until a more convenient season.

Twenty-five acres of land, with such a cabin and other improvements upon it as "poor white people" are now generally content with in Virginia, could not have been, at the time of the Revolution, worth, on an average, more than one hundred dollars. The property of a majority of the able-bodied, tax-paying men in the State, was then less than this.[1]

Mr. Jefferson says, the poorer class are accustomed to live almost entirely on animal food, "although a free use of vegetables is indispensable to their health and comfort." It is probable that but few of them were habituated to regular labor, and that a large part still lived by hunting, and were but slightly elevated, if any at all, above the savages they had displaced.

The father of American Democracy, believing in his heart that these men were unjustly denied the right of taking part in the election of their rulers, yet acknowledging the danger of intrusting power in the hands of

[1] Jefferson's Notes, comp. pp. 171, 172, 225.

men so grossly ignorant, was anxious that measures should be taken, simultaneously with those he advocated for the removal of the slave-laborers, to elevate their children, and, at all events, to draw out from them a fully educated class of free citizens—men who should understand and sympathize with their wants, yet be fully competent for the highest offices of State. He was too true to himself, however, to advocate any marked distinctions of classes in the laws, such as characterize the present school laws of Virginia.

He proposed that the whole State should, as soon as practicable, be divided into districts, each, at most, of six miles square, in every one of which a schoolhouse, and competent teacher should be provided: that *all residents* in the district should be entitled to send their children to this school for three years, without payment, and by payment of a fixed moderate tuition fee, as much longer as they pleased: That out of the scholars whose parents were unable to give their children more complete education, the boy showing most genius, in each school district, should be chosen annually, to be advanced at the public expense, to a classical and mathematical, or High school: that from among the High school scholars, a certain number should be annually selected for promotion to a superior institution, where they should remain six years. This institution was intended to answer the purpose of a normal college, in supplying competent teachers for the common schools: but also from among its graduates, one-half of the most talented were to be offered three years' additional support by the State, while they pursued the study of arts and sciences at the University. This University—the present University of Virginia, at Charlottesville—is the only part of this scheme which has yet been realized. It is a school for the rich —for the sons of slave-holders almost exclusively.

"The general objects of this law," said Mr. Jefferson, "are to provide an education adapted to the years, to the capacity, and the condition of every one, and directed to their freedom and happiness." "Of the views of this law, none is more important, none more legitimate than that of rendering the people the safe, as they are the ultimate, guardians of their own liberty. The people themselves are the only safe depositories of government. And to render them safe, their minds must be improved to a certain degree. This, indeed, is not all that is necessary, though it be essentially necessary."

The proposal met with no greater favor than that for the education and gradual emancipation of the slaves. However earnest Mr. Jefferson was, nothing can be more evident than that, even then, there was no sincere purpose on the part of the planters—that is, the rich and powerful—to constitute a truly Democratic government, or even to prepare the ground for it. Yet the results of what he was able to accomplish by the power of his eloquence, over their egotism and illiberality, are such as to encourage us never to fear, when we have an opportunity to legislate in advance of our age. The people of Virginia have not, to this day, as a body, approached to Jefferson's sound, practical and Christian views of governmental and social science. Yet, to his limited success in embodying those views in their Constitution and laws, they are indebted for most of their present limited prosperity.

Before the Revolution, there were, in Virginia, beside the temporary servile class, four distinct legal and social orders of the people: first, the aristocracy proper; second, the common free men; third, the poor whites, or non-freeholders, who had no vote on the matters of the Commonwealth; fourth, the slaves proper. The history of Virginia, since the Revolution, is a record of the industrial advantages resulting from the downfall of the old aristocracy and the formation of a younger—and, therefore, more vigorous,—broader—and, therefore, freer and less sharply defined—modern aristocracy. By comparing the industrial progress of the state with that of others, more democratically organized and managed, and entirely or nearly free from Slavery proper, an index is also given us of the injury the Commonwealth has experienced from Slavery, and from morbid pro-slavery conservatism.

Neither the condition nor the character of the poor people of the east was, on the whole, much improved by the Revolution. The class of well-to-do planters, the wealthier yeomen of the country, were chiefly elevated and benefited by it.[1] Its effect on the old aristocracy

---

[1] In the first Bill for organizing a militia, drawn up by Patrick Henry, the people of the State were designated, as they would be in England, "gentlemen and yeomen," the distinction of class being, even at such a time, and by such a man, distinctly recognized.

was not directly ruinous; it merely exposed its essential weakness, and revealed the heavy expense to the Commonwealth by which it had hitherto been sustained. A generation passed away, before payment of the debt it had been running up for nearly two centuries was demanded, and its pride distinctly brought low.

The interval needs no particular account. The system of husbandry—so to dignify the pernicious method of extracting the wealth of the land, which prevailed—had necessarily, already, been somewhat modified. The great size of the plantations was a principal hindrance to any extended improvement. The cultivated land was divided into "in-fields" and "out-fields;" the former, being those nearest the central establishment, received all the manure that was made, and were planted with tobacco; the out-fields, were those at such a distance that manure could not be afforded to be carried to them. If not thought to be rich enough, without the aid of manure, to produce a single crop of tobacco when first cleared up (after having been thrown out for many years), they were planted with maize, several years in succession, and, afterwards, cropped with maize and wheat alternately; or, if the wheat crop fell to less than three (3!) bushels an acre, with maize alone. Occasionally a "rest," of a year or two, would be permitted, during which the spontaneous growth of weeds was closely pastured. This process was continued as long as the land would produce five bushels of maize to the acre; when the crop fell below that, the land would be left alone twenty or thirty years (the length of time depending on the number of negroes the planter owned in proportion to the size of his plantation), when it would be again subjected to the same course.[1]

It was estimated that the crops of the whole State, just previous to the Revolution, were worth respectively—*per annum, communibus annis*—as follows:

Tobacco,	$1,650,000	Pork,	$40,000
Wheat,	666,666	Brandy and Whisky,	6,666
Maize,	200,000	Horses,	6,666
All other agricultural productions,			14,667

The tobacco-crop being still, if we except the small items of horses and distilled spirits, more than twice the value of all other agricultural productions, and ten times the value of all the shipping, lumber, naval stores, peltry, and other productions of the forest, fisheries, mines, and manufactures.

But its production was falling off, and Mr. Jefferson, commenting on the above statement, rejoices in the hope that it will soon be necessarily given up altogether. It is important to remember this; and I shall again refer to it—that the culture of tobacco was *already* so little profitable that the amount grown was rapidly declining—and, that the philosophical statesman, who was the author of the bills for abrogating entails and primogeniture, saw, in the prospect of its entire discontinuance, subject for congratulation, rather than regret.

I can find no distinct statements or estimates, with

[1] See Ruffin's Essay on Calcareous Manures.

regard to the material interests of Virginia, for a long time after the Revolution. It is certain that, owing to the causes I have mentioned, the culture of tobacco became necessarily less and less, on the Eastern Virginia plantations, and the labor owned upon them was necessarily devoted increasingly to the culture of wheat and maize. The income from the land and labor became constantly smaller; not because of the substitution of grain for tobacco, but because of the gradual but constant deterioration of the soil, which that substitution marked.

I use the awkward term, "income from property in land and labor," instead of the simple one, "profits of agriculture," because there never had yet been any legitimate profit of agriculture, in Virginia. From the beginning the planting aristocracy had merely been living on its capital; the whole labor of the country had been, and still, at the Revolution, continued to be engaged in nothing else but transmuting the soil of the country into tobacco—which was sent to England to purchase luxuries for its masters—and into bread for the bare support of its inhabitants, without making any return. Some manure, it is true, was occasionally deposited; but it was not, probably, one per cent. of the value of the capital of fertility which was washed into the sea between the periods at which it was applied. Entail, primogeniture, and Slavery, had been sufficient to hide the increasing poverty of the country under the ostentatious hospitality and pompous airs of the aristocracy. This extravagance, however, could not, under the most favorable circumstances, have lasted much longer. If the Revolution had not occurred, if these laws had not been changed, it is probable that a very much longer period would not have elapsed, before their repeal would have been desired by the aristocracy itself, as was the "Encumbered Estates Act" in Ireland, by its fine-blooded gentlemen, of Old Virginia habits, a few years since. Such pitiable calamity as Ireland suffered in the famine, is, perhaps, not possible in a country like Virginia; but, if the old system had been pursued on a short time longer, there would have been nothing left for the people but to emigrate in a body, or be reduced to a common level of extreme destitution.

But the revolutionary penance could only mitigate, not arrest, punitive justice, and, at length—at the close of the second war with England, which has occasioned a protracted dulness in the demand for tobacco—the hand of inevitable Nemesis is manifest. Many of the old Colonial proprietors are now dead, the plantations are generally divided according to the new laws. The young men, brought up among the negroes—"nursed, educated, and daily exercised in tyranny," as Mr. Jefferson described them to be—with luxurious and vicious propensities, and irrestrainable passions, are not able to meet the demands of their habits, much less to pay the interest of the long accumulating debts of their families. The law no longer protects them from the honest claims of the despised merchants. Lands and negroes have been mortgaged. The sale of negroes, from time to time, to traders, who are now beginning to ship them off in considerable number, to the cotton plantations of the Southern Slave States, satisfies the most pressing demands for a few years, but only makes the ultimate catastrophe more accumulative and overwhelming. The end of the rope is finally reached, and the worn out and used up old plantations are going a begging for purchasers, like foundered horses, at any price which shall give bare freedom to the poor young cavaliers. The iniquity of aristocracy is visited upon the children and upon the children's children, unto the third and fourth generations, and, in the world's open market, the exact value of grandfathers is at length ascertained.

The story is thus told by a Virginian in the *Southern Planter:*

"Every farm was greatly impoverished—almost every estate was seriously impaired—and some were involved in debt to nearly their value. Most of the proprietors had died, leaving families in reduced circumstances, and in some cases in great straits. No farm, whether of a rich or a poor proprietor, had escaped great exhaustion, and no property great dilapidation, unless because the proprietor had at first been too poor to join in the former expensive habits of his wealthier neighbors."

* * * "There was nothing left to waste, but time and labor; and these continued to be wasted in the now fruitless efforts to cultivate to profit, or to replace the fertility of soil which had been destroyed. Luxury and expense had been greatly lessened. But on that account the universal prostration was even the more apparent. Many mansions were falling into decay. Few received any but trivial and indispensable repairs. No new mansion was erected, and rarely any other farm-building of value. There was still generally prevailing idleness among proprietors; and also an abandonment of hope, which made every one desirous to sell his land and move to the fertile and far West, and a general emigration and dispersion was only prevented by the impossibility of finding purchasers for the lands, even at half the then low estimate of market prices."

And thus by Mr. Palfrey:

"By-and-by the father dies, and the land and the hundred negroes, more or less, are divided equally among the children. The sons cannot live — at all events as they have been used to living — on a piece of exhausted tobacco-lands with a dozen or two of hands to till it. The professions are full; the trades too vulgar for them; they have no way to get a subsistence. They sell off the human-stock, and live off the proceeds, as long as they last; and then become borrowing loafers about the Court-House tavern, or take their departure for parts unknown. Or they take to the Capitol, their only capital, long so well accredited there, of 'belonging to one of the first families in Virginia,' and get some small clerkship in one of the public offices,——."

The Democratic system, so far as it was established by the Revolution, was limited in its scope to what had been previously the middle white class, and the aristocracy. Its first effect upon the latter I have shown to have been disastrous, but upon the great mass its operation must have been elevating and encouraging. Even during this very same period of aristocratic dispersion, now known as the dark days of Virginia, because many flashing lights of her old gentry were then extinguished, I believe the condition of the major part of the people (leaving out of view, for the present, the slaves, and the politically debased whites), was steadily improving. There were more rising than falling men.

Notwithstanding a constant emigration of the decayed families, and of the more enterprising of the poor, the population steadily augmented, though not so rapidly as in the adjoining more democratic States.[1] If the apparent wealth of the country was not increasing, the foundation of a greater material prosperity was being laid, in the increase of the number of small, but intelligent proprietors, and in the constantly growing necessity to abandon tobacco, and substitute grains, or varied crops, as the staple productions of the country. The very circumstance that reduced the old pseudo-weathy proprietors, was favorable to this change, and to the application of intelligence to a more profitable disposal of the remaining elements of wealth in the land.

While multitudes abandoned their ancestral acres in despair, or were driven from them by the recoil of their fathers' inconsiderate expenditures, they were taken possession of by "new men," endowed with more hopefulness and energy, if not more intelligence than the old. Movement, though it be apparently downward, is evidence of life, and is stimulating to the mind. Every man who thought about it, saw that either tobacco must be given up, or its method of culture essentially modified, or that his land must continue to decrease in productive value. With the new proprietors this was a matter of more consequence than it

---

[1] 1790 to 1810, population to sq. mile in Virginia increased from 10.68 to 13.92
" " " " New York " 7.56 to 21.31
" " " " Pennsylvania " 9.28 to 17.3

had formerly been, because a larger proportion of their capital was now absorbed in the land they owned, proportionately to that in slaves. In an address of Mr. Madison, President of the Confederacy, 1809–1817, before an Agricultural Society in Albemarle County, in 1819, the change then progressing in the economy of Virginia is thus alluded to:

"Whilst there was an abundance of fresh and fertile soil, it was the interest of the cultivator to spread his labor over as great a surface as possible. Land being cheap, and labor dear, and the land coöperating powerfully with the labor, it was profitable to draw as much as possible from the land. Labor is now comparatively cheaper, and land dearer. It might be profitable, therefore, now, to contract the surface over which labor is spread, even if the soil retained its freshness and fertility. But this is not the case. Much of the fertile soils are exhausted, and unfertile soils are brought into cultivation; and both coöperating less with labor in producing the crop, it is necessary to consider how far labor can be profitably exerted on them: whether it ought not to be applied towards making them fertile, rather than in further impoverishing them; or whether it might not be more profitably applied to mechanical operations, or domestic manufactures."

Among men of capital, intelligence, and social habits—for, without the stimulus of conversation or reading, improvements are accepted slowly—certain systematic methods of sustaining and improving landed estate began to prevail, immediately after the second war. Tobacco was given up, or cultivated only in its proper turn of a rotation; artificial grasses were introduced, and, with the aid of gypsum, clover was made to grow upon the exhausted lands, and made use of as a green manure, to resuscitate them; ambulatory pens, shifted yearly from field to field, came into use upon large farms, instead of the stationary central stockyards, thus saving the great labor of hauling fodder and manure between them and distant fields, and doing away with the "in and out-field" system. Cattle and horses were fed a much longer period of the year than formerly, and by some they were excluded from the tillage lands altogether, the growth of weeds and grasses having been found to be of more value to plough in as manure, than to be pastured.

Among American patriots of this period of our history, should always be classed John Taylor, of Caroline county, Virginia, the author of "Arator," and John S. Skinner, who, in 1819, commenced at Baltimore, in Maryland, the publication of the first special agricultural journal in America. Other men, many of whose names are enrolled among those of our national statesmen, were then united with them, in strenuous and concerted exertion, to give a better direction to the labor and agricultural capital of those States.

The convalescence of Virginia agriculture, however, if convalescent it may be considered ever to have been, should more especially be dated from the introduction of lime, as an application, in connection with better tillage, judicious rotations, and more frequent applications of dung and green crops, for the improvement of the land. And for this, Virginia is chiefly indebted to the study, experiments, preaching, and publications of Edmund Ruffin. Mr. Ruffin was, for many years, the editor of the *Virginia Farmers' Register*, but is best known as the author of "A Treatise on Calcareous Manures," than which no work on a similar subject has ever been published in Europe or America based on more scientifically careful investigation, and trusty, personal experience, or of equal practical value to those for whose benefit it was designed.

But, cotemporaneously with the invigoration of the planting class, the depression of the tobacco market, and the introduction of these improvements in agriculture which promised so much for the future of the State, there entered a still more potent element into the direction of her destiny. This was occasioned by the increasing profit and extending culture of cotton in the more Southern States, which gave rise to a demand for additional labor, increased the value of slaves, and, the African Slave Trade having been declared piracy, led to a great extension of the internal Slave Trade.

The value of the cotton exported from the United States was:

In 1794,	$500,000
1800,	5,000,000
1810,	15,000,000
1820,	22,000,000
1830,	30,000,000
1840,	64,000,000
1850,	72,000,000

Closely corresponding to the increase in the exportation of cotton, was the growth of the demand for labor; and as, in any slave-holding community, experience shows no other labor can be extensively made use of but that of slaves, the value of slaves *for sale* has steadily advanced in Virginia, with the extension of cotton fields over the lands conquered or purchased for that purpose of the Indians in Alabama and Florida; of France, in the valley of the Mississippi; and of Mexico, in Texas.[1]

The effect of this demand for slaves was directly contrary to those influences which I have described as being the foundation of renewed agricultural energy in Virginia. It concentrated the interest of the planter in his slaves, as in old times it had been concentrated in tobacco; the improvement, or even the sustentation of the value of his lands became a matter of minor importance; the taste for improving husbandry, except among the men of leisure, capital, and highly-cultivated minds, was fatally checked. Mr. Ruffin, a gentleman of ultra, and, it seems to a stranger, fanatical devotion to the perpetuation of slavery, yet otherwise a most sensible and reliable observer and thinker, unintentionally gives his evidence against the Slave Trade, by describing the effect of the increased value it gave to negroes:

"A gang of slaves on a farm will increase to four times their original number in thirty or forty years. If a farmer is only able to feed and maintain his slaves, their increase in value may double the whole of his capital originally invested in

---

[1] That the people of California should have decided not to permit slaves to be sold also in that great acquisition to our territory, has been an intense disappointment to Virginia slaveholders; and the influence of the State, for some time after this was determined, was very undecided with regard to further schemes of annexation.

farming before he closes the term of an ordinary life. But few farms are able to support this increasing expense, and also furnish the necessary supplies to the family of the owner; whence very many owners of large estates, in lands and negroes, are, throughout their lives, too poor to enjoy the comforts of life, or to incur the expenses necessary to improve their unprofitable farming. A man so situated may be said to be a slave to his own slaves. If the owner is industrious and frugal, he may be able to support the increasing numbers of his slaves, and to bequeath them undiminished to his children. But the income of few persons increases as fast as their slaves, and, if not, the consequence must be that some of them will be sold, that the others may be supported, and the sale of more is perhaps afterwards compelled to pay debts incurred in striving to put off that dreaded alternative. The slave at first almost starves his master, and at last is eaten by him—at least, he is exchanged for his value in food."

What a remarkable state of things is here pictured—the labor of a country almost exclusively applied to agriculture, and yet able to supply *itself*, but in few cases, with the coarsest food!

The interest of the slaves' owners being withdrawn, by their increasing value as transferable property, from their land, a gradual but rapid amelioration of their condition followed, as respects physical comfort. Since 1820, there has been a constant improvement in this respect. They are now worked no harder, in general, than is supposed to be desirable to bring them into high muscular and vital condition; they are better fed, clothed, and sheltered, and the pliant strap and scientific paddle have been substituted, as instruments of discipline, for the scoring lash and bruising cudgel.[1]

[1] Hon. Humphrey Marshall, of Kentucky, in his defence of Mat. Ward, thus describes the strap:

"The strap, gentlemen, you are probably aware, is an in-

No similar progress, it is to be observed, has been made in the mental and moral economy of Slavery in Virginia; the laws and customs being a good deal less favorable, than formerly, to the education of the race, which is sufficiently explainable. The opinion being prevalent—and, I suppose, being well-founded—that negro property, as it increases in intelligence, decreases in security; as it becomes of greater value, and its security more important, more regard is naturally paid to the means of suppressing its ambition and dwarfing its intellect.

Of course, this increased care of the slaves' physical well-being adds to the current expenditure of their master, and makes all operations, involving labor, cost more than formerly; and, as its effect is to force more rapid breeding, and the number of slaves does not diminish, no corresponding encouragement is obtained from it for free-labor. Consequently, the internal slave-

---

strument of refined modern torture, ordinarily used in whipping slaves. By the old system, the cow-hide — a severe punishment — cut and lacerated them so badly as to almost spoil their sale when brought to the lower markets. But this strap, I am told, is a vast improvement in the art of whipping negroes; and, it is said, that one of them may be punished by it within one inch of his life, and yet he will come out with no visible injury, and his skin will be as smooth and polished as a peeled onion!"

The paddle is a large, thin ferule of wood, in which many small holes are bored; when a blow is struck, these holes, from the rush and partial exhaustion of air in them, act like diminutive cups, and the continued application of the instrument has been described to me to produce precisely such a result as that attributed to the strap by Mr. M.

The Experience of Virginia

trade makes the cost of labor greater, and its quality worse, precisely in proportion to its activity. This, as I pointed out in the last chapter, is the grand reason of the excessively low market value of all real estate, and has occasioned the slow and stingy application of capital to mining and other industrial enterprises, in all other elements for the success of which Virginia is so exceedingly rich.

It was, for a long time, generally expected that the demand of the cotton-planters would gradually draw off all the slaves from Virginia, and that the State would thus be redeemed to freedom. The objection which had been chiefly urged against Jefferson's scheme of emancipation, certainly would have had less weight, during thirty years past, against a requirement that all slaves below mature age, remaining, after a certain future time, in the State, should be educated, freed, and transported; for the owners, who could not afford to lose the value of their property, could, at any time, have sold away their slaves, at very much more than their cost price, before the requirement went into effect.

It, therefore, became advisable to stigmatize such a proposition as tyrannical — to claim for a class the power of thus continuing to ruin the State, so long as they found in it their private profit, as a legal and vested right. On January 18, 1832, a member of the legislature, Mr. Gholson, proclaimed this, in the following cunning language. Be it observed that all existing nuisances, and those that are a part of them, are always called old-fashioned; which, oddly enough under such circumstances, is considered equivalent to respectable.

> "It has always (perhaps erroneously) been considered, by steady and old-fashioned people, that the owner of land had a reasonable right to its annual profit, the owner of orchards to their annual fruits, * * * and the owner of female slaves to their increase. * * * It is on the justice and inviolability of this maxim that the master foregoes the service of the female slave, has her nursed and attended during the period of gestation, and raises the helpless infant offspring. The value of the property justifies the expense; and I do not hesitate to say, that in its increase consists much of our wealth."

That is to say, no law providing for the freedom of unborn generations is to be considered just; consequently, Mr. Jefferson's scheme was agrarian and preposterous.

The value of slaves for sale has, since then, pretty steadily advanced; the exportation has as steadily augmented; while the stock kept on hand is some three thousand more than it then was. The amiable letter-writer, whom the State of Jefferson now delights to honor, tells our simple New York Democrats, that if they had not been so foolish as to favor the admission of California as a Free State—*if they had been able, as he desired, to force it to become a Slave State*—it would have opened such a market for slaves as would have soon drained them all out of Virginia.

I do not believe, if prime field-hands should ever sell for ten thousand dollars a head, there would be one negro less kept in Virginia than there is now, when they are worth but one thousand.

How would this increasing demand be met, then?

Very easily: by the re-importation of breeding-slaves from the consuming States. Connecticut exports bullocks and barren cows by the thousand annually; and the drovers who take the working and fatted stock out, often drive back heifers from the districts in which the breeding of cattle is made less a matter of business, and is, therefore, less profitable than it is in that region of bleak pastures.

It is an assertion often made, and generally credited, that it is only since the rise of the abolition agitation that the people of the South have shown a determined disposition to perpetuate Slavery — that in Virginia, especially, the people would, ere this, have abolished, or greatly modified it, if they had not been exasperated to folly by the calumnious and impertinent meddling in the matter of those who had no business with it.

I have always, until recently, taken the truth of this assertion for granted; and have often, I am afraid, somewhat foolishly, repeated it. No doubt there is a certain basis of truth in it; no doubt the abolition agitation in the Free States has been, and is in many respects, injudicious; but I am induced to think this charge against it requires to be made with some reservation and explanation.

It certainly is a curious coincidence — and it can hardly be thought a mere coincidence, it seems to me — that the general indisposition to emancipate slaves has been very closely proportionate to the expense, or loss of cash property, which would attend it. If an accurate yearly price-current of slaves since the Revolution could be had, it would indicate the fluctuating probabilities of their general emancipation more exactly than the value of the English consolidated debt follows the varying prospects of peace or war.

From the day in which Jefferson inaugurated the agitation for the emancipation of the slaves, up to 1820, the Abolition party in Virginia, though it never succeeded in accomplishing the smallest of its legislative purposes, was strong in talent if not in number, and was in close fraternity and affiliation with the more successful party in the States now free.[1] At this time the internal slave traffic was first recognized as a phenomena of pregnant importance; and Randolph and other Virginians lamented it, and deplored its probable consequences in Congress.

There were then (1820) in Virginia no men of education and influence who were not slave-owners—and as such, pecuniarily interested, more or less, in restraining legislation unfavorable to Slavery. During the next fifteen years, the Southern demand for slaves, and, consequently, their value as stock, constantly increasing, there would appear to have been a struggle between the consciences and the interests, or between the selfishness and the good judgment, of those who had constituted the anti-slavery influence of the State.

[1] Benjamin Franklin was President, and George Washington and Thomas Jefferson correspondents, of the Abolition Society of Pennsylvania, of which Passmore Williamson, lately lying in jail, in Philadelphia, is the present Secretary.

Gradually the older and more powerful opponents of the perpetuation of the system passed off the field of action, and the younger were induced to accept what they found so increasingly profitable—at least, to be quiet, and leave its determined supporters to govern and represent the State.

In 1830, Daniel Webster said, in the Senate:

"I know full well, that it is, and has been, the settled policy of some persons in the South, *for years*, to represent the people of the North as disposed to interfere with them in their own exclusive and peculiar concerns. This is a delicate and sensitive point in Southern feeling; and of late years, it has always been touched, and generally with effect, whenever the object has been to unite the whole South against Northern men or Northern measures. This feeling, *always carefully kept alive*, and maintained at too intense a heat to admit discrimination or reflection, is a lever of great power in our political machine. It moves vast bodies, and gives to them one and the same direction. But it is without adequate cause, and the suspicion which exists is wholly groundless."

Remember that slave property still grew daily less productive, but more valuable.

Two years after the above declaration of Mr. Webster, an important debate occurred in the Virginia Legislature, with regard to Slavery. The Anti-Slavery party may be said to have then made its last demonstration, and final protest, against the policy which now, far more distinctly than formerly, was defended and maintained as an established permanent policy: whether most from a spirit of resistance to an abolition agitation at the North, or at home, or from the increasing value of slaves, the reader will judge.

On that occasion (in the Virginia Legislature, in the city of Richmond, fifty-six years after the Declaration of Independence), there were still not wanting some men who saw the evil of Slavery, and the rights of slaveholders in the same light that Jefferson, and Madison, and Mason, and Monroe, and Henry, and all the real statesmen of Virginia had done, and who were brave and magnanimous enough to utter their convictions. Thus, one Mr. Faulkner used the following language, especially significant in the italicized passage, of what he considered to be then the real obstacle in the way of measures for emancipation:

"Slavery, it is admitted, is an evil. It is an institution which presses heavily against the best interests of the State. It banishes free white labor—it exterminates the mechanic, the artisan, the manufacturer. It converts the energy of a community into indolence; its power into imbecility; its efficiency into weakness. Being thus injurious, have we not a right to demand its extermination? *Shall society suffer that the slaveholder may continue to gather his vigintial crop of human flesh?* What is his mere pecuniary claim, compared with the great interests of the common weal? Must the country languish and die, that the slaveholder may flourish? Shall all interests be subservient to one? Have not the middle classes their rights—rights incompatible with the existence of Slavery?"

MR. BRODNAX: "That Slavery in Virginia is an evil, and a transcendent evil, it would be more than idle for any human being to doubt or deny. It is a mildew, which has blighted every region it has touched, from the creation of the world. Illustrations from the history of other countries and other times might be instructive; but we have evidence nearer at hand, in the short histories of the different States of this great confederacy, which are impressive in their admonitions, and conclusive in their character."

MR. SUMMERS: "Will gentlemen inform us when this subject will become less delicate—when it will be attended with fewer difficulties than at present—and at what period we shall be better enabled to meet them? Shall we be more adequate to the end proposed, after the resources of the State have been yet longer paralyzed by the withering, desolating influence of our present system? *Sir, every year's delay but augments the difficulties of this great business, and weakens our ability to compass it.*"[1]

Having suffered twenty-three years longer since this protest against her cherished policy was made in her Legislature, now at length has Virginia acquired the necessary strength and courage to undergo the painful operation necessary to free her from that chronic malady which, from the earliest period of her colonial infancy, has constantly debilitated and paralyzed her?

She is further from it than ever. Like a poor man, rendered prematurely imbecile by his long endurance of pain, and who, conscious that every pretext against the application of the surgeon's relieving knife has been long since exhausted, finally, in unconquerable cowardice, discharges his faithful old family physician, feigns to despise his judgment, and throws himself, in a flood of grateful tears, into the embrace of some contemptible, bragging quack, who pretends that his disease has hitherto been entirely misunderstood — who predicts that, under his care, he will soon be the strongest man in town—who diverts him with expensive nostrums, and amuses him by humorous descriptions of his own

---

[1] Speeches delivered in the House of Delegates of Virginia, in relation to her colored population, January, 1832. Richmond, printed by Thomas W. White.

debilitated form and palsied movements; so **Virginia** now insultingly spurns from her councils all who suggest that slavery is *ever* to be eradicated, and not one man is allowed to enter her Legislature who dares to declare and demand "the rights of the middle class," nay, even to supplicate for them; and if one should now petition for the passage of the amendment proposed by Jefferson, he would actually be in danger of losing his life. Such has been the influence of the extension of cotton culture and the demand for slaves in Virginia —such is the power of organized capital and educated wisdom, in a republic.

Virginia has this year passed through an exciting election—the most so, probably, of any since the discussion of the Alien and Sedition Acts. It was preceded by a prolonged and very thorough canvass, with personal appeals to the conscience, the patriotism, and especially to the pecuniary interests of the people, by the rival candidates and their friends. The successful candidate is said to have made more than sixty addresses, in person, to large assemblages of the electors convened to hear him describe the policy he desired to pursue, and his reasons for it.

I have read with attention all the reports which I could obtain of these expositions, in order to judge from them what the people of Virginia now want or expect of their public servants. Among the passages which are represented by the reporters to have been received with great applause by the intelligent audience, on one occasion, are the following:

"Commerce has long ago spread her sails, and sailed away from you. You have not, as yet, dug more than coal enough to warm yourselves at your own hearths; you have set no tilt-hammer of Vulcan to strike blows worthy of gods in your own iron-foundries; you have not yet spun more than coarse cotton enough, in the way of manufacture, to clothe your own slaves.

"You have had no commerce, no mining, no manufactures.

"You have relied alone on the single power of agriculture—and such agriculture! Your sedge-patches outshine the sun. Your inattention to your only source of wealth has scared the very bosom of mother earth. Instead of having to feed cattle on a thousand hills, you have had to chase the stump-tailed steer through the sedge-patches to procure a tough beef-steak. (Laughter and applause.)

"The present condition of things has existed too long in Virginia. The landlord has skinned the tenant, and the tenant has skinned the land, until all have grown poor together. I have heard a story—I will not locate it here or there—about the condition of the prosperity of our agriculture. I was told by a gentleman in Washington, not long ago, that he was travelling in a county not a hundred miles from this place, and overtook one of our citizens on horseback, with, perhaps, a bag of hay for a saddle, without stirrups, and the leading line for a bridle, and he said: 'Stranger, whose house is that?' 'It is mine,' was the reply. They came to another. 'Whose house is that?' 'Mine, too, stranger.' To a third: 'And whose house is that?' 'That's mine, too, stranger; but don't suppose that I'm so darned poor as to own all the land about here.' (Laughter and applause.) We may own land, we may own slaves, we may own roadsteads and mines, we may have all the elements of wealth; but unless we apply intelligence, unless we adopt a thorough system of instruction, it is utterly impossible that we can develop, as we ought to develop, and as Virginia is prepared now to do, and to take the line of march towards the very eminence of prosperity." (Applause and continued merriment.)

And how does the fiddling Nero propose, it will be wondered, to remedy this so very amusing stupidity, poverty, and debility? Very simply and pleasantly. By building railroads and canals, ships and mills; by establishing manufactories, opening mines, and setting up smelting-works and foundries. And "Hurrah!" shout the tickled electors; "that's exactly what we want."

Indeed, it is what they want; but how are they going to get it? one is next anxious to ascertain. This question is neither asked nor answered. The confirmed paralytic and dyspeptic pauper is told: "All you want is a good digestion. Take plenty of exercise, walk twenty miles a day, swing dumb-bells, box, fence, row, and hunt; live generously; breakfast on cutlets *à la victime;* dine on salmon and venison with truffles; sup on canvas-backs, and don't spare pure old port." "Ah! that's it; I'm satisfied you understand my complaint," whispers the poor, bed-ridden wretch; "I put myself in your hands." "Good," returns the laughing charlatan; "you are now prepared to develop."

The same sagacious candidate, in a similar strain of eloquent mockery, depicts the intense ignorance which characterizes the people of Virginia; and affects to deplore it, though when a member of Congress he used publicly to boast of it, and congratulate himself upon it, as preventing disagreeable dissensions in his constituency. Now he laments it, and ridicules it, and promises, if they will make him governor, he will set about remedying it. How?

Actually, he has the impudence, as he stands there laughing at them, to pretend an admiration for the educational scheme of Jefferson, and to promise to recommend its adoption by the State.

And the poor mob appears to be imposed upon again; and, having a traditional confidence in the sincerity of Jefferson's democracy, they actually cheer him as if he was in earnest.

"He was in earnest," will the reader say, if about the time this book comes out, his first message will be reported in the newspapers, as containing a recommendation redeeming his promise?

Unless he also recommends—which I think would make an "activity" for a day or two in Wall street—Jefferson's sister scheme for the emancipation of the slaves, I should say, he was not in earnest, but was cruelly imposing again upon the ignorance of the poor, quack-ridden "Democracy;" for the Democratic scheme of education, proposed by Jefferson, is as impracticable and fallacious when disconnected from that sister scheme of his, as, when associated with it, it is admirable and necessary to a truly Democratic system of political economy.

Every Virginian possessing the average American development of brain, and not quite demented with avarice, or doctrinarianism, must know this, if he has ever had any interest in the workings of the wretched attempts at public education employed in his State.

In the year ending Sept. 30, 1851, there were in ninety-eight counties, the School Commissioners of which made reports as required by law, 55,312 indigent children, between eight and eighteen years old, needing special State aid, to enable them to attend any school. Besides this number, there were those of forty counties, and the towns of Norfolk, Portsmouth, Williamsburg, and Wheeling, of which report was neglected to be made. In 125 counties but 30,324, less than half the immense body of pauper-children living in them, were enabled or induced to attend school at all; and these (namely, the poor children mainly living nearest schools already established and supported by the wealthy for their own children), each on an average only eleven weeks and one day (less than one-quarter of the year). This pitiable result was obtained at a cost to the State of sixty-nine thousand dollars.

The Second Auditor's General Report on Education, from which I compile these facts, contains abstracts of sub-reports touching the working of the system then in operation, and which, I was assured by several worthy gentlemen in Richmond, was working most satisfactorily. These sub-reports were drawn up by the County School Commissioners and Superintendents, through whose hands what is called the Literary Fund is distributed. From them I shall make a few extracts, which will show how entirely impracticable—while the white population is so excessively distributed, as it needs must be, where there are many slaves—it will always be to contrive any *valuable* system of education for the families of those not able to pay for each scholar at a very high rate of tuition.

ALBEMARLE (White Population, 11,875; Slave do., 13,338).—"The Board of Commissioners state, that with the present appropriation to the county, they must be dependent upon the schools established by individual enterprise. They can, of course, proffer their assistance only where such schools exist."

"Your Superintendent would bring to your consideration the importance of recommending an increased per diem rate of tuition from four to five cents, as many of the best qualified teachers in the county object to take the indigent children into their schools on account of the reduced price per diem. He cannot furnish a synopsis of the proceedings of the Commissioners in the county, as very few reports have been furnished him."

AMELIA (Whites, 2,785; Slaves, 6,819; number of indigent children registered, 120; number of do., who attended school at any time within a year, 68).—No remarks.

BUCKINGHAM (White Population, 5,426; Slave, 8, 161).— "The Board of School Commissioners report, that some of the Commissioners are unable, for the want of schools, to expend the money allotted to their districts. They have no regular system of visiting the schools, nor do they, as a body, formally examine the teachers, leaving that to be done by those who patronize the schools. Neither have they established schools where none existed. The quota to this county is not sufficient to educate all the poor children. The number of children and the time they are sent to school, is discretionary with the district commissioners."

CHARLOTTE (White Population, 4,615; Slave, 8,988).—"The Superintendent states that *in three or four of the districts, schools could not be obtained, and in others the children could not be induced to go;* that it is utterly impossible to induce the district commissioners to have the accounts and reports made out according to form; the consequence is, that *there is a great difficulty in making the returns in due time."*

CLARKE (Whites, 3,614; Slaves, 3,614).— "The Board has no regulations of a general character for the government of the district commissioners, as they have only acted in sessions of the Board. The schools are not visited by them, nor can they judge of the qualifications of the teachers, because, from the insufficiency of their quota, they are obliged to send the indigent children to such established schools as are most convenient to the residence of the children."

FAUQUIER (Whites, 9,875; Slaves, 10,350).—"The Commissioners would call attention to the inadequacy of the school quota of this county, for the tuition of the indigent children within its limits. They would further state, as the reason why they have not returned the number of poor children in their respective districts, that the duty is a very onerous one, and such as they are not able to perform without compensation, but that in the discharge of their duties they endeavor to aid the cause of education as much as they can, consistent with their own private interests, and are at all times ready to resign their trust to any who will perform the duties of the office more faithfully than themselves."

GLOUCESTER (Whites, 4,290; Slaves, 5,557).—"Some of the Commissioners have visited the schools in their districts, and are happy to state that there is a considerable improvement in the pupils, as well as in the management and the course of instruction on the part of the teachers. The school quota of this county is entirely insufficient to educate the indigent children. No preference is given to either sex."

GOOCHLAND (Whites, 3,863; Slaves, 5,845).—No remarks by board of school commissioners.

"The superintendent, as usual, has visited some of the schools, and has to say, that at some of them the scholars were progressing very well, whilst at others they were not doing so well as is desirable."

HALIFAX (Whites, 10,976; Slaves, 14,452; poor children, 803; attended school, 378).—"The individual commissioners have occasionally visited the schools to which they entered indigent children, and found that the poor children were improving in their studies as well as other children. The teachers are well qualified to teach spelling, reading, writing, and arithmetic, which is all that can be hoped for that class. The annual appropriation from the treasury, to the primary schools of this county, is not more than half enough to educate all the indigent children.

"They have no alterations to suggest in the present system. If any were made, it would not be to amend, but to make an entire alteration of the present system; but they do not believe that the county would adopt such a system as they would recommend."

HANOVER (Whites, 6,539; Slaves, 8,393).—"The school commissioners have paid some attention to visiting the schools in their districts. The teachers are generally persons of good moral character, and capable of conducting schools of respectable grades. Indigent children improve as well as others, and are generally making good progress.

"The commissioners have established several schools. They have aided in establishing others in neighborhoods where they could not otherwise have been established; and others might have been established to great advantage but for the want of funds. There appears to be an increasing desire among indigent persons to have their children educated, but the quota of the Literary fund for this county is not half sufficient to educate all of them. We have found but little difficulty in getting indigent children to attend school, except amongst the most ignorant or degraded class. No general rule has been adopted by them for the selection of children to be sent to school, except what the law requires."

RAPPAHANNOCK (Whites, 5,642; Slaves, 3,844).—"The board of school commissioners state that the appropriation from the treasury is insufficient to educate all the poor of the county, yet as *there are many indigent children, whose parents cannot be prevailed upon to send them to school*, they generally enter all the indigent children who will attend school."

KING WILLIAM (Whites, 2,701; Slaves, 5,731).—"The commissioners report that such of the commissioners as have schools in their districts have visited them. They find the teachers well qualified to give instruction in the common branches of an English education, and that the indigent children, for the time they attend school, learn as well as other children. The appropriation from the treasury is fully sufficient for all who are entered, and the commissioners enter as many of that class as they or the teachers can get to attend school." (Number of poor children returned, 246; number sent to school within the year, 66.)

NANSEMOND (Whites, 5,424; Slaves, 4,715).—"A majority of the school commissioners find difficulty in getting indigent children to attend school regularly, *principally owing to the schools not being located near them;* they sometimes send children to another district. Some of the commissioners have visited the schools, and are well satisfied with the qualifications of the teachers. The children that attend make very fair improvement. Children from eight to eighteen have been admitted to school without regard to sex. The commissioners have not established any more schools, for want of funds; they send to schools that have been established heretofore."

SUSSEX (Whites, 3,086; Slaves, 5,992).—"The commissioners state that they have no power in regulating the government of the schools. The qualifications of the teachers they believe to be as good as the small sum which they possess will command. They have no choice generally in the selection of teachers — the scholars entered are taken by the teachers as objects of charity, and not for the compensation they receive. The fund being insufficient to educate the poor of the county, the commissioners have made selections from among the children, giving the preference to those who would be most likely to attend the schools regularly."

SOUTHAMPTON (Whites, 5,940; Slaves, 5,755).—"The commissioners state, that the funds appropriated are very inadequate to the education of the poor children of the county; that not one-half of them attend school at all, and of those the most of them were at school but a small portion of the year; that the parents of many were willing and anxious for their children to attend, but the teachers would not receive them, because there was nothing to pay for their tuition. They further state, that *the irregular attendance of the poor children still continues to be one of the greatest difficulties they labor under in judiciously applying the funds allotted them;* and, in consequence of this, the school commissioner is very much embarrassed in distributing his quota among the schools of his district, and consequently in determining the number of days he should enter to each teacher, as he can form no correct idea, from the number of children, how many days they are likely to make."

POWHATAN (Whites, 2,513; Slaves, 5,282).—No remarks. Number of poor children, 150; attended school, 60.

I do not mean to say that, if the people will submit to the necessary taxation, some enormously expensive system of education may not be adopted, which will be of great benefit to the State, and lead to a more rapid development of her resources, even though Slavery should still continue to separate, distract, and debilitate the associative energies of the indigent whites. I have not a doubt this can be done, and I sincerely trust it will be tried. But, except as an indirect step towards the abolition of Slavery, it will do hardly anything towards raising Virginia to an equality of intelligence with the Free States, or to that position of power and attractiveness which is indicated by her natural elements of wealth.

Nor can anything do this, but a free, self-dependent, self-supporting, and self-respecting, intelligent laboring people. Whether the negroes can be made a part of such a people, I need not here give an opinion; but I will say that I can see no evidence that they are advancing towards it, or that it is the general intention that they shall advance towards it. Whether, if the negroes were free, and remained as stupid, as helpless, as contented, as unhopeful and unambitious, and as indolent, as it is claimed they are at present, it would be possible to have any general population of white people of such a kind, I do not now care to answer. But I declare, with confidence, that it is evidently an absolute impossibility to have such a people, and such a development of the State, or such a degree of intelligence among the mass of free people as, under a republic, it is of vital importance to secure to them, while a peculiar, degraded, pitiable, or despicable class, capable of being used only as the instruments of labor in the hands of a more intelligent, is by law expressly provided for, and not merely left unfurnished with education by the State, but expressly prevented from being educated, expressly prevented from striving to improve its own capacity of usefulness through the impulse to improve its status in society. While such a class is carefully conserved for the purposes of labor, good, careful, high-spirited and high-purposed men, disposed to turn their own honest labor to good account, will avoid or go out from such a labor-market; and only bad, mean, low-minded, careless, and poor laboring people will come to it, or stay in it. So it always has been: so it is now.

So much for the remedies which the new governor imposes upon the people of Virginia, for the evils under which the State suffers.

What little he has time to say, directly of Slavery, he says only as the champion and advocate, before the electors at large, of the interests of the slaveholders, and in denunciation and defiance of those who may dare doubt the necessity of making that interest paramount to all others in the nation. But to the slaveholders themselves he especially commends himself, by the assertion, that if he could have had his way, California would have been a Slave State, and in that case slaves would have been worth five thousand dollars a-piece!

I know not much about Louis Blanc, except that he is very much detested by most people, and especially by the aristocracy and the stock-brokers of Europe, but I saw something which he said lately to the continental democratic refugees in England, which seems to me in itself true and good.

> "The republican form of government is not the object: the object is, to restore to the dignity of human nature those whom the excess of poverty degrades, and to enlighten those whose intelligence, from want of education, is but a dim, vacillating lamp, in the midst of darkness; the object is to make him that works enjoy all the fruits of his work; the object is to enfranchise the people, by endeavoring gradually to abolish this double slavery—ignorance and misery. A very difficult task, indeed, the accomplishment of which requires long study, deep meditation, and something more than discipline! As to the republican form of government, it is a means, most valuable, certainly, and which we ought to strive to conquer, even at the cost of life, but which it is very imprudent to mistake for the aim, as the consequence might be to make us take the shadow for the substance, and run through a heap of ruins to fatal delusions."

I think this mistake has been made by the Virginia experimenters: the republican form of government has certainly failed to restore to much dignity of human nature that part of her population degraded by excess of poverty, or to very materially enlighten those whose intelligence, for want of education, was dim and vacillating. I think, also, the people of Virginia have been running very fast through their "heap of ruins, towards fatal delusions"—fatal delusions, already warmly embraced, as will presently be seen.

The *Richmond Examiner* and the *Richmond Enquirer* are the chief organs of those who lead the long dominant party of Virginia. They are conducted with more talent than any other journals of the State, and each receives a very much larger income from its subscribers than does any newspaper in the State which now ever distinctly admits Slavery to be an evil, desirable or possible to be remedied.

From the Richmond Enquirer, Sept. 6, 1855.

"We are happy to find that others of our Southern cotemporaries are willing to discuss (?) the true and great question of the day—*The existence of Slavery as a permanent institution in the South.*

"Every moment's additional reflection but convinces us of the absolute impregnability of the Southern position on this subject. Facts, which cannot be questioned, come thronging in support of the true doctrine—that Slavery is the best condition of the black race in this country, and that the true philanthropists should rather desire that race to remain in a state of servitude, than to become free, with the privilege of becoming worthless. * * * The Virginians need not be told that, as a class, there is not a more worthless or dissolute set of men than these free negroes. Our slaves, even, look upon most of them with contempt, and speak of them with a sneer. They deserve it. There are some few honorable exceptions — but, as a class, they are the most despicable characters our State contains. This is not peculiar to Virginia. In the Northern States as well as in the Southern — indeed, everywhere — this is the true state of facts; and we were not surprised, therefore, to see a *free* State refuse admission to the Randolph negroes. Without, then, going the length of declaring that Slavery *in the abstract*— Slavery everywhere—is a blessing to the laboring classes, may we not candidly and calmly, and upon the maturest and soberest reflection, say that to the black race of the Union it is a blessing, and perhaps the greatest blessing we can now confer upon them?"

From the Richmond Examiner, 1854.

"It is all a hallucination to suppose that we are ever going to get rid of African Slavery, or that it will ever be desirable to do so. It is a thing that we cannot do without, that is *righteous, profitable*, and permanent, and that belongs to Southern society as inherently, intricately, and durably as the white race itself. Yea, the white race will itself emigrate from the Southern States to Africa, California, or Polynesia, sooner than the African.

"Let us make up our minds, therefore, to put up with and make the most of the institution. Let us not bother our brains about what *Providence* intends to do with our negroes in the distant future, but glory in and profit to the utmost by what He has done for them in transplanting them here, and setting them to work on our plantations. Let the politicians and planters of the South, while encouraging the 'Baptists and Methodists,' (and other denominations having a less number of votes), in Christianizing the negro, keep their slaves at hard work, under strict discipline, out of idleness and mischief, while they live; and, when they come to die, instead of sending them off to Africa, or manumitting them to a life of "freedom," licentiousness, and nuisance, will them over to their children, or direct them to be sold where they will be made to work hard, and be of service to their masters, and to the country. True philanthropy to the negro, begins, like charity, at home; and if Southern men would act as if the canopy of heaven were inscribed with a covenant, in letters of fire, that *the negro is here, and here forever; is our property, and ours forever; is never to be emancipated; is to be kept hard at work, and in rigid subjection all his days;* and is never to go to Africa, to Polynesia, or to Yankee Land (far worse than either), they would accomplish more good for the race in five years than they boast the institution itself to have accomplished in two centuries, and cut up by the roots a set of evils and fallacies that threaten to drive the white race a wandering in the western wilderness, sooner than Cuffee will go to preach the Gospel in Guinea."

I think these notions, if the policy of the State shall continue in accordance with them, will be proved to the satisfaction of all Northerners—all who do not trade with Virginia, at least—to be delusions, and fatal ones, before another seventy-nine years of the Republic is accomplished.

And that these papers do give a fair expression to

the views and purposes of the present governing influence in Virginia, there is every reason to believe. Not of the majority of the people—they are not quite so demented yet—but of the majority of those whose monopoly of wealth and knowledge has a governing influence on a majority of the people: in a word, of those among the educated and wealthy slaveholders, whose combined patronage and talent, applied with an energy and facility for political labor, unknown to the more conscientious and liberal, is sufficient to make everybody else's interest dependent upon and subservient to their own.

There are certainly, in the State of Virginia, a very large number of voters, strongly desirous, either from selfish or other motives, that the State should be freed from Slavery. I have conversed with enough myself almost to form a respectable party; and if a party, for that purpose, could once be thoroughly organized and equipped, and its aims well advertised, I have not the least doubt that a majority of the voters of the State would rejoice to enlist in it. But, suppose a man could have been found, with the necessary audacity to offer himself as a candidate to the people on this ground, in opposition alike to the Know Nothings and those who, with artful absurdity, assumed the name of Democrats, at the late election. There is not, probably, one newspaper in the State that could have afforded to support him. If there is, it is published at a manufacturing town, and within a stone's throw of a free State, and where, consequently, there are few, if any, resident slave-owners. If he had attempted to make the rural population acquainted with his plan, he would have had to do so, literally, by hunting them up, one by one. All the ordinary means of collecting assemblages would have been denied him, or he would have been able to make use of them only at very unusual expense. The poor traders and mechanics could not generally have afforded to listen to him, much less to vote for him, because, there being no vote by ballot in Virginia, it would be immediately known; they would be denounced as Abolitionists, and, at least, the slave-holders, who are their most valued customers, would decline employing men who so opposed their interests. Under these circumstances, with all the newspapers and bar-room orators, and many of the pulpits industriously coupling the audacious candidate's purposes with every ridiculous and detestable doctrine, scheme, and "ism," to which a name has ever been fixed, it would appear, to the most conscientious and earnest opponent of Slavery, who yet gives himself the vexation and loss of remaining in the State, a perfect waste of his vote to give it to a man so evidently unable to command a general vote of any significance; and he would determine, probably, to give it where it would tell against the least objectionable of the candidates who stood some chance of being successful. If I had been a Virgininan, I should have voted myself for the gasconading mountebank who was elected governor, ambitious and expert for mischief as he certainly is, because I should have been conscientiously bound to prevent, as far as my vote would do it, the success of a party more directly opposed to Democratic principles than is that which disgraced itself by allowing him to be nominated as the exponent of its strength.

It can only be by affiliating itself with a party of great strength and success at the North, that a party opposed to the interest of the Slave stock-jobbers can get upon its legs in any Slave State. It must have a prestige of national success, to encourage the immense labor of sufficient organization for local success. Only by a resolute determination of the thinking men of the Democratic party in the free States, not to be driven from the Jeffersonian creed upon Slavery, can the Democratic party in Virginia be made responsive to the wants of the common people, or otherwise than obstructive in its action to their prosperity.

Railroads and guano seem, just now, to give much life and improvement to Virginia.

Railroads, badly as they are managed, must encourage activity and punctuality in the people, besides increasing the value of exports of the country through which they pass, and diminishing the cost of imports by lessening the above-sea freightage expenses. Beside which, they cannot be prevented from disseminating intelligence and stirring thought, and in this way they will do more than any school-system at present possible.

Guano not only increases the immediate crops, to which it is applied, very profitably, but may be made the means of rapidly and permanently restoring the fertility of exhausted soils. Where judiciously employed, as it is by most men of wealth and education, it will do much good; where ignorantly or improvidently employed, with a thought only of immediate returns, it will probably lead to a still greater exhaustion of the soil, and lessen the real wealth of the poor farmer. Thus it would seem likely to better the wealthy and intelligent, and eventually injure the lower class. It must be added that there is now a very strong and most judiciously conducted State Agricultural Society, and one of the best agricultural journals in the United States (the *Southern Planter*) is published at Richmond.

The Constitution of the State has been democratized lately, so that poor people may vote, but no sufficient system of instruction has been instituted; and, though great promises are now made, it is probable, as I have shown, that, while Slavery lasts, there never can be. The majority of the people will, therefore, continue to be amused and used by greedy and ambitious speculators in politics; and, unless the West is more intelligent than it has thus far shown itself to be, the State will yet, for an indefinite time, be wholly ruled by the slave-holders, and everything else will continue, as heretofore, to be sacrificed to what they suppose to be their interests.

But, on the whole, the condition of the people has certainly improved, since the Revolution, both in comfort and in intelligence; less so, very much, than in the Free States, yet very distinctly.

The diffusion of intelligence, and, with it, of wealth, is likely to be even more rapid in future, and must be expected, eventually, to result in a revolution and reorganization of society, with Free Trade in Labor as its corner-stone. Whether this process shall be spasmodic and bloody, or gradual and peaceful, will depend on the manner in which it is resisted. It may come this century, it may come the next. The sooner the better, if broader and more important interests are not too greatly endangered. For, if soon, Virginia might yet be the most attractive field of enterprise and industry in America, and would rapidly be occupied by an ambitious and useful laboring population—the parent of an intelligent and respectable people.

As things are, citizens of the free States, especially needing good land on which to use their labor, with a mild climate, and other advantages available in Virginia, might, perhaps, colonize in the vicinity of railroads, or of the Ohio, and its navigable tributaries, with advantage, if they could settle together in sufficient numbers to give business to various kinds of industry. Under no other circumstances can I recommend any one in the free States to choose in Virginia a residence for a family, unless a move southward be deemed peculiarly desirable, as offering a chance to prolong life, imperilled in our harsher atmospheres.

CHAPTER V

NORTH CAROLINA

The largest and best hotel in Norfolk had been closed, shortly before I was there, from want of sufficient patronage to sustain it, and I was obliged to go to another house which, though quite pretending, was very shamefully kept. The landlord paid scarcely the smallest attention to the wants of his guests, turned his back when inquiries were made of him, and replied insolently to complaints and requests. His slaves were far his superiors in manners and morals; but, not being one quarter in number what were needed, and consequently not being able to obey one quarter of the orders that were given them, their only study was to disregard, as far as they would be allowed to, all requisitions upon their time and labor. The smallest service could only be obtained by bullying or bribing. I had to make a bargain for every clean towel that I got during my stay.

I was first put in a very small room, in a corner of the house, next under the roof. The weather being stormy, and the roof leaky, water was frequently dripping from the ceiling upon the bed and driving in at the window, so as to stand in pools upon the floor.

There was no fire-place in the room; the ladies' parlor was usually crowded by ladies and their friends, among whom I had no acquaintance, and, as it was freezing cold, I was obliged to spend most of my time in the stinking bar-room, where the landlord, all the time, sat with his boon companions, smoking and chewing and talking obscenely.

This crew of old reprobates frequently exercised their indignation upon Mrs. Stowe, and other "Infidel abolitionists;" and, on Sunday, having all attended church, afterwards mingled with their ordinary ribaldry laudations of the "evangelical" character of the sermons they had heard.

On the night I arrived, I was told that I would be provided, the next morning, with a room in which I could have a fire, and a similar promise was given me every twelve hours, for five days, before I obtained it; then, at last, I had to share it with two strangers.

When I left, the same petty sponging operation was practised upon me as at Petersburg. The breakfast, for which half a dollar had been paid, was not ready until an hour after I had been called; and, when ready, consisted of cold salt fish; dried slices of bread and tainted butter; coffee, evidently made the day before and half re-warmed; no milk, the milkman not arriving so early in the morning, the servant said; and no sooner was I seated than the choice was presented to me, by the agitated book-keeper, of going without such as this, or of losing the train and so being obliged to stay in the house twenty-four hours longer.

Of course I dispensed with the breakfast, and hurried off with the porter, who was to take my baggage on a wheelbarrow to the station. The station was across the harbor, in Portsmouth. Notwithstanding all the haste I could communicate to him, we reached the ferry-landing just as the boat left, too late by three seconds. I looked at my watch; it lacked but twenty minutes of the time at which the landlord and the book-keeper and the breakfast-table waiter and the railroad company's advertisements had informed me that the train left. "Nebber mine, masser," said the porter, "dey won't go widout 'ou—Baltimore boat haant ariv yet; dey doan go till dat come in, sueh."

Somewhat relieved by this assurance, and by the arrival of others at the landing, who evidently expected to reach the train, I went into the market and bought a breakfast from the cake and fruit stalls of the negro-women.

In twenty minutes the ferry-boat returned, and after waiting some time at the landing, put out again; but when midway across the harbor, the wheels ceased to revolve, and for fifteen minutes we drifted with the tide. The fireman had been asleep, the fires had got low, and the steam given out. I observed that the crew, including the master or pilot, and the engineer, were all negroes.

We reached the railroad station about half an hour after the time at which the train should have left. There were several persons, prepared for travelling, waiting about it, but there was no sign of a departing train, and the ticket-office was not open. I paid the porter, sent him back, and was added to the number of the waiters.

The delay was for the Baltimore boat, which arrived in an hour after the time the train was advertised, unconditionally, to start, and the first forward movement was more than an hour and a half behind time. A brakeman told me this delay was not very unusual, and that an hour's waiting might be commonly calculated upon with safety.

The distance from Portsmouth to Weldon, N. C., eighty miles, was run in three hours and twenty minutes—twenty-five miles an hour. The road, which was formerly a very poor and unprofitable one, was bought up a few years ago, mainly, I believe, by Boston capital, and reconstructed in a substantial manner. The grades are light, and there are few curves. Fare 2¾ cents a mile.

At a way-station, a trader had ready a company of negroes, intended to be shipped South; but the "servants' car" being quite full already, they were obliged to be left for another train. As we departed from the station, I stood upon the platform of the rear car with two other men. One said to the other:

"That's a good lot of niggers."

"Damn'd good; I only wish they belonged to me."

I entered the car and took a seat, and presently they followed, and sat near me. Continuing their conversation thus commenced, they spoke of their bad luck in life. One appeared to have been a bar-keeper; the other an overseer. One said the highest wages he had ever been paid were two hundred dollars a year, and that year he had n't laid up a cent. Soon after, the other, speaking with much energy and bitterness, said:

"I wish to God old Virginny was free of all the niggers."

"It would be a good thing if she was."

"Yes, sir; and, I tell you, it would be a damn'd good thing for us poor fellows."

"I reckon it would, myself."

When we stopped at Weldon, a man was shouting from a stage-coach, "Passengers for Gaston! Hurry up! Stage is waiting!" As he repeated this the third time, I threw up to him my two valises, and proceeded to climb to the box, to take my seat.

"You are in a mighty hurry, aint ye!"

"Did n't you say the stage was waiting?"

"If ye'r goin' ter get any dinner to-day, you'd better get it here; won't have much other chance. Be right smart about it, too."

"Then you are not going yet?"

"You can get yer dinner, if ye want to."

"You'll call me, will you, when you are ready to go?"

"I shan't go without ye, ye need n't be afeard—go 'long in, and get yer dinner; this is the place, if any-war;—don't wan't to go without yer dinner, do ye?"

Before arriving at Weldon, a handbill, distributed by the proprietors of this inn, had been placed in my hands, from which I make the following extracts:

"We pledge our word of honor, as gentlemen, that if the fare at our table be inferior to that on the table of our enterprising competitor, we will not receive a cent from the traveller, but relinquish our claims to pay, as a merited forfeit, for what we would regard as a wanton imposition upon the rights and claims of the unsuspecting traveller.

"We have too much respect for the Ladies of our House, to make even a remote allusion to their domestic duties in a public circular. It will not, however, be regarded indelicate in us to say, that the duties performed by them have been, and are satisfactory to us, and, as far as we know, to the public. And we will only add, in this connection, that we take much pleasure in superintending both our 'Cook-House' and Table in person, and in administering in person to the wants of our guests.

"We have made considerable improvements in our House of late, and those who wish to remain over at Weldon, will find, with us, airy rooms, clean beds, brisk fires, and attentive and orderly servants, with abundance of FRESH OYSTERS during the season, and every necessary and luxury that money can procure.

"It is not our wish to deceive strangers nor others; and if, on visiting our House, they do not find things as here represented, they can publish us to the world as impostors, and the ignominy will be ours."

Going into the house, I found most of the passengers by the train at dinner, and the few negro boys and girls in too much of a hurry to pay attention to any one in particular. The only palatable viand within my reach was some cold sweet-potatoes; of these I made a slight repast, paid the landlord, who stood like a sentry in the doorway, half a dollar, and in fifteen minutes, by my watch, from the time I had entered, went out, anxious to make sure of my seat on the box, for the coach was so small that but one passenger could be conveniently carried outside. The coach was gone.

"O, yes, sir," said the landlord, hardly disguising

his satisfaction; "gone—yes, sir, some time ago; you was in to dinner, was you, sir—pity! you 'll have to stay over till to-morrow now, won't you?"

"I suppose so," said I, hardly willing to give up my intention to sleep in Raleigh that night, even to secure a clean bed and fresh oysters. "Which road does the stage go upon?"

"Along the county road."

"Which is that—this way through the woods?"

"Yes, sir.—Carried off your baggage, did he?—Pity Suppose he forgot you. Pity!"

"Thank you—yes, I suppose he did. Is it a pretty good road?"

"No, sir, 't aint first-rate—good many pretty bad slews. You might go round by the Petersburg Railroad to-morrow. You 'd overtake your baggage at Gaston."

"Thank you. It was not a very fast team, I know. I 'm going to take a little run; and, if I should n't come back before night, you need n't keep a bed for me. Good-day, sir."

I am pretty good on the legs for a short man, and it did n't take me long, by the *pas gymnastique*, to overtake the coach.

As I came up, the driver hailed me:—

"Hallo! that you?"

"Why did not you wait for me, or call me when you wanted to go, as you promised?"

"Reckoned ye was inside—did n't look in, coz I asked if 't was all right, and somebody—this 'ere gentleman, here"—(who had got my seat) "'Yes,' says he, 'all right;' so I reckoned 't was, and driv along. Must n't blame me. Ort n't to be so long swallerin' yer dinner—mind, next time!"

The road was as bad as anything, under the name of a road, can be conceived to be. Wherever the adjoining swamps, fallen trees, stumps, and plantation fences would admit of it, the coach was driven, with a great deal of dexterity, out of the road. When the wheels sunk in the mud, below the hubs, we were sometimes requested to get out and walk. An upset seemed every moment inevitable. At length, it came; and the driver, climbing on to the upper side, opened the door, and asked, with an irresistibly jolly drawl:

"Got mixed up some in here then, did n't ye? Ladies, hurt any? Well, come, get out here; don't wan't to stay here all night I reckon, do ye?—Aint nothing broke, as I see. We 'll right her right up. Nary durn'd rail within a thousan' mile, I don't s'pose; better be lookin' roun'; got to get somethin' for a pry."

In four hours after I left the hotel at Weldon, the coach reached the bank of the Roanoke, a distance of fourteen miles, and stopped. "Here we are," said the driver, opening the door.

"Where are we—not in Gaston?"

"Durned nigh it. That ere 's Gaston, over thar; and you just holler, and they 'll come over arter you in the boat."

Gaston was a mile above us, and on the other side of the river. Nearly opposite to where we were was a house, and a scow drawn up on the beach; the distance across the river was, perhaps, a quarter of a mile. When the driver had got the luggage off, he gathered his reins, and said:

"Seems to me them gol-durned lazy niggers aint a goin' to come over arter you now; if they won't, you 'd better go up to the railroad bridge, some of ye, and get a boat, or else go down here to Free-town; some of them cussed free niggers 'll be glad of the job, I no doubt."

"But, confound it, driver! you are not going to leave us here, are you? we paid to be carried to Gaston."

"Can't help it; you are close to Gaston, anyhow, and if any man thinks he 's goin' to hev me drive him up to the bridge to-night, he 's damnably mistaken, he is, and I ain't a goin' to do it, not for no man, I ain't."

And away he drove, leaving us, all strangers, in a strange country, just at the edge of night, far from any house, to "holler."

The only way to stop him was to shoot him; and, as we were all good citizens, and travelled with faith in the protection of the law, and not like knights-errant, armed for adventure, we could not do that.

Good citizens? No, we were not; for we have all, to this day, neglected to prosecute the fellow, or his employers. It would, to be sure, have cost us ten times any damages we should have been awarded; but, if we had been really good citizens, we should have been as willing to sacrifice the necessary loss as knights-errant of old were to risk life to fight bloody giants. And, until many of us can have the nobleness to give ourselves the trouble and expense of killing off these impudent highwaymen of our time, at law, we have all got to suffer in their traps and stratagems.

We soon saw the " gol-durned lazy niggers " come to their scow, and after a scrutiny of our numbers, and a consultation among themselves, which evidently resulted in the conclusion that the job would n't pay, go back.

When it began to grow dark, leaving me as a baggage-guard, the rest of the coach's company walked up the bank of the river, and crossed by a railroad bridge to Gaston. One of them afterwards returned with a gang of negroes, whom he had hired, and a large freight-boat, into which, across the snags which lined the shore, we passed all the baggage. Among the rest, there were some very large and heavy chests, belonging to two pretty women, who were moving, with their effects; and, although they remained in our company all the next day, they not only neglected to pay their share of the boat and negro-hire, but forgot to thank us, or even gratefully to smile upon us, for our long toil in the darkness for them.

Working up the swollen stream of the Roanoke, with setting-poles and oars, we at length reached Gaston. When I bought my tickets at the station in Portsmouth, I said: " I will take tickets to any place this side of Raleigh at which I can arrive before night. I wish to avoid travelling after dark." " You can go straight through to Raleigh, before dark," said the clerk. "You are sure of that?" "Yes, sir." On reaching Gaston, I inquired at what time the train for Raleigh had passed: "At three o'clock." According to the advertisement, it should have passed at two o'clock; and, under the most favorable circumstances, it could not have been possible for us, leaving Portsmouth at the time we did, to reach Gaston before four o'clock, or Raleigh in less than twenty-eight hours after the time promised. The next day, I asked one of the railroad men how often the connection occurred, which is advertised in the Northern papers, as if it were a certain thing to take place at Gaston. "Not very often, sir; it hain't been once, in the last two weeks." Whenever the connection is not made, all passengers whom these railroad freebooters have drawn into their ambush, are obliged to remain over a day, at Gaston; for, as is to be supposed, with such management, the business of the road will support but one train a day.

The route by sea, from Baltimore to Portsmouth, and thence by these lines, is advertised as the surest, cheapest, and most expeditious route to Raleigh. Among my stage companions, were some who lived beyond Raleigh. This was Friday. They would now not reach Raleigh till Saturday night, and such as could not conscientiously travel on Sunday, would be detained from home two days longer than if they had come the land route. One of them lived some eighty miles beyond Raleigh, and intended to proceed by a coach, which was to leave Saturday morning. He would probably be now detained till the following Wednesday, as the coach left Raleigh but twice a week.

The country from Portsmouth to Gaston, eighty miles, partly in Virginia, and partly in North Carolina, is almost all pine forest, or cypress swamp; and on the little land that is cultivated, I saw no indication of any other crop than maize. The soil is light and poor. Between Weldon and Gaston there are heavier soils, and we passed several cotton fields, and substantial planters' mansions. On the low, flat lands bordering the banks of the Roanoke, the soil is of the character of that of James River, fine, fertile, mellow loam; and the maize crop seemed to have been heavy.

Gaston is a village of some twenty houses, shops and cabins, besides the railroad store-houses, the hotel, and a nondescript building, which may be either a fancy barn, or a little church, getting high. From the manner in which passengers are forced, by the management of the trains arriving here, to patronize it, the hotel, I presume, belongs to the railroad companies. It is ill-kept, but affords some entertainment from its travesty of certain metropolitan vulgarities. I was chummed with a Southern gentleman, in a very small room. Finding the sheets on both our beds had been soiled by previous occupants, he made a row about it with the servants, and, after a long delay, had them changed; then, observing that it was probably the mistress's fault, and not the servants', he paid the negro whom he had been berating, for his trouble.

Among our inside passengers, in the stage-coach, was a free colored woman; she was treated in no way differently from the white ladies. My roommate said this was entirely customary at the South, and no Southerner would ever think of objecting to it. Notwithstanding which, I have known young Southerners to get very angry because negroes were not excluded from the public conveyances in which they had taken passage themselves, at the North; and I have always supposed that when they were so excluded, it was from fear of offending Southern travellers, more than anything else.

A South Carolina View of the Subject. (*Correspondence of Willis's Musical World, New York*).

"CHARLESTON, Dec. 31.

"I take advantage of the season of compliments (being a subscriber to your invaluable sheet), to tender you this scrap, as a reply to a piece in your paper of the 17th ult., with the caption: 'Intolerance of colored persons in New York.' The piece stated that up-town families (in New York) objected to hiring colored persons as servants, in consequence of 'conductors and drivers refusing to let them ride in city cars and omnibuses,' and colored boys, at most, may ride on the top. And after dwelling on this, you say, 'shame on such intolerant and outrageous prejudice and persecution of the colored race at the North!' You then say, 'Even the slaveholder would cry shame upon us.' You never made a truer assertion in your life. For you first stated that they were even rejected when they had white children in their arms. My dear friend, if this was the only persecution that your colored people were compelled to yield submission to, then I might say nothing. Are they allowed (if they pay) to sit at the tables of your fashionable hotels? Are they allowed a seat in the 'dress circle,' at your operas? Are they not subject to all kinds of ill-treatment from the whites? Are they not pointed at, and hooted at by the whites (natives of the city), when dressed up a little extra, and if they offer a reply, are immediately overpowered by gangs of whites? You appear to be a reasonable writer, which is the reason I put these queries, knowing they can only be answered in the affirmative.

"We at the South feel proud to allow them to occupy seats in our omnibuses (public conveyances), while they, with the affection of mothers, embrace our white children, and take them to ride. And in our most fashionable carriages, you will see the slaves sitting alongside of *their owner*. You will see the slave clothed in the most comfortable of wearing apparel. And more. Touch that slave, if you dare, and you will see the owner's attachment. And thus, in a very few words, you have the contrast between the situation of the colored people at the North and South. Do teach the *detestable* Abolitionist of the North his duty, and open his eyes to the misery and starvation that surrounds his own home. *Teach him* to love his brethren of the South, and teach him to let Slavery alone in the South, while starvation and destitution surrounds him at the North; and oblige,

"BARON."

Listening to a conversation among some men lounging on the river-bank, and who were, probably, brakemen or engineers on the railroads, I took notes of the following interesting information:

"Nitrate of silver is a first-rater; you can get it at the 'pothecary shops in Richmond. But the best medicine there is, is this here Idee of Potasun. It's made out of two minerals; one on 'em they gets in the mountains of Scotland—that's the Idee; the other's steel-filings, and they mixes them eschemically until they works altogether into a solid stuff like saltpetre. Now, I tell you that's the stuff for medicine. It's the best thing a man can ever put into his self. It searches out every narve in his body."

The train by which we were finally able to leave Gaston arrived the next day an hour and a half after its advertised time. The road was excellent and speed good, a heavy U rail having lately been substituted for a flat one. A new equipment of the road, throughout, is nearly complete. The cars of this train were very old, dirty, and with dilapidated and moth-eaten furniture. They furnished me with a comfort, however, which I have never been able to try before—a full-length lounge, on which, with my overcoat for a pillow, the car being warmed, and, unintentionally well ventilated, I slept soundly after dark. Why night-trains are not furnished with sleeping apartments, has long been a wonder to me. We have now smoking-rooms and water-closets on our trains; why not sleeping, dressing, and refreshment rooms? With these additions, and good ventilation, we could go from New York to New Orleans by rail without stopping: as it is, a man of ordinary constitution cannot go a quarter that distance without suffering serious indisposition. Surely such improvements could not fail to be remunerative, particularly on lines competing with water communication.

The country passed through, so far as I observed, was almost entirely covered with wood; and such of it as was cultivated, very unproductive.

The city of Raleigh (old Sir Walter), the capital of North Carolina, is a pleasing town—the streets wide and lined with trees, and many white wooden mansions, all having little courtyards of flowers and shrubbery around them. The State-House is, in every way, a noble building, constructed of brownish-gray granite, in Grecian style. It stands on an elevated position, near the centre of the city, in a square field, which is shaded by some tall old oaks, and could easily be made into an appropriate and beautiful little park; but which, with singular negligence, or more singular economy (while $500,000 has been spent upon the simple edifice), remains in a rude state of undressed nature, and is used as a hog-pasture. A trifle of the expense, employed with doubtful advantage, to give a smooth exterior face to the blocks of stone, if laid out in grading, smoothing, and dressing its ground base, would have added indescribably to the beauty of the edifice. An architect should always begin his work upon the ground.

There are several other public buildings and institutions of charity and education, honorable to the State. A church, near the Capitol, not yet completed, is very beautiful; cruciform in ground plan, the walls of stone, and the interior wood-work of oiled native pine, and with, thus far, none of the irreligious falsities in stucco and paint that so generally disenchant all expression of worship in our city meeting-houses.

It is hard to admire what is common; and it is, perhaps, asking too much of the citizens of Raleigh, that they should plant for ornament, or even cause to be retained about such institutions as their Lunatic Asylum, the beautiful evergreens that crowd about the town; but can any man walk from the Capitol oaks to the pine grove, a little beyond the Deaf and Dumb Institution, and say that he would not far rather have the latter than the former to curtain in his habitation? If he can in summer, let him try it again, as I did, on a soft winter's day, when the evergreens fill the air with a balsamic odor, and the green light comes quivering through them, and the foot falls silently upon the elastic carpet they have spread, deluding one with all the feelings of spring.

The country, for miles about Raleigh, is nearly all pine forest, unfertile, and so little cultivated, that it is a mystery how a town of 2500 inhabitants can obtain sufficient supplies from it to exist.

The public-house at which I stayed was, however, not only well supplied, but was excellently well kept, for a house of its class, in all other respects. The landlord superintended his business personally, and was always attentive and obliging to his guests; and the servants were sufficiently numerous, intelligent, and well instructed. Though I had no acquaintances in Raleigh, I remained, finding myself in such good quarters, several days. I think the house was called "The Burlinghame."

After this stay, rendered also partly necessary for the repair of damages to my clothing and baggage on the Weldon stage, I engaged a seat one day on the coach, advertised to leave at nine o'clock for Fayetteville. At half-past nine, tired of waiting for its departure, I told the agent, as it was not ready to start, I would walk on a bit, and let them pick me up. I found a rough road—for several miles a clayey surface and much water—and was obliged to pick my way a good deal through the woods on either side. Stopping frequently, when I came to cultivated land, to examine the soil and the appearance of the stubble of the maize—the only crop—in three different fields I made five measurements at random, of fifty feet each, and found the stalks had stood, on an average, five feet by two feet one inch apart, and that, generally, they were not over an inch in diameter at the butt. In one old field, in process of clearing for new cultivation, I examined a most absurd little plough, with a share not more than six inches in depth, and eight in length on the sole, fastened by a socket to a stake, to which was fitted a short beam and stilts. It was drawn by one mule, and its work among the stumps could only be called scratching. A farmer told me that he considered twenty-five bushels of corn a large crop, and that he generally got as much as fifteen. He said that no money was to be got by raising corn, and very few farmers here " made " any more than they needed for their own force. It cost too much to get it to market, and yet sometimes they had had to buy corn at a dollar a bushel, and wagon it home from Raleigh, or further, enough not having been raised in the country for home consumption. Cotton was the only crop they got any money for. I, nevertheless, did not see a single cotton-field during the day. He said that the largest crop of corn that he knew of, reckoned to be fifty bushels to the acre, had been raised on some reclaimed swamp, while it was still so wet that horses would mire on it all the summer, and most of it had been tended entirely with hoes.

A very fine oak tree, standing by itself on some elevated ground, having attracted me to a considerable distance from the road, I found that the spread of its branches covered a circle of the diameter of forty-two paces.

After walking a few miles, the country became more flat, and was covered with old forests of yellow pine, and, at nine miles south of Raleigh, there were occasionally young long-leaved pines: exceedingly beautiful they are while young, the color being more agreeable than that of any other pine, and the leaves, or *straw*, as its foliage is called here, long, graceful, and lustrous. As the tree gets older, it becomes of a stiffer character and darker color.

I do not think I passed, in ten miles, more than half a dozen homesteads, and of these but one was above the character of a hut or cabin.

A little after one o'clock I reached "Banks's," a plantation where the stage horses are changed, eleven miles from Raleigh; and the coach not having arrived, I asked for something to eat. A lunch was prepared for me in about fifteen minutes. There was nothing on the table, when I was invited to it, except some cold salt pork and pickled beets; but as long as I remained, at intervals of two or three minutes, additions would be made, till at last there had accumulated five different preparations of swine's flesh, and two or three of corn, most of them just cooked; the only vegetable, pickled beets.

Before I finished my repast, the coach arrived, and I took my seat.

"All right?" asked the driver.

"You have n't changed your horses."

"Goin' ter change the wheelers on top the hill; horses in the field there."

Having reached the hill top, the change was effected —a change, but no improvement. The fresh horses could do but little more than stand up; there was not one among them that would have sold for twenty-five dollars in New York. "There ain't a man in North Car'lina could drive them horses up the hills without a whip," said the driver. "You ought to get yeself a whip, massa," said one of the negroes. "*Durnation!* think I 'm going to buy whips; the best whip in North Car'lina would n't last a week on this road." "Dat's a fac—dat ar is a fac; but look yeah, massa, ye let me hab yer stick, and I 'll make a whip for ye; ye nebber can make Bawley go widout it, nohow." The stick was a sapling rod, of which two or three lay on the coach top; the negro fastened a long leather thong to it. "Dah! ye can fetch old Bawley wi' dat." "Bawley" had been tackled in as the leader of the "spike team;" but, upon attempting to start, it was found that he could n't be driven in that way at all, and the driver took him out and put him to the pole, within reach of the butt of his stick, and another horse was put on the lead.

One negro now took the leader by the head, and applied a stick lustily to his flanks; another, at the near wheeler, did the same; and the driver belabored Bawley from the box. But as soon as they began to move forward, and the negro let go the leader's head, he would face about. After this had been repeated many times, a new plan of operations was arranged that proved successful. Leaving the two wheelers to the care of the negroes, the driver was enabled to give all his attention to the leader. When the wheelers started, of course he was struck by the pole, upon which he would turn tail and start for the stable. The negroes kept the wheelers from following him, and the driver with his stick, and another negro with the bough of a tree, thrashed his face; he would then turn again, and, being hit by the pole, start ahead. So, after ten minutes of fearful outcry, we got off.

"How far is it to Mrs. Barclay's?" a passenger had asked. "Thirteen miles," answered a negro; "but I tell 'ou, massa, dais a heap to be said and talk 'bout 'fore 'ou see Missy Barclay's wid dem hosses." There was, indeed.

"Bawley—*you!* Bawley—Bawley! wha' 'bout?—ah!"

"*Rock!* wha' you doin'?—(durned sick horse—an't fit to be in a stage, nohow)."

"Bawley! you! g'up!"

"Oh! you dod-rotted Bob—*Bob!*—(he don't draw a pound, and he an't a goin' to)—*you*, Bob!—(well, he can't *stop, can he*, as long as the wheelers keep movin'?) Bob! I'll break yer legs, you don't git out the way."

"Oh, Bawley!—(no business to put such a lame hoss

into the stage.) Blamnation, Bawley! Now, if you stop, I'll kill you."

"Wha' 'bout, Rock? Dod burn that Rock! You stop if you dare! (I'll be durned to Hux if that ere hoss arn't all used up.)"

"You, *Bob!* get out de way, or I'll be——."

"Oh! d'rot yer soul, Bawley—y're goin' to stop! G'up! G'up! *Rock!* You all-fired ole villain! Wha' 'bout? (If they jus' git to stoppin', all hell could n't git the mails through to-night.)"

After about three miles of this, they did stop. The driver threw the reins down in despair. After looking at the wheels, and seeing that we were on a good piece of road, nothing unusual to hinder progress, he put his hands in his pockets, and sat quietly a minute, and then began, in a business-like manner, to swear, no longer confining himself to the peculiar idiomatic profanity of the country, but using real, outright, old-fashioned, uncompromising English oaths, as loud as he could yell. Then he stopped, and, after another pause, began to talk quietly to the horses:

"You, Bob, you won't draw? Did n't you git enough last night? (I jabbed my knife into his face twice when we got into that fix last night;" and the wounds on the horse's head showed that he spoke the truth.) "I swar, Bob, if I have to come down thar, I'll *cut your throat.*"

He stopped again, and then sat down on the foot-board, and began to beat the wheelers as hard and as rapidly as possible with the butt of his stick. They started, and, striking Bob with the pole, he jumped and turned round; but a happy stroke on "the raw" in his face brought him to his place; and the stick being applied just in time to the wheelers, he caught the pole and jumped ahead. We were off again.

"Turned over in that 'ere mire hole last night," said the driver. "Could n't do anythin' with 'em—passengers camped out—thar's where they had their fire, under that tree; did n't get to Raleigh till nine o'clock this mornin'. That 's the reason I wern't along arter you any sooner—had n't got my breakfast; that 's the reason the hosses don't draw no better to-day, too, I s'pose. *You*, Rock!—*Bawley!*—BOB!

After two miles more, the horses stopped once more. The driver now quietly took the leader off (he had never drawn at all), and tied him behind the coach. He then began beating the near-wheeler, a passenger did the same to Bawley—both standing on the ground —while I threw off my overcoat and walked on. For a time I could occasionally hear the cry, "Bawl— Rock!" and knew that the coach was moving again; gradually I outwalked the sound.

I was now fairly in the Turpentine region of North Carolina. The road was a mere opening through a forest of the long-leafed pine; the trees from eight to eighteen inches in diameter, with straight trunks bare for nearly thirty feet, and their evergreen foliage forming a dense dark canopy at that height, the surface of the ground undulating with long swells, occasionally low and wet. In the latter case, there was generally a mingling of deciduous trees and a water-course crossing the road, with a thicket of shrubs. The soil sandy, with occasionally veins of clay; the latter more commonly in the low ground, or in the descent to it. Very little grass, herbage, or under-wood; and the ground covered, except in the road, with the fallen pine-leaves. Every tree, on one, two, or three sides, was scarified for turpentine. In ten miles, I passed half a dozen cabins, one or two small clearings, in which corn had been planted, and one turpentine distillery, with a dozen sheds and cabins clustered about it.

In about an hour after I left the coach, the driver, mounted on Bob, overtook me: he was going on to get fresh horses.

After dark, I had some difficulty in keeping the road, there being frequent forks, and my only guide the telegraph wire. I had to cross three or four brooks, which were now high, and had sometimes floated off the logs which, in this country, are commonly placed, for the teamsters, along the side of the road, where it runs through water. I could generally jump from stump to stump; and, by wading a little at the edges in my staunch Scotch shooting boots, get across dry-shod. Where, however, the water was too deep, I always found, by going up or down stream, a short way, a fallen trunk across it, by which I got over.

I met the driver returning with two fresh horses; and at length, before eight o'clock, reached a long one-story cabin, which I found to be Mrs. Barclay's. It was right cheerful and comforting to open the door, from the dark, damp, chilly night, into a large room, filled with blazing light from a great fire of turpentine pine, by which two stalwart men were reading newspapers, a door opening into a background of supper-table and kitchen, and a nice, stout, kindly-looking, Quaker-like old lady coming forward to welcome me.

As soon as I was warm, I was taken out to supper: seven preparations of swine's flesh, two of maize, wheat cakes, broiled quails, cold roast turkey, coffee, and tea.

My bed-room was a house by itself, the only connection between it and the main building being a platform, or gallery, in front. A great fire burned here also in a broad fire-place; a stuffed easy-chair had been placed before it, and a tub of hot water, which I had not thought to ask for, to bathe my weary feet.

And this was a piny-woods stage-house! But genius will find its development, no matter where its lot is cast; and there is as much a genius for hospitality as for poetry. Mrs. Barclay is a Burns in her way, and with even more modesty; for, after twenty-four hours of the best entertainment that could be asked for, I was only charged one dollar. I paid two dollars for my stage-coach privileges—to wit, riding five miles and walking twenty-one.

At three o'clock in the morning, the three gentlemen that I had left ten miles back at four o'clock the previous day, were dragged, shivering in the stage-coach, to the door. They had had no meal since breakfasting at Raleigh; and one of them was now so tired that he could not eat, but lay down on the floor before the fire and slept the half hour they were changing horses, or rather resting horses, for there was nothing left to change to.

I afterwards met one of the company in Fayetteville. Their night's adventure after I left them, and the continued cruelty to the horses, were really most distressing. The driver once got off the box, and struck the poor, miserable, sick "Rock" with a rail, and actually knocked him down in the road. At another time, after having got the fresh horses, when they, too, were "stalled," he took them out of the harness and turned them loose, and, refusing to give any answer to the inquiries of the passengers, looked about for a dry place, and laid down and went to sleep on the ground. One of the passengers had then walked on to Mrs. Barclay's, and obtained a pair of mules, with which the coach was finally brought to the house. The remainder kindled a fire, and tried to rest themselves by it. They were sixteen hours in coming thirty miles, suffering much from cold, and without food.

The next day I spent in visiting turpentine and rosin works, piny-wood farms, etc., under the obliging guidance of Mrs. Barclay's son-in-law, and in the evening again took the coach. The horses were better than on the previous stage: upon my remarking this to the driver, he said that the reason was, that they took care of this team themselves (the drivers); on the last stage the horses were left to negroes, who would not feed them regularly, nor take any decent care of them. "Why, what do you think?" said he, "when I got to

Banks's, this morning, I found my team had n't been fed all day; they had n't been rubbed nor cleaned, nary durned thing done to 'em, and thar the cussed darkey was, fast asleep. Reckon I did n't gin him a wakin' up!"

"You don't mean the horses that you drove up?"

"Yes, I do, and they had n't a cussed thing to eat till they got back to Barclay's!"

"How was it possible for you to drive them back?"

"Why, I don't suppose I could ha' done it if I'd had any passengers: (you *Suze!*) shall lose a mail again to-night, if this mare don't travel better, (durn ye, yer ugly, I believe). She's a good mare—a heap of go in her, but it takes right smart of work to get it out. *Suze!*"

So we toiled on, with incessant shouting, and many strange piny-wood oaths, and horrid belaboring of the poor horses' backs, with the butt-end of a hickory whip-stalk, till I really thought their spinal-columns must break. The country, the same undulating pine forest, the track tortuous among the trees, which frequently stood so close that it required some care to work between them. Often we made detours from the original road to avoid a fallen tree, or a mire-hole, and all the time we were bouncing over protruding roots and small stumps. There was but little mud, the soil being sand, but now and then a deep slough. In one of these we found a wagon, heavily laden, stuck fast, and six mules and five negroes tugging at it. With our help it was got out of the way, and we passed on.

Soon afterwards we met the return coach, apparently in a similar predicament; but one of the passengers, whom I questioned, replied: "No, not stalled, exactly, but somehow *the horses won't draw.* We have been more than three hours coming about four miles."

"How is it you have so many balky horses?" I asked the driver.

"The old man buys 'em up cheap, 'cause nobody else can do anything with 'em."

"I should not think you could do much with them, either—except to kill them."

"Well, that's what the old man says he buys 'em for. He was blowing me up for losing the mail t'other night; I told him, says I, 'you have to a'most kill them horses, 'fore you can make 'em draw a bit,' says I. 'Kill 'em, damn 'em, kill 'em, then; that's what I buy 'em for,' says he. 'I buy 'em a purpose to kill; that's all they are good for, ain't it?' says he. 'Don't s'pose they're going to last forever, do ye?' says he."

We stopped once, nearly half an hour, for some unexplained reason, before a house on the road. The door of the house was open, an enormous fire was burning in it, and, at the suggestion of the driver, I went in to warm myself. It was a large log-cabin, of two rooms, with beds in each room, and with an apartment overhead, to which access was had by a ladder. Among the inmates were two women; one of them sat at the chimney-corner, smoking a pipe, and rocking a cradle; the other sat directly before the fire, and full ten feet distant. She was apparently young, but her face was as dry and impassive as a dead man's. She was doing nothing, and said but little; but, once in about a minute, would suddenly throw up her chin, and spit with perfect precision across the ten feet range, into the hottest embers of the fire. The furniture of the house was more scanty and rude than I ever saw before in any house, with women living in it, in the United States. Yet these people were not so poor but that they had a negro woman cutting and bringing wood for their fire.

It must be remembered that this is a long-settled country, having been occupied by Anglo-Saxons as early as any part of the Free States.

There is nothing that is more closely connected, both as cause and effect, with the prosperity and wealth of a country, than its means and modes of travelling, and of transportation of the necessities and luxuries of life. I saw this day, as I shall hereafter describe, three thousand barrels, of an article worth a dollar and a half a barrel in New York, thrown away, a mere heap of useless offal, because it would cost more to transport it than it would be worth. There was a single wagon, with a ton or two of sugar, and flour, and tea, and axes, and cotton cloths, unable to move, with six mules and five negroes at work upon it. Raleigh is a large distributing post-office, getting a very heavy mail from the North; here was all that is sent by one of its main radii, travelling one day two miles an hour, the next four miles, and on each occasion failing to connect with the conveyances which we pay to scatter further the intelligence and wealth transmitted by it. Barbarous is too mild a term to apply to the manner in which even this was done. The improvidence, if not the cruelty, no sensible barbarian could have been guilty of.

Afterwards, merely to satisfy my mind (for there is a satisfaction in seeing even scoundrelism consistently carried out, if attempted at all in a business), I called on the agent of the line at Fayetteville, stated the case, and asked if any part of what I had paid for my passage would be returned me, on account of the disappointment and delay which I had suffered from the inability of the proprietor to carry out his contract with me. The impudence of the suggestion, of course, only created amusement; and I was smilingly informed that the business was not so "lucky" that the proprietor could afford to pay back money that he had once got into his hands.

At one of the stations for changing horses, an old colored man was taken into the coach. I ascertained from him that he was a blacksmith, and had been up the line to shoe the horses at the different stables. Probably he belonged (poor fellow) to the man who bought horses to be killed in doing his work. After answering my inquiries, he lay down in the bottom of the coach, and slept until we reached Fayetteville. The next time we changed, the new driver inquired of the old one what passengers he had. "Only one gentleman, and old man Ned."

"Oh! is old man along—that's good—if we should turn over, or break down, or anything, reckon the could nigh about pray us up — he's right smart at prayin'."

"Well, I tell you, now, ole man can trot out as smart a prayer, when he's a mind to go in for't, as any man I ever heerd, durned if he can't."

The last ten miles we came over rapidly, smoothly, and quietly, by a plank-road, reaching Fayetteville about twelve, of a fine, clear, frosty night.

Entering the office or bar-room of the stage-house, at which I had been advised to stay while in Fayetteville, I found it occupied by a group of old soakers, among whom was one of perhaps sixteen years of age. This lad, without removing the cigar which he had in his mouth, went to the bar, whither I followed him, and, without saying a word, placed an empty tumbler before me.

"I don't wish anything to drink," said I; "I am cold and tired, and I would like to go to a room. I intend to stay here some days, and I should be glad if you could give me a private room, and I should like to have a fire in it."

"Room with a fire in it?" he inquired, as he handed me the registry-book.

"Yes, and I will thank you to have it made immediately, and let my baggage be taken up."

He closed the book, after I had written my name, and returned to his seat at the stove, leaving me standing, and immediately engaged in conversation, without paying any attention to my request. I waited some time, during which a negro came into the room, and went out again. I then repeated my request, necessarily aloud, and in such a way as to be understood, not only by the boy, but by all the company. Immediately all conversation ceased, and every head was turned to look at me. Some faces showed evident signs of amusement. The lad paused a moment, spit upon the stove, and then:

"Want a room to yourself?"

"Yes, if convenient, and with a fire in it."

No answer and no movement, all the company staring at me as if I was a detected burglar.

"Perhaps you can't accommodate me?"

"Want a fire made in your room?"

"Why, yes, if convenient; but I should like to go to my room, at any rate; I am very tired."

After puffing and spitting for a moment, he rose and pulled a bell; then took his seat again. In about five minutes a negro came in, and during all this time there was silence.

"What 'll you drink, Baker," said the lad, rising and going to the bar, and taking no notice of the negro's entrance. A boozy man followed him, and made some reply; the lad turned out two glasses of spirits, added water to one, and drank it in a gulp.[1]

---

[1] The mother of this young man remonstrated with a friend of mine, for permitting his son to join a company of civil engineers, engaged, at the time, in surveying a route for a road—he would be subject to such fatiguing labor, and so much exposure to the elements; and congratulated herself that her own child was engaged in such an easy and gentleman-like employment as that of hotel-clerk and bar-keeper.

"Can this boy show me to my room?" I asked.

"Anybody in number eleven, Peter?"

"Not as I knows on, sar."

"Take this man's baggage up there."

I followed the negro up to number eleven, which was a large back room, in the upper story, with four beds in it.

"Peter," said I, "I want a fire made here."

"Want a fire, sar?"

"Yes, I want you to make a fire."

"Wan' a fire, master, this time o' night?"

"Why, yes! I want a fire! Where are you going with the lamp?"

"Want a lamp, massa?"

"Want a lamp? Certainly, I do."

After about ten minutes, I heard a man splitting wood in the yard, and, in ten more, Peter brought in three sticks of green wood, and some chips; then, the little bed-lamp having burned out, he went into an adjoining room, where I heard him talking to some one, evidently awakened by his entrance to get a match; that failing, he went for another. By one o'clock, my fire was made.

"Peter," said I, "are you going to wait on me, while I stay here?"

"Yes, sar; I 'tends to dis room."

"Very well; take this, and, when I leave, I 'll give you another, if you take good care of me. Now, I want you to get me some water."

"I 'll get you some water in de morning, sar."

"I want some to-night—some water and some towels; don't you think you can get them for me?"

"I reckon so, massa, if you wants 'em. Want 'em 'fore you go to bed?"

"Yes; and get another lamp."

"Want a lamp?"

"Yes, of course."

"Won't the fire do you?"

"No; bring a lamp. That one won't burn without filling; you need not try it."

The water and the lamp came, after a long time.

In the morning, early, I was awakened by a knock at the door.

"Who's there?"

"Me, massa; I wants your boots to black."

I got up, opened the door, and returned to bed. Falling asleep, I was soon again awakened by Peter throwing down an armful of wood upon the floor. Slept again, and was again awakened, by Peter's throwing up the window, to empty out the contents of the wash-bowl, etc. The room was filled with smoke of the fat light-wood: Peter had already made a fire for me to dress by; but I again fell asleep, and, when I next awoke, the breakfast-bell was ringing. Peter had gone off, and left both the window and the door open. The smoke had been blown out, and the fire had burned out. My boots had been taken away, and not returned; and the bell-wire was broken. I dressed, and walked to the bar-room in my stockings, and asked the bar-keeper—a polite, full-grown man—for my boots. He did not know where they were, and rang the bell for Peter. Peter came, was reprimanded for his forgetfulness, and departed. Ten minutes elapsed, and he did not return. I again requested that he should be called; and, this time, he came with my boots. He had had to stop to black them; having, he said, been too busy to do it before breakfast.

The following evening, as it grew too cold to write in my room, I went down, and found Peter, and told him I wanted a fire again, and that he might get me a couple of candles. When he came up, he brought one of the little bed-lamps, with a capacity of oil for fifteen minutes' use. I sent him down again to the office, with a request to the proprietor that I might be furnished with candles. He returned, and reported that there were no candles in the house.

"Then, get me a larger lamp."

"Aint no larger lamps, nuther, sar; — none to spare."

"Then go out, and see if you can't buy me some candles, somewhere."

"Aint no stores open, Sunday, massa, and I don't know where I can buy 'em."

"Then go down, and tell the bar-keeper, with my compliments, that I wish to write in my room, and I would be obliged to him if he would send me a light, of some sort; something that will last longer, and give more light, than these little lamps."

"He won't give you none, massa—not if you hab a fire. Can't you see by da light of da fire? When a gentleman hab a fire in his room, dey don't count he wants no more light 'n dat."

"Well, make the fire, and I 'll go down and see about it."

As I reached the foot of the stairs, the bell rang, and I went in to tea. The tea-table was moderately well lighted with candles. I waited till the company had generally left it, and then said to one of the waiters:

"Here are two dimes: I want you to bring me, as soon as you can, two of these candles to number eleven; do you understand?"

"Yes, sar; I 'll fotch 'em, sar."

And he did.

About eight o'clock, there was an alarm of fire. Going into the street, I was surprised to observe how leisurely the people were walking towards the house in flames, standing very prominently, as it did, upon a hill, at one end of the town. As I passed a church, the congregation was coming out; but very few quickened their step above a strolling pace. Arrived near the house, I was still more astonished to see how few, of the crowd assembled, were occupied in restraining the progress of the fire, or in saving the furniture, and at the prevailing stupidity, confusion, and want of system and concert of action, in the labor for this purpose. A large majority of those who were thus engaged were negroes. As I returned towards the hotel, a gentleman, walking, with a lady, before me, on the sidewalk, accosted a negro whom he met:

"What! Moses! That you? Why were you not here sooner?"

"Why, Mass Richard, I was a singing, an' I didn' her de bells and——I see twant in our ward, sar, and so I didn' see as dar was zactly 'casion for me to hurry mysef to def. Ef eed a been in our ward, Mass Richard, I 'd a rallied, you knows I would. Mose would ha rallied, ef eed a been in our ward—ha! ha! ha!—you knows it, Mass Richard!"

And he passed on, laughing comically, without further remark.

Turpentine is the crude sap of pine-trees. It varies somewhat, in character and in freedom of flow, with the different varieties; the long-leafed pine (*Pinus Palustris*) yielding it more freely than any other.

There are very large forests of this tree in North and South Carolina, Georgia, and Alabama; and the turpentine business is carried on, to some extent, in all these States. In North Carolina, however, much more largely than in the others; because, in it, cotton is rather less productive than in the others, in an average of years. Negroes are, therefore, in rather less demand; and their owners oftener see their profit in employing them in turpentine orchards than in the cotton-fields.

In the region in which the true turpentine-trees grow, indeed, there is no soil suitable for growing cotton; and it is only in the swampy parts, or on the borders of streams flowing through it, that there is any attempt at agriculture. The farmer, in the forest, makes nothing for sale but turpentine, and, when he cultivates the land, his only crop is maize; and of this, I was often told, not more than five bushels from an acre is usually obtained. Of course, no one would continue long to raise such crops, if he had wages to pay for the labor; but, having inherited or reared the laborers, the farmer does not often regard them as costing him anything more than what he has to pay for their clothes and food—which is very little.

Few turpentine-farmers raise as much maize as they need for their own family; and those who carry on the business most largely and systematically, frequently purchase all the food of their hands. Maize and bacon are, therefore, very largely imported into North Carolina, chiefly from Ohio, by the Baltimore and Wheeling railroad, and from Baltimore to Wilmington or Newbern, by sea.

The turpentine forest is from thirty to eighty miles wide, and extends from near the north-line of North Carolina to the Gulf of Mexico. Until lately, even in North Carolina, the business of collecting turpentine has been confined to such parts of the forest as were situated most conveniently to market—the value of the commodity not warranting long inland transportation. Recently, the demand has increased, owing, probably, to the enlarged consumption of spirits of turpentine in "burning fluids;" and the business has been extended into the depths of the forest. It is yet thought a hazardous venture to start the business where more than thirty miles of wagoning is required to bring the spirits of turpentine to a railroad, or navigable water.[1]

If we enter, in the winter, a part of a forest that is about to be converted into a "turpentine orchard," we come upon negroes engaged in making boxes, in which the sap is to be collected the following spring. They continue at this work from November to March, or until, as the warm weather approaches, the sap flows freely, and they are needed to remove it from the boxes into barrels. These "boxes" are not made of boards, nailed together in a cubical form, as might be supposed; nor are they log-troughs, such as, at the North, maple-sap is collected in. They are cavities dug in the trunk of the tree itself. A long, narrow ax, made in Connecticut, especially for this purpose, is used for this wood-pecking operation; and some skill is required to use it properly. We may see the green hands doing 'prentice work upon any stray oaks, or other *non*-turpentine trees they can find in the low grounds.

The boxes are made at from six inches to a foot above the roots, and are shaped like a distended waistcoat-pocket. The lower lip is horizontal—the upper, arched; the bottom of the box is about four inches below the lower lip, and eight or ten below the upper. On a tree of medium size, a box should be made to hold a quart. The less the ax approaches towards the centre of the tree, to obtain the proper capacity in the box, the better, as the vitality of the tree is less endangered; but this is little thought about.

[1] Since this was written, a great decline of prices has occurred.

An expert hand will make a box in less than ten minutes; and seventy-five to a hundred—according to the size and proximity of the trees—is considered a day's work.

The boxes being made, the bark, and a few of the outer rings of the wood of the tree, are cut off ("hacked") along the edge of the upper lip. From this excoriation, the sap begins to flow about the fifteenth of March, and gradually fills the boxes, from which it is taken by a spoon or ladle, of a peculiar form, and collected into barrels.

The turpentine barrels are made by negro coopers; the staves split from pine-logs, shaved and trimmed. They are hooped with split oak-saplings. Coopers' wages, when hired out, are from $1.50 to $2.00 a day. A good cooper is expected to make six or seven barrels a day. They are of the rudest construction possible—the staves being straight, and forming a simple cylinder—thirty inches long and eighteen inches diameter, headed up at both ends, with a square hole in one end, where the turpentine is poured in.

In from seven to ten days after the first hacking, the trees are again scarified. This is done with a hatchet, or with an instrument made for the purpose. A very slight chip, or shave, above the former, is all that is needed to be removed; the object being merely to expose a new surface of the cellular tissue—the flow from the former being clogged by congelations of the sap.

These hackings being made three or four times a month, the excoriation is constantly advancing higher up the trunk. The slighter the cut, the less the tree is injured, and the slower the advance, and the longer and the more conveniently may the process be carried on: nevertheless, in ninety-nine "orchards" out of a hundred, you will see that the chip has always been much broader and deeper than, with the slightest care to restrict it, it needed to have been. If the "dipping" has commenced when you visit the orchard, you will notice that the turpentine collected has much rubbish—chips and leaves—in it, considerably injuring its value. The greater part of this might have been avoided, by having the negroes clean out the boxes in which it had fallen, in the winter; but they seldom take this trouble.

In some orchards, you will see that many trees have been killed by fire. The wire-grass, which grew among the trees the previous year, is frequently set on fire, either accidentally or purposely, when dead and dry, in the spring. It burns slowly, and with little flame, and the living trees, the bark of which is not very inflammable, are seldom injured. But where a tree has been boxed, and the chips lie about it, these take fire, and burn with more flame; so that freqently the turpentine in the box, and on the scarified wood above it, also takes fire, and burns with such intensity as to kill the tree. The danger might be avoided by raking away the chips and leaves, for a foot or two about the roots; but I nowhere saw this precaution taken. I mention these things, by the way, as further illustration of the general inefficient direction of slave-labor; or as indicating, as might be rather claimed by the owners, that the high cost of the labor prevents its direction to these minor points of economy.

By the middle of March, the turpentine is flowing abundantly, and the negroes must be employed in hacking, as each tree requires to be freshly scarified once in a week, or ten days. Soon afterwards, it is necessary to commence dipping, or the removal of the turpentine from the boxes to barrels. There are two ways of arranging the labor for this purpose used by the larger proprietors. In one, all the negroes employed are divided into two classes—"hackers" and "dippers." The hackers are wholly employed in scarifying the trees. A task, of a certain number of trees, is given to each, which he is required to go over, hacking each tree, once in seven or eight days. The dippers are constantly employed in emptying the boxes, as they fill with turpentine. The other way—and this is more common—is to give each hand a task of trees, each of which he is required to both hack and dip statedly. Twenty-five hundred trees give a man five days' employment hacking, and one day dipping, in a week.

From one to four boxes are made in each tree, according to its size; a few inches of bark being left between them. The greater number of trees, from which turpentine is now obtained, are from a foot to eighteen inches in diameter, and have three boxes each. The hacking is carried on year after year, until, in the oldest orchards, it is extended twelve or fifteen feet, and ladders have to be used to carry it farther up the trunks of the trees. The turpentine flows from the most recent hack, down over the previously scarified wood of the tree, towards the box, a considerable proportion of it congealing by the way, and remaining attached to the wood. From this adhering portion, a part of the spirits or oil has evaporated in the process of drying; it is, therefore, of less value than that which is taken, in a more liquid condition, from the box. It is occasionally—perhaps but once a year—scraped off, and barrelled by itself. It is, therefore, known in market as "scrape;" while that which is dipped from the box, and which is of considerably higher value, is termed "dip." The flow of the first year, having but a small surface of wood to traverse, and being, therefore, less exposed to evaporation than the flow of later years, is of higher value than the ordinary dip. It is called "virgin dip." In many of the orchards, at a distance from market, and where, of course, all classes of turpentine are of less value, I observed that the trees had never been scraped—the proprietor having boxed and hacked more trees than he could apply force enough to both dip and scrape. The dip is lessened, however, by allowing the scrape to accumulate; for much of the flow is thus often made to drop outside of the box. The price of turpentine being now much higher than usual, many of the small proprietors are this year scraping their trees, that have not scraped before. This old "scrape" will be of inferior quality.

A considerable amount of turpentine is shipped in barrels to Northern ports, where it is distilled; a larger amount is distilled in the State. The proprietors of the large turpentine orchards, themselves, have stills; and those collecting but a small quantity sell to them, or to custom distilleries, owned by those who make distilling alone their business.

The stills used for making spirits or oil of turpentine from the crude gum, are of copper, not materially different in form from common ardent-spirit stills, and have a capacity of from five to twenty barrels; an average size being, perhaps, ten barrels.

The forest distilleries are usually placed in a ravine or valley, where water can be brought to them in troughs, so as to flow, at an elevation of fifteen feet from the ground, into the condensing tank. At a point at which the ground will decline from it in one direction, the still is set in a brick furnace. A floor or scaffold is erected on a level with the bottom of the still-head, and a roof covers all. The still-head is taken off, and barrels of turpentine, full of rubbish as it is collected by the negroes, are emptied in. When the still is full, or nearly so, the still-head is put on, and the joint made tight with clay; fire is made, and soon a small, transparent stream of spirits begins to flow from the mouth of the worm, and is caught directly in the barrel in which it finally comes to market. When all the spirits which can be profitably extracted, are thus drawn off, the fire is raked out of the furnace, a spigot is drawn from a spout at the bottom of the still, and the residuum flows out—a dark, thick fluid, appearing, as it runs, like molasses.

This residuum is resin, or the rosin of commerce. There is not a sufficient demand for rosin, except of the first qualities, to make it worth transporting from the inland distilleries; it is ordinarily, therefore, conducted off to a little distance, in a wooden trough, and allowed to flow from it to waste upon the ground. At the first distillery I visited, which had been in operation but one year, there lay a congealed pool of rosin, estimated to contain over three thousand barrels. Its appearance was very beautiful; firm and glairy; varying in color, and glistening like polished porphyry. The rosin from "virgin dip" turpentine, only, was saved here. At the distilleries on the river-banks, a second quality is also saved, while a poorer description is still let run to waste. When it is intended to save the rosin, it is drawn off into a vat of water, which separates the chips and other rubbish, that were contained in the gum, and it is then barrelled for market.

To prevent the spirits soaking through the wood and evaporating, the barrels are all washed on the inside with glue. They are made as carefully as possible, and are often brought from the North, and sold at three or four dollars a-piece. Notwithstanding all precaution, the waste from leakage and evaporation is often great, owing to the exceedingly subtile nature of the fluid.

The turpentine lands that I saw were valued at from $5 to $20 an acre. They have sometimes been sold at $2 an acre; and those of Georgia and Alabama can be purchased, to any extent, at that price. From 500 to

1000 trees (or 2000 boxes), I judged, stand usually upon an acre. The quantity of turpentine that would flow from these, in a year, I cannot state reliably. According to some statements given me, it would be about fourteen barrels of dip, and two barrels of scrape. Fourteen barrels of dip would give, in distillation, two barrels of spirits, and eight of resin.

At a fifteen barrel still, I found one white man and one negro employed under the oversight of the owner. It kept employed twenty-five men hacking and dipping; running twice, that is, using thirty barrels crude turpentine, a day. Besides these hands, were two coopers, and several wagoners. The wages of ordinary practised turpentine hands (slaves) are about $120 a year, with board, clothing, etc., as usual.

A North Carolina turpentine orchard, with the ordinary treatment, lasts fifty years. The trees are subject to the attack of an insect which rapidly kills them. Those most severely hacked are chiefly liable to this danger.

The turpentine business is considered to be extremely favorable to health and long life. It is sometimes engaged in by persons afflicted with pulmonary complaints, with the belief that it has a remedial effect.

When the original long-leafed pine has been destroyed, and the ground cultivated a few years, and then "turned out," a bastard variety springs up, which grows with rapidity, but is of no value for turpentine, and of but little for timber. The true variety, rich in turpentine, is of very slow growth. On one trunk, seven inches in diameter, I counted eighty-five rings. Whether there will be a renewed spontaneous growth of the true long-leafed pine, where they are allowed to gradually decay on the ground, I am unable to say.

Tar is an extract from the pine-wood obtained by charring it. It is made wholly from the heart or "light wood" of the long-leafed pine, which is split into billets of a size convenient for handling and arranging in the tar-kiln. Trees which have been used up in the turpentine business, are the best to use for making tar. The billets are piled in a conical heap, which is covered with turf, much as coal-pits are made at the North. The kiln is usually made upon a hillock, and trenches are made under it, having a mouth a little below it on the hillside. The proper burning of the kiln to produce the most tar, is an art to be learned by practice. It is made to burn very slowly, to gradually roast out the juices of the pine, so that they will run down, collect in the trench, and flow out at its mouth, where, in the commingled condition known as tar, they are ladled into barrels.

This is an exceedingly slovenly process, the tar being mixed with sand, and collecting other impurities as it flows through the kiln, and searches a way out on and through the ground. It is for the reason that it is prepared with more care, so as to be free from the admixture of sand, that the tar of Northern Europe always stands at a higher value, and competes with the Carolina tar, even in our own ports. A new patent process of roasting the pine in iron ovens, the fire not being in contact with it, has lately been introduced, and gives good promise of removing this reproach. The tar is said to be of much superior quality and to be obtained more expeditiously and economically than by the old method.

Pitch is a concentration of tar obtained by boiling it. I was unable to obtain any particulars of the process of manufacturing it.

The negroes employed in this branch of industry, seemed to me to be unusually intelligent and cheerful. Decidedly they are superior in every moral and intellectual respect to the great mass of the white people inhabiting the turpentine forest. Among the latter there is a large number, I should think a majority, of entirely uneducated, poverty-stricken vagabonds. I mean by vagabonds, simply, people without habitual, definite occupation or reliable means of livelihood. They are poor, having almost no property but their own bodies; and the use of these, that is, their labor, they are not accustomed to hire out statedly and regularly, so as to obtain capital by wages, but only occasionally by the day or job, when driven to it by necessity. A family of these people will commonly hire, or "squat" and build, a little log cabin, so made that it is only a shelter from rain, the sides not being chinked, and having no more furniture or pretension to comfort than is commonly provided a criminal in the cell of a prison. They will cultivate a little corn, and possibly a few roods of potatoes, cow-peas and coleworts. They will own a few swine, that find their living in the forest; and pretty certainly, also, a rifle and dogs; and the men, ostensibly, occupy most of their time in hunting.

A gentleman of Fayetteville told me that he had, several times, appraised, under oath, the whole household property of families of this class at less than $20. If they have need of money to purchase clothing, etc., they obtain it by selling their game or meal. If they have none of this to spare, or an insufficiency, they will work for a neighboring farmer for a few days, and they usually get for their labor fifty cents a day, *finding themselves*. The farmers say, that they do not like to employ them, because they cannot be relied upon to finish what they undertake, or to work according to directions; and because, being white men, they cannot "drive" them. That is to say, their labor is even more inefficient and unmanageable than that of slaves.

That I have not formed an exaggerated estimate of the proportion of such a class, will appear to the reader more probable from the testimony of a pious colporteur, given before a public meeting in Charleston, in February, 1855. I quote from a Charleston paper's report. The colporteur had been stationed at —— county, N. C.:—"*The larger portion* of the inhabitants seemed to be totally given up to a species of mental hallucination, which carried them captive at its will. They nearly all believed implicitly in witchcraft, and attributed everything that happened, good or bad, to the agency of persons whom they supposed possessed of evil spirits."

The majority of what I have termed turpentine-farmers—meaning the small proprietors of the long-leafed pine forest land, are people but a grade superior, in character or condition, to these vagabonds. They have habitations more like houses—log-cabins, commonly, sometimes chinked, oftener not—without windows of glass, but with a few pieces of substantial old-fashioned heir-loom furniture; a vegetable garden, in which, however, you will find no vegetable but what they call "collards" (colewort) for "greens"; fewer dogs; more swine, and larger clearings for maize, but no better crops than the poorer class. Their property is, nevertheless, often of considerable money value, consisting mainly of negroes, who, associating intimately with their masters, are of superior intelligence to the slaves of the wealthier classes.

The larger proprietors, who are also often cotton planters, cultivating the richer low lands, are, sometimes, gentlemen of good estate—intelligent, cultivated, and hospitable. The number of these, however, is extremely small.

The shad and herring fisheries upon the sounds and inlets of the North Carolina coast are an important branch of industry, and a source of considerable wealth. The men employed in them are mainly negroes, slave and free; and the manner in which they are conducted is interesting, and in some respects novel.

The largest sweep seines in the world are used. The gentleman to whom I am indebted for the most of my information, was the proprietor of a seine over two miles in length. It was manned by a force of forty negroes, most of whom were hired at a dollar a day, for the fishing season, which usually commences between the tenth and fifteenth of March, and lasts fifty days. In favorable years the profits are very great. In extremely unfavorable years, many of the proprietors are made bankrupt.

Cleaning, curing, and packing-houses are erected on the shore, as near as they conveniently may be to a point on the beach suitable for drawing the seine. Six or eight windlasses, worked by horses, are fixed along the shore, on each side of this point. There are two large seine-boats, in each of which there is one captain, two seine-tenders, and eight or ten oarsmen. In making a cast of the net, one-half of it is arranged on the stern of each of the boats, which, having previously been placed in a suitable position—perhaps a mile off shore, in front of the buildings—are rowed from each other, the captains steering, and the seine-tenders throwing off, until the seine is all cast between them. This is usually done in such a way that it describes the arc of a circle, the chord of which is diagonal with the shore. The hawsers attached to the ends of the seine are brought first to the outer windlasses, and are wound in by the horses. As the operation of gathering in the seine occupies several hours, the boat-hands, as soon as they have brought the hawsers to the shore, draw their boats up, and go to sleep.

As the wings approach the shore, the hawsers are from time to time carried to the other windlasses, to contract the sweep of the seine. After the gaff of the net reaches the shore, lines attached toward the bunt are carried to the windlasses, and the boats' crews are awakened, and arrange the wing of the seine, as fast as it comes in, upon the boat again. Of course, as the cast was made diagonally with the shore, one wing is beached before the other. By the time the fish in the bunt have been secured, both boats are ready for another cast, and the boatmen proceed to make it, while the shore-gang is engaged in sorting and gutting the " take."

My informant, who had $50,000 invested in his fishing establishment, among other items of expenditure, mentioned that he had used seventy kegs of gunpowder the previous year, and amused himself for a few moments with letting me try to conjecture in what way villainous saltpetre could be put to use in taking fish.

There is evidence of a subsidence of this coast, in many places, at a comparatively recent period; many stumps of trees, evidently standing where they grew, being found some way below the present surface, in the swamps and salt marshes. Where the formation of the shore and the surface, or the strength of the currents of water, which have flowed over the sunken land, has been such as to prevent a later deposit, the stumps of great cypress trees, not in the least decayed, yet protrude from the bottom of the sounds. These would obstruct the passage of a net, and must be removed from a fishing-ground.

The operation of removing them is carried on during

the summer, after the close of the fishing season. The position of a stump having been ascertained by divers, two large seine-boats are moored over it, alongside each other, and a log is laid across them, to which is attached, perpendicularly, between the boats, a spar, fifteen feet long. The end of a chain is hooked to the log, between the boats, the other end of which is fastened by divers to the stump which it is wished to raise. A double-purchase tackle leads from the end of the spar to a ring-bolt in the bows of one of the boats, with the fall leading aft, to be bowsed upon by the crews. The mechanical advantages of the windlass, the lever, and the pulley being thus combined, the chain is wound on to the log, until either the stump yields, and is brought to the surface, or the boats' gunwales are brought to the water's edge.

When the latter is the case, and the stump still remains firm, a new power must be applied. A spile, pointed with iron, six inches in diameter, and twenty feet long, is set upon the stump by a diver, who goes down with it, and gives it that direction which, in his judgment, is best, and driven into it by mauls and sledges, a scaffold being erected between the boats for men to stand on while driving it. In very large stumps, the spile is often driven till its top reaches the water; so that when it is drawn out, a cavity is left in the stump, ten feet in depth. A tube is now used, which is made by welding together three musket-barrels, with a breech at one end, in which is the tube of a percussion breech, with the ordinary position of the nipple reversed, so that when it is screwed on with a detonating cap, the latter will protrude within the barrel. This breech is then inserted within a cylindrical tin box, six inches in diameter, and varying in length, according to the supposed strength of the stump; and soap or tallow is smeared about the place of insertion, to make it water-tight. The box contains several pounds of gunpowder.

The long iron tube is elevated, and the diver goes down again, and guides it into the hole in the stump, with the canister in his arms. It has reached the bottom—the diver has come up, and is drawn into one of the boats—an iron rod is inserted in the mouth of the tube—all hands crouch low, and hold hard—the rod is let go—crack!—whoo—oosch! The sea swells, boils, and breaks upward. If the boats do not rise with it, they must sink: if they rise, and the chain does not break, the stump must rise with them. At the same moment the heart of cypress is riven; its farthest rootlets quiver; the very earth trembles, and loses courage to hold it; "up comes the stump, or down go the niggers!"

If I owned a yacht, I think I would make a trip to Currituck next summer, to witness this Titanic dentistry. Who could have invented it? Not a Carolinian; it is too ingenious: not a Yankee; it is too reckless: not a sailor; it is too hard upon the boats.

The success of the operation evidently depends mainly on the discretion and skill of the diver. My informant, who thought that he removed last summer over a thousand stumps, using for the purpose seventy kegs of gunpowder, employed several divers, all of them negroes. Some of them could remain under water, and work there to better advantage than others; but all were admirably skilful, and this, much in proportion to the practice and experience they had had. They wear, when diving, three or four pairs of flannel drawers and shirts. Nothing is required of them when they are not wanted to go to the bottom, and, while the other hands are at work, they may lounge, or go to sleep in the boat, which they do, in their wet garments. Whenever a diver displays unusual hardihood, skill, or perseverance, he is rewarded with whisky; or, as they are commonly allowed, while diving, as much whisky as they want, with money. Each of them would generally get every day from quarter to half-a-dollar in this way, above the wages paid for them, according to the skill and industry with which they had worked. On this account, said my informant, "the harder the work you give them to do, the better they like it." His divers very frequently had intermittent fevers, but would very rarely let this keep them out of their boats. Even in the midst of a severe "shake," they would generally insist that they were "well enough to dive."

What! slaves eager to work, and working cheerfully, earnestly and skilfully? Even so. Being for the time managed as freemen, their ambition stimulated by wages, suddenly they, too, reveal sterling manhood, and honor their Creator.

In the vicinity of Fayetteville, there are many Scotch Highlanders. The emigration of these people to North Carolina commenced in the early Colony days, and has been continued, at intervals, to the present time. They come direct, in a small class of vessels, to Wilmington.[1]

Very few Highlanders come to New York, or to other parts of the United States; the largest proportion of those emigrating arrive at Quebec, and remain in Canada. In this they are led simply by their clannishness; like sheep, they follow one another without looking right or left for an easier leap; the stream once started, there is no diverting it. I remember to have found the Highlanders at home familiar with the names of districts and towns in Canada, though they had no knowledge whatever of the United States, and used the names Canada and America synonymously. Probably, in some districts of the Highlands, no one knows of any other port in America than Wilmington. You frequently find people who can speak Gaelic, in North Carolina; and, sometimes, a small settlement where it is the common tongue: there are even one or two churches in the State, in which the services are performed in Gaelic.

The immigrants of the present generation have, nearly all, come to Fayetteville. Most of them are very poor, and obtain employment as laborers, as soon as they can get it, after their arrival. In a year or two, they will have saved money enough from their wages

[1] There is a credible tradition that Flora Macdonald once lived in North Carolina.

to purchase a few acres of piny-wood land, upon which they raise a cabin, make a clearing, and go to raising corn and a family. They are distinguished for frugality and industry; and, unless they are very intemperate—as too many of them are—are certain in a few years to acquire money enough to buy a negro, which they are said to be invariably ambitious to possess. Before they die, they will have got a family or two of young negroes about them, to be divided as a patrimony among their children. With a moderate competence they are content, and seldom become wealthy. Their children do not appear, generally, to retain their thrifty habits. I saw a number of girls, of Highland blood, employed in a cotton factory near Fayetteville. In modesty, cleanliness, and neatness of apparel, though evidently poor, they certainly compared favorably with the girls employed in a cotton mill that I visited near Glasgow, a few years ago; but the proprietor told me that they very seldom laid up anything, and spent the greater part of their earnings very foolishly, as fast as they received them.

A young man, employed in this factory, to whom the proprietor, having told me he was more intelligent and trustworthy than most of his class, had introduced me, finding that I was from the North, voluntarily told me that Slavery was a great weight upon poor people here, and he wished that he lived in a Free State.

Having observed, from my room in the hotel at Fayetteville, a number of remarkable, bright lights, I walked out, about eleven o'clock, in the direction in which they had appeared, and found, upon the edge of an old field, near the town, a camp of wagoners, with half-a-dozen fires, around some of which were clustered groups of white men and women and negroes cooking and eating their suppers (black and white from the same kettle, in many cases), some singing Methodist songs, and some listening to a banjo or fiddle-player. A still larger number appeared to be asleep, generally lying under low tents, about as large as those used by the French soldier. There were thirty or forty great wagons, with mules, cattle, or horses, feeding from troughs set upon their poles. The grouping of all among some old sycamore trees, with the fantastic shadows and wavering lights, the free flames and black brooding smoke of the pitch-pine fires, produced a most interesting and attractive spectacle, and detained me long in admiration. I could easily imagine myself to be on the Oregon or California trail, a thousand miles from the realm of civilization—not readily realize that I was within the limits of one of the oldest towns on the American continent.

These were the farmers of the distant highland districts, and their slaves, come to market with their produce. Next morning I counted sixty of their great wagons in the main street of the little town. They would generally hold, in the body, as much as seventy-five bushels of grain, were very strongly built, and drawn by from two to six horses; the near wheeler always having a large Spanish saddle on his back, for their driver. The merchants stood in the doors of their stores, or walked out into the street to observe their contents—generally of corn, meal, flour, or cotton—and to traffic for them. I observed that the negroes often took part in the bargaining, and was told by a merchant, that both the selling of the produce, and the selection and purchase of goods for the farmer's family, was often left entirely to them.

Several of the wagons had come, I found, from a hundred miles distant; and one of them from beyond the Blue Ridge, nearly two hundred miles. In this tedious way, until lately, nearly all the commerce between the back country and the river towns and sea-ports of Virginia and North Carolina has been carried on, strong teams of horses toiling on, less than a score of miles a day, with the lumbering wagons, the roads running through a sparsely settled district of clay soil, and much worse, even, than those of the sandy lands I have described. Every night, foul or fair, the driver and attendants, often including the farmer himself, and part of his family, camp out on the road-side.

At Gaston I had seen a number of long, narrow, canoe-like boats, of light draft, in which the produce of the country along the head waters of the Roanoke was brought to market. They were generally manned by three men each, who were sheltered at night under a hood of canvas, stretched upon poles, in the stern of the boat. The mouth of this hood opened upon a bed of clay, laid upon the boat's bottom, on which a fire was made, that would keep them warm, and cook their food. An equally picturesque scene with that of the wagon camp was a collection of these boats, moored at night under the steep river bank, the negroes reclining under the dusky hoods, or sitting on the gunwales, cooking and eating their hoe-cake, smoking, singing, or telling of their adventures on the passage. The cargoes of these boats were chiefly composed of meal, hides, and tobacco, and at Gaston they were transhipped, by rail, to some of the Virginia ports.

Until within a recent period, much tobacco has been brought to market, from the more remote districts of North Carolina and Virginia, by a very rude method, called "rolling," which was performed in this wise. Felloes, like those of cart-wheels, were hewn with an axe, and fitted to a cask of tobacco, at a little distance each side the bilge; holes were bored with an auger, and long wooden pins driven in, fastening them to the cask; a large hole was then bored in the middle of each head, and a spar driven through, which formed an axle-tree. To this, long poles, used as shafts, were attached, holes being bored through the ends of them, which slipped over the axle-tree, and they were secured by linch-pins. One horse was tackled in between the poles, and another attached tandem, before him. On the leader's back, a kettle and a bag of meal were hung; and on the shaft-horse was strapped a blanket, or bear-skin, which served as a saddle for the driver by day, and a bed-cover by night. Small farmers themselves often brought in their tobacco in this way; but there were also a set of men who made it their principal occupation, and whose calling was that of "tobacco-rollers." They contracted with the large planters to take their whole crop to the market-town at a certain price, furnishing horses, felloes, etc., themselves. It was their custom to so arrange their starting, that many would come together on the road, and so proceed, making a considerable camp, wherever they stopped for the night; and many such companies, by a previous agreement, would arrive in the towns together. A hard set they must have been—for the citizens now tell how, when they were young, all quiet housekeepers were kept in a state of excited alarm during the seasons when the tobacco-rollers were in town; and they well remember with what respect and consideration they were treated by all discreet people; for the quarrel of one, was made that of the whole body.

Railroads and canals, running westward from the navigable water at Baltimore, Richmond, Petersburg, and Charleston, now shorten the distance to which it is necessary for the horse transportation of the products of much of the upper country to be carried. A large district of Central and Western North Carolina, however, is still unpierced by either railroad or serviceable canal; and much of this finds its readiest communication with the sea, and by that to the rest of the world, by the Cape Fear river. Fayetteville is the point of transfer from wagon to boat, being at the head of navigation.

In 1820, a company was chartered, to make the river above Fayetteville navigable for boats, with a capital of $100,000. About $80,000 were raised and spent, probably without good judgment; certainly without accomplishing anything; and this failure operated for a long time to discourage the further employment of capital (which is much less concentrated in this than in the adjoining States), in public works. The Cape Fear river improvements have been persevered in with fluctuating energy at different periods, and are now directed by the State. The main object in view at present, is to obtain a boat-transportation from certain coal-beds to the ocean. The coal is bituminous—some of it of a very desirable quality, would be readily and cheaply mined, and the beds are of exhaustless extent. If it could be brought from the mines to the ocean with but one transhipment, and untaxed with heavy tolls, it could, without doubt, be sold with a good profit in New York and New England. It is calculated, also, that it would bear railroad freight to Fayetteville, and thence two handlings to get it to sea; and for this purpose a railroad had been projected, and a charter obtained, shortly before my visit. Gentlemen interested told me then, that they had scarcely any hopes of getting a sufficient amount of stock taken to proceed, but they should try to get a loan from the corporations of Fayetteville and Wilmington. When I returned through Western North Carolina, some months afterwards, I was informed that when about one-sixth of the amount of stock required to be taken by a certain date, before any use could be made of the charter, had been subscribed for, and when it was thought no more subscriptions could be obtained, a stranger had suddenly subscribed, in behalf of certain New Yorkers, for all the remainder. It was reported to be the design of these capitalists, if it should be found practicable upon careful survey, to carry the road to a point on the coast where they had discovered a neglected harbor, with great natural advantages for commerce, the charter having, by accident, been so loosely worded as to admit of this change in the terminus of the road. The New Yorkers were supposed to have made large purchases of land in the vicinity of this new harbor, and probably at other points, where the value of land would be favorably influenced by the work. How much truth there was in this report, I do not know, but my informant, having just come from Fayetteville, told me that the people there believed it, and were in transports of delight with the prospect it afforded them. Not one word was said about the "impudent intermeddling of Northerners," not the slightest indignation expressed, that the "profits of their own legitimate business should thus be stolen from them by the mercenary New Yorkers."

Paragraphs like the following may often be seen in juxtaposition, in the Southern papers:

"The Farmersville coal field, on Deep river, Chatham county, N. C., which was purchased some four years ago for $8,000, was sold last week to a Northern Company, for $91,000, cash. There are 900 acres of land in the tract."

* * * "It is plain that a new and glorious destiny awaits the South, and beckons us onward to a career of independence. Shall we train and discipline our energies for the coming crisis, or *shall we continue the tributary and dependent vassals of*

Northern brokers and money-changers? Now is the time for the South to begin in earnest the work of self-development! Now is the time to break asunder the fetters of commercial subjection, and to prepare for that more complete independence that awaits us!"—*Richmond Enquirer*.

A railroad from Charlotte to Raleigh, from which the line to navigable waters is already complete, is now building, and will much shorten the necessary wagoning of produce to market from the central district of the State, and will, doubtless, stimulate a greatly increased production.

The advantages offered by railroads, to the farmers of inland districts, are strikingly shown by the following fact: A gentleman, near Raleigh, who had a quantity of wheat to dispose of, seeing it quoted at high prices, in a paper of Petersburg, Va., and seeing, at the same time, the advertisement of a commission-house there, wrote to the latter, making an offer of it. The next day he received a reply, by mail, and by the train a bundle of sacks, in which he immediately forwarded the wheat, and, by the following return mail, received his pay, at the rate of $1.20 a bushel, the top price of the winter. At the same time, only forty miles from where he lived, off the line of the railroad, wheat was selling at 60 cents a bushel. There was one county, during the time I was in North Carolina, to and through which the roads were absolutely impassable, and out of which, I was told, no intelligence had been received, at the capital, for more than a month. It is not, therefore, incredible that it should cost 60 cents to move a bushel of wheat forty miles.

Railroads do not, however, so readily and entirely change the channels in which farmers have been accustomed for a long time to float their trade, especially in thinly settled districts, as might be expected. I was told of a farmer who persisted in wagoning his produce one hundred miles, making several trips during the winter to do so, for several years after he had the opportunity of using a cheap and direct communication, with a better market, by railroad. The farmer, unaccustomed to the usual mercantile forms, shrinks from them, and is afraid to deal in a large way. He does not like to trust agents, particularly strangers at a distance, and many in North Carolina are unable to deal at all by correspondence. He enjoys much more, after the Fall ploughing is done, and the horses are no longer required for field-work, to hitch them to the big wagon, load it with a little of everything he has made, and bring it to town, under his own guard and guidance, camping o' nights, on the road; and then, to talk over the news of the year, and trade with his old town cronies, as his father used to when he was a boy, and he began to go down with him. Then, with some new store goods for his family and his "people;" molasses, sugar, and coffee, and a new coffee-mill, or other Downeast notion, to return leisurely as he went, so that, when he reaches home, two or three weeks' absence shall make his arrival something of an event.

Plank-roads, it will be obvious, from these considerations, are admirably adapted to all the circumstances of this country. They suit the habits of the people, and the value of land being small, and the country heavily timbered, they may be built at a low cost. On them the farmer may drive his wagon, as he has been accustomed in the Winter, but carrying double his usual load, and in less time, and with much less liability to accidents.

The first plank-road in the State of New York was laid, I believe, in 1844, and in 1846 there were several in operation; and the public, generally, began to be informed of their mode of construction and their advantages.

It is creditable to the citizens of North Carolina, that they so soon appreciated the peculiar advantages offered them in the invention, and took measures to avail themselves of it. In 1847 an engineer was procured from New York, and, under his direction, a plank-road commenced, running westwardly from Fayetteville, into the middle of the productive region I have referred to.

The road so commencing, now forms a great trunk road, running northwest more than a hundred miles. From this trunk there are many laterals, drawing from districts which in the winter season are almost inaccessible by the old earth roads. The plank-roads are as good in winter, when the farmer has leisure to drive to market, as they are in summer; and he can take upon them a much heavier load, thirty-five miles a day, than he formerly wore out his horses and exhausted his patience to drag seventeen. So well are the advantages appreciated in the State, that over forty new companies, for building plank-roads, have been incorporated by one legislature.

North Carolina has a proverbial reputation for the ignorance and torpidity of her people; being, in this respect, at the head of the Slave States. I do not find the reason of this in any innate quality of the popular mind; but, rather, in the circumstances under which it finds its development. Owing to the general poverty of the soil in the Eastern part of the State, and to the almost exclusive employment of slave-labor on the soils productive of cotton; owing, also, to the difficulty and expense of reaching market with bulky produce from the interior and western districts, population and wealth is more divided than in the other Atlantic States; industry is almost entirely rural, and there is but little communication or concert of action among the small and scattered proprietors of capital. For the same reason, the advantages of education are more difficult to be enjoyed, the distance at which families reside apart preventing children from coming together in such numbers as to give remunerative employment to a teacher. The teachers are, generally, totally unfitted for their business; young men, as a clergyman informed me, themselves not only unadvanced beyond the lowest knowledge of the elements of primary school learning, but often coarse, vulgar, and profane in their language and behavior, who take up teaching as a temporary business, to supply the demand of a neighborhood of people as ignorant and uncultivated as themselves.

The native white population of North Carolina is, . 550,267
The whole white population under 20 years is, . . 301,106
Leaving white adults over 20, ... 249,161
Of these there are natives who cannot read and write, 73,226[1]

Being more than one fourth of the native white adults.

But the aspect of North Carolina with regard to slavery, is, in some respects, less lamentable than that of Virginia. There is not only less bigotry upon the subject, and more freedom of conversation, but I saw here, in the institution, more of patriarchal character than in any other State. The slave more frequently appears as a family servant—a member of his master's family, interested with him in his fortune, good or bad. This is a result of the less concentration of wealth in families or individuals, occasioned by the circumstances I have described. Slavery thus loses much of its inhumanity. It is still questionable, however, if, as the subject race approaches civilization, the dominant race is not proportionately detained in its onward progress. One is forced often to question, too, in viewing slavery in this aspect, whether humanity and the accumulation of wealth, the prosperity of the master, and the happiness and improvement of the subject, are not in some degree incompatible.

I left Fayetteville in a steamboat (advertised for 8 o'clock, left at 8.45) bound down Cape Fear river to Wilmington. A description of the river, with incidents of the passage, will serve to show the character of most

[1] Official Census Report, pp. 299, 309, 317.

of the navigable streams of the cotton States, flowing into the Atlantic and the Gulf, and of the manner of their navigation.

The water was eighteen feet above its lowest summer stages; the banks steep, thirty feet high from the present water surface—from fifty to one hundred feet apart—and covered with large trees and luxuriant vegetation; the course crooked; the current very rapid; the trees overhanging the banks, and frequently falling into the channel — making the navigation hazardous. The river is subject to very rapid rising. The master told me that he had sometimes left his boat aground at night, and, on returning in the morning, found it floating in twenty-five feet water, over the same spot. The difference between the extremes of low stages and floods is as much as seventy feet. In summer, there are sometimes but eighteen inches of water on the bars: the boat I was in drew but fourteen inches, light. She was a stern-wheel craft—the boiler and engine (high pressure) being placed at opposite ends, to balance weights. Her burden was three hundred barrels, or sixty tons measurement. This is the character of most of the boats navigating the river—of which there are now twelve. Larger boats are almost useless in summer, from their liability to ground; and even the smaller ones, at low stages of water, carry no freight, but are employed to tow up "flats," or shallow barges. At this season of the year, however, the steamboats are loaded close to the water's edge.

The bulk of our freight was turpentine; and the close

proximity of this to the furnaces suggested a danger fully equal to that from snags or grounding. On calling the attention of a fellow-passenger to it, he told me that a friend of his was once awakened from sleep, while lying in a berth on one of these boats, by a sudden, confused sound. Thinking the boiler had burst, he drew the bed-clothing over his head, and lay quiet, to avoid breathing the steam; until, feeling the boat ground, he ran out, and discovered that she was on fire near the furnace. Having some valuable freight near by, which he was desirous to save, and seeing no immediate danger, though left alone on the boat, he snatched a bucket, and, drawing water from alongside, applied it with such skill and rapidity as soon to quench the flames, and eventually to entirely extinguish the fire. Upon the return of the crew, a few repairs were made, steam was got up again, and the boat proceeded to her destination in safety. He afterwards ascertained that three hundred kegs of gunpowder were stowed beneath the deck that had been on fire—a circumstance which sufficiently accounted for the panic-flight of the crew.

Soon after leaving, we passed the *Zephyr*, wooding-up: an hour later, our own boat was run to the bank, men jumped from her fore and aft, and fastened head and stern lines to the trees, and we also commenced wooding.

The trees had been cut away so as to leave a clear space to the top of the bank, which was some fifty feet from the boat, and moderately steep. Wood, cut, split, and piled in ranks, stood at the top of it, and a shoot of plank, two feet wide and thirty long, conveyed it nearly to the water. The crew rushed to the woodpiles—master, passengers, and all, but the engineer and chambermaid, deserting the boat—and the wood was first passed down, as many as could, throwing into the shoot, and others forming a line, and tossing it, from one to another, down the bank. From the water's edge it was passed, in the same way, to its place on board, with great rapidity—the crew exciting themselves with yells. They were all blacks, but one.

On a tree, near the top of the bank, a little box was nailed, on which a piece of paper was tacked, with this inscription:

"Notic
"to all persons takin wood from this landin pleas to leav a ticket payable to the subscriber, at $1,75 a cord as heretofore,

"Amos Sikes."

and the master—just before the wood was all on board—hastily filled a blank order (torn from a book, like a check-book, leaving a memorandum of the amount, etc.) on the owner of the boat for payment, to Mr. SIKES, for two cords of pine-wood, at $1.75, and two cords of light-wood, at $2—and left it in the box. The wood used had been measured in the ranks with a rod, carried for the purpose, by the master, at the moment he reached the bank.

Before, with all possible haste, we had finished wooding, the *Zephyr* passed us; and, during the rest of the day, she kept out of our sight. As often as we met a steamboat, or passed any flats or rafts, our men were calling out to know how far ahead of us she was; and when the answer came back each time, in an increasing number of miles, they told us that our boat was more than usually sluggish, owing to an uncommonly heavy freight; but, still, for some time, they were ready to make bets that we should get first to Wilmington.

Several times we were hailed from the shore, to take on a passenger, or some light freight; and these requests, as long as it was possible, were promptly complied with—the boat being run up, so as to rest her bow upon the bank, and then shouldered off by the men, as if she had been a skiff.

There were but three through-passengers, besides myself. Among them, was a glue-manufacturer, of Baltimore—getting orders from the turpentine-distillers—and a turpentine-farmer and distiller. The glue-manufacturer said that, in his factory, they had formerly employed slaves; had since used Irishmen, and now employed Germans altogether. Their operations were carried on night and day, and one gang of the men had to relieve another. The slaves they had employed never would be *on hand*, when the hour for relieving came. It was also necessary to be careful that certain operations should be performed at a certain time, and some judgment and watchfulness was necessary, to fix this time: the slaves never could be made to care enough for the matter, to be depended upon for discretion, in this respect; and great injury was frequently done in consequence. Some of the operations were disagreeable, and they would put one another up to thinking and saying that they ought not to be required to do such dirty work—and try to have their owners get them away from it.

Irishmen, he said, worked very well and, to a certain extent, faithfully, and, for a time, they liked them very much; but they found that, in about a fortnight, an Irishman always thought he knew more than his master, and would exercise his discretion a little too much, as well as often directly disregard his orders. Irishmen were, he said, "*too* faithful"—that is, self-confident and officious.

At length, at a hurried time, they had employed one or two Germans. The Irishmen, of course, soon quarrelled with them, and threatened to leave, if they were kept. Whereupon, they were, themselves, all discharged, and a full crew of Germans, at much less wages, taken; and they proved excellent hands—steady, plodding, reliable, though they never pretended to know anything, and said nothing about what they could do. They were easily instructed, obeyed orders faithfully, and worked fairly for their wages, without boasting or grumbling.

The turpentine-distiller gave a good account of some of his men; but said he was sure they never performed half so much work as he himself could; and they sometimes would, of their own accord, do twice as much, in a day, as could usually be got out of them. He employed a Scotchman at the "still;" but he never would have white people at ordinary work, because he could n't drive them. He added, with the utmost simplicity—and I do not think any one present saw, at the time, how much the remark expressed more than it was intended to—"I never can drive a white man, for I know I could never bear to be driven myself, by anybody."

The other passenger was "a North of England man," as I suspected from the first words I heard from him—though he had been in this country for about twenty years. He was a mechanic, and employed several slaves; but testified strongly of the expensive character of their labor; and declared, without any reserve, that the system was ruinous in its effects upon the character of all classes of working-men.

The country on the river-bank was nearly all wooded, with, occasionally, a field of corn, which, even in the low alluvial meadows, sometimes overflowed by the river, and enriched by its deposit, had evidently yielded but a very meagre crop—the stalks standing singly, at great distances, and very small. The greater part, even of these once rich low lands, that had been in cultivation, were now "turned out," and covered, either with pines, or broom-sedge and brushwood.

At some seventy or eighty miles, I should think, below Fayetteville, the banks became lower, and there was much swamp land, in which the ground was often covered with a confusion of logs and sawn lumber, mingled with other rubbish, left by floods of the river. The standing timber was very large, and many of the trees were hung with the long, waving drapery of the *Tillandsia*, or Spanish moss, which, as well as the mistletoe, I here first saw in profusion. There was also a thick network among the trees, of beautiful climbing plants. I observed some very large grape-vines, and many trees of greater size than I ever saw of their species before. I infer that this soil, properly reclaimed, and protected from floods of the river, might be most profitably used in the culture of the various half-tropical trees and shrubs, of whose fruits we now import so large and costly an amount. The fig, I have been informed, grows and bears luxuriantly at Wilmington, seldom or never suffering in its wood, though a crop of fruit may be occasionally injured by a severe late spring frost. The almond, doubtless, would succeed equally well, so also the olive; but of none of these is there the slightest commercial value produced in North Carolina, or in all our country.

In the evening we passed many boats and rafts, blazing with great fires, made upon a thick bed of clay, and their crews singing at their sweeps. Twenty miles above Wilmington, the shores became marshy, the river wide, and the woody screen that had hitherto, in a great degree, hid the nakedness of the land, was withdrawn, leaving open to view only broad, reedy savannahs, on either side.

We reached Wilmington, the port at the mouth of the river, at half-past nine. Taking a carriage, I was driven first to one hotel, and afterwards to another. They were both so crowded with guests, and excessive business duties so prevented the clerks from being tolerably civil to me, that I feared if I remained in either of them, I should have another Norfolk experience. While I was endeavoring to ascertain if there was a third public-house, in which I might, perhaps, obtain a private room, my eye fell upon an advertisement of a new railroad line of passage to Charleston. A boat, to take passengers to the railroad, was to start every night from Wilmington, at ten o'clock. It was already something past ten, but being pretty sure that she would not get off punctually, and having a strong resisting impulse to being packed away in a close room, with any chance stranger the clerk of the house might choose to couple me with, I shouldered my baggage, and ran for the wharves. At half-past ten I was looking at Wilmington over the stern of another little wheelbarrow-steamboat, pushing back up the river. When or how I was to be taken to Charleston, I had not yet been able to ascertain. The captain assured me it was all right, and demanded twenty dollars. Being in his power, I gave it to him, and received in return a pocketful of tickets, guaranteeing the bearer passage from place to place; not one of which places had I ever heard of before, except Charleston.

The cabin was small, dirty, crowded, close and smoky. Finding a warm spot in the deck, over the furnace, and to leeward of the chimney, I pillowed myself on my luggage, and went to sleep.

The ringing of the boat's bell awoke me, after no great lapse of time, and I found we were in a small creek, heading southward. Presently we reached a wharf, near which stood a locomotive and train. A long, narrow plank having been run out, half a dozen white men, including myself, went on shore. Then followed as many negroes, who appeared to be a recent purchase of their owner. Owing, probably, to an unusually low tide, there was a steep ascent from the boat to the wharf, and I was amused to see the anxiety of this gentleman for the safe landing of his property, and especially to hear him curse them for their carelessness, as if their lives were of much greater value to him than to themselves. One of them was a woman. All carried over their shoulders some little baggage, probably all their personal effects, slung in a blanket; and one had a dog, whose safe landing caused him nearly as much anxiety as his own did *his* owner.

"Gib me da dog, now," said the dog's owner, standing half way up the plank.

"Damn the dog," said the negro's owner; "give me your hand up here. Let go of the dog; d'ye hear! Let him take care of himself."

But the negro hugged the dog, and brought him safely on shore.

After a short delay, the train started: the single passenger car was a very fine one (made at Wilmington, Delaware), and just sufficiently warmed. I should have slept again if it had not been that two of the six inmates were drunk—one of them uproariously, and the other blandly. The latter had got possessed with the idea that I was the conductor—probably because I wore a cap—and in whatever part of the car I seated myself, would, as often as once in five minutes, come to make some inquiry of me, usually first apologizing with, "Hope I don't intrude, sir, as the immortal says."

END OF VOL. I.

BOOK JUNGLE

Bringing Classics to Life

www.bookjungle.com email: sales@bookjungle.com fax: 630-214-0564 mail: Book Jungle PO Box 2226 Champaign, IL 61825

The Two Babylons
Alexander Hislop
You may be surprised to learn that many traditions of Roman Catholicism in fact don't come from Christ's teachings but from an ancient Babylonian "Mystery" religion that was centered on Nimrod, his wife Semiramis, and a child Tammuz. This book shows how this ancient religion transformed itself as it incorporated Christ into its teachings....

Religion/History   Pages:358
ISBN: *1-59462-010-5*   MSRP *$22.95*   QTY ☐

The Power Of Concentration
Theron Q. Dumont
It is of the utmost value to learn how to concentrate. To make the greatest success of anything you must be able to concentrate your entire thought upon the idea you are working on. The person that is able to concentrate utilizes all constructive thoughts and shuts out all destructive ones...

Self Help/Inspirational   Pages:196
ISBN: *1-59462-141-1*   MSRP *$14.95*   ☐

Rightly Dividing The Word
Clarence Larkin
The "Fundamental Doctrines" of the Christian Faith are clearly outlined in numerous books on Theology, but they are not available to the average reader and were mainly written for students. The Author has made it the work of his ministry to preach the "Fundamental Doctrines." To this end he has aimed to express them in the simplest and clearest manner..

Religion   Pages:352
ISBN: *1-59462-334-1*   MSRP *$23.45*   ☐

The Law of Psychic Phenomena
Thomson Jay Hudson
"I do not expect this book to stand upon its literary merits; for if it is unsound in principle, felicity of diction cannot save it, and if sound, homeliness of expression cannot destroy it. My primary object in offering it to the public is to assist in bringing Psychology within the domain of the exact sciences. That this has never been accomplished..."

New Age   Pages:420
ISBN: *1-59462-124-1*   MSRP *$29.95*   ☐

Beautiful Joe
Marshall Saunders
When Marshall visited the Moore family in 1892, she discovered Joe, a dog they had nursed back to health from his previous abusive home to live a happy life. So moved was she, that she wrote this classic masterpiece which won accolades and was recognized as a heartwarming symbol for humane animal treatment...

Fiction   Pages:256
ISBN: *1-59462-261-2*   MSRP *$18.45*   ☐

The Codes Of Hammurabi And Moses - W. W. Davies
The discovery of the Hammurabi Code is one of the greatest achievements of archaeology, and is of paramount interest, not only to the student of the Bible, but also to all those interested in ancient history...

Religion   Pages:132
ISBN: *1-59462-338-4*   MSRP *$12.95*   ☐

The Thirty-Six Dramatic Situations
Georges Polti
An incredibly useful guide for aspiring authors and playwrights. This volume categorizes every dramatic situation which could occur in a story and describes them in a list of 36 situations. A great aid to help inspire or formalize the creative writing process...

Self Help/Reference   Pages:204
ISBN: *1-59462-134-9*   MSRP *$15.95*   ☐

The Go-Getter
Kyne B. Peter
The Go Getter is the story of William Peck. He was a war veteran and amputee who will not be refused what he wants. Peck not only fights to find employment but continually proves himself more than competent at the many difficult test that are throw his way in the course of his early days with the Ricks Lumber Company...

Business/Self Help/Inspirational   Pages:68
ISBN: *1-59462-186-1*   MSRP *$8.95*   QTY ☐

Self Mastery
Emile Coue
Emile Coue came up with novel way to improve the lives of people. He was a pharmacist by trade and often saw ailing people. This lead him to develop autosuggestion, a form of self-hypnosis. At the time his theories weren't popular but over the years evidence is mounting that he was indeed right all along...

New Age/Self Help   Pages:98
ISBN: *1-59462-189-6*   MSRP *$7.95*   ☐

The Awful Disclosures Of Maria Monk
"I cannot banish the scenes and characters of this book from my memory. To me it can never appear like an amusing fable, or lose its interest and importance. The story is one which is continually before me, and must return fresh to my mind with painful emotions as long as I live.."

Religion   Pages:232
ISBN: *1-59462-160-8*   MSRP *$17.95*   ☐

As a Man Thinketh
James Allen
"This little volume (the result of meditation and experience) is not intended as an exhaustive treatise on the much-written-upon subject of the power of thought. It is suggestive rather than explanatory, its object being to stimulate men and women to the discovery and perception of the truth that by virtue of the thoughts which they choose and encourage..."

Inspirational/Self Help   Pages:80
ISBN: *1-59462-231-0*   MSRP *$9.45*   ☐

The Enchanted April
Elizabeth Von Arnim
It began in a woman's club in London on a February afternoon, an uncomfortable club, and a miserable afternoon when Mrs. Wilkins, who had come down from Hampstead to shop and had lunched at her club, took up The Times from the table in the smoking-room...

Fiction   Pages:368
ISBN: *1-59462-150-0*   MSRP *$23.45*   ☐

Holland - The History Of Netherlands
Thomas Colley Grattan
Thomas Grattan was a prestigious writer from Dublin who served as British Consul to the US. Among his works is an authoritative look at the history of Holland. A colorful and interesting look at history....

History/Politics   Pages:408
ISBN: *1-59462-137-3*   MSRP *$26.95*   ☐

A Concise Dictionary of Middle English
A. L. Mayhew
Walter W. Skeat
The present work is intended to meet, in some measure, the requirements of those who wish to make some study of Middle-English, and who find a difficulty in obtaining such assistance as will enable them to find out the meanings and etymologies of the words most essential to their purpose...

Reference/History   Pages:332
ISBN: *1-59462-119-5*   MSRP *$29.95*   ☐

www.bookjungle.com email: sales@bookjungle.com fax: 630-214-0564 mail: Book Jungle PO Box 2226 Champaign, IL 61825

BOOK JUNGLE

Bringing Classics to Life

www.bookjungle.com email: sales@bookjungle.com fax: 630-214-0564 mail: Book Jungle PO Box 2226 Champaign, IL 61825

The Witch-Cult in Western Europe
Margaret Murray QTY

The mass of existing material on this subject is so great that I have not attempted to make a survey of the whole of European "Witchcraft" but have confined myself to an intensive study of the cult in Great Britain. In order, however, to obtain a clearer understanding of the ritual and beliefs I have had recourse to French and Flemish sources...

Occult Pages: 308
ISBN: *1-59462-126-8* MSRP *$22.45*

Philosophy Of Natural Therapeutics
Henry Lindlahr QTY

We invite the earnest cooperation in this great work of all those who have awakened to the necessity for more rational living and for radical reform in healing methods...

Health/Philosophy/Self Help Pages: 552
ISBN: *1-59462-132-2* MSRP *$34.95*

The Science Of Psychic Healing
Yogi Ramacharaka

This book is not a book of theories it deals with facts. Its author regards the best of theories as but working hypotheses to be used only until better ones present themselves. The "fact" is the principal thing the essential thing to uncover which the tool, theory, is used...

New Age/Health Pages: 180
ISBN: *1-59462-140-3* MSRP *$13.95*

A Message to Garcia
Elbert Hubbard

This literary trifle, A Message to Garcia, was written one evening after supper, in a single hour. It was on the Twenty-second of February, Eighteen Hundred Ninety-nine, Washington's Birthday, and we were just going to press with the March Philistine...

New Age/Fiction Pages: 92
ISBN: *1-59462-144-6* MSRP *$9.95*

Bible Myths
Thomas Doane

In pursuing the study of the Bible Myths, facts pertaining thereto, in a condensed form, seemed to be greatly needed, and nowhere to be found. Widely scattered through hundreds of ancient and modern volumes, most of the contents of this book may indeed be found; but any previous attempt to trace exclusively the myths and legends...

Religion/History Pages: 644
ISBN: *1-59462-163-2* MSRP *$38.95*

The Book of Jasher
Alcuinus Flaccus Albinus

The Book of Jasher is an historical religious volume that many consider as a missing holy book from the Old Testament. Particularly studied by the Church of Later Day Saints and historians, it covers the history of the world from creation until the period of Judges in Israel. It's authenticity is bolstered due to a reference to the Book of Jasher in the Bible in Joshua 10:13

Religion/History Pages: 276
ISBN: *1-59462-197-7* MSRP *$18.95*

Tertium Organum
P. D. Ouspensky

A truly mind expanding writing that combines science with mysticism with unprecedented elegance. He presents the world we live in as a multi dimensional world and time as a motion through this world. But this isn't a cold and purely analytical explanation but a masterful presentation filled with similes and analogies...

New Age Pages: 356
ISBN: *1-59462-205-1* MSRP *$23.95*

The Titan
Theodore Dreiser

"When Frank Algernon Cowperwood emerged from the Eastern District Penitentiary, in Philadelphia he realized that the old life he had lived in that city since boyhood was ended. His youth was gone, and with it had been lost the great business prospects of his earlier manhood. He must begin again..."

Fiction Pages: 564
ISBN: *1-59462-220-5* MSRP *$33.95*

Advance Course in Yogi Philosophy
Yogi Ramacharaka

"The twelve lessons forming this volume were originally issued in the shape of monthly lessons, known as "The Advanced Course in Yogi Philosophy and Oriental Occultism" during a period of twelve months beginning with October, 1904, and ending September, 1905."

Philosophy/Inspirational/Self Help Pages: 340
ISBN: *1-59462-229-9* MSRP *$22.95*

Biblical Essays
J. B. Lightfoot

About one-third of the present volume has already seen the light. The opening essay "On the Internal Evidence for the Authenticity and Genuineness of St John's Gospel" was published in the "Expositor" in the early months of 1890, and has been reprinted since...

Religion/History Pages: 480
ISBN: *1-59462-238-8* MSRP *$30.95*

Ambassador Morgenthau's Story
Henry Morgenthau

"By this time the American people have probably become convinced that the Germans deliberately planned the conquest of the world. Yet they hesitate to convict on circumstantial evidence and for this reason all eye witnesses to this, the greatest crime in modern history, should volunteer their testimony..."

History Pages: 472
ISBN: *1-59462-244-2* MSRP *$29.95*

The Settlement Cook Book
Simon Kander

A legacy from the civil war, this book is a classic "American charity cookbook," which was used for fundraisers starting in Milwaukee. While it has transformed over the years, this printing provides great recipes from American history. Over two million copies have been sold. This volume contains a rich collection of recipes from noted chefs and hostesses of the turn of the century...

How-to Pages: 472
ISBN: *1-59462-256-5* MSRP *$29.95*

The Aquarian Gospel of Jesus the Christ
Levi Dowling

A retelling of Jesus' story which tells us what happened during the twenty year gap left by the Bible's New Testament. It tells of his travels to the far-east where he studied with the masters and fought against the rigid caste system. This book has enjoyed a resurgence in modern America and provides spiritual insight with charm. Its influences can be seen throughout the Age of Aquarius.

Religion Pages: 264
ISBN: *1-59462-321-X* MSRP *$18.95*

My Life and Work
Henry Ford

Henry Ford revolutionized the world with his implementation of mass production for the Model T automobile. Gain valuable business insight into his life and work with his own auto-biography... "We have only started on our development of our country we have not as yet, with all our talk of wonderful progress, done more than scratch the surface. The progress has been wonderful enough but..."

Biographies/History/Business Pages: 300
ISBN: *1-59462-198-5* MSRP *$21.95*

www.bookjungle.com email: sales@bookjungle.com fax: 630-214-0564 mail: Book Jungle PO Box 2226 Champaign, IL 61825

BOOK JUNGLE

Bringing Classics to Life

www.bookjungle.com email: sales@bookjungle.com fax: 630-214-0564 mail: Book Jungle PO Box 2226 Champaign, IL 61825

QTY

- **The Rosicrucian Cosmo-Conception Mystic Christianity** by *Max Heindel* — ISBN: 1-59462-188-8 — **$38.95**
  The Rosicrucian Cosmo-conception is not dogmatic, neither does it appeal to any other authority than the reason of the student. It is not controversial, but is sent forth in the hope that it may help to clear...
  New Age/Religion Pages 646

- **Abandonment To Divine Providence** by *Jean-Pierre de Caussade* — ISBN: 1-59462-228-0 — **$25.95**
  "The Rev. Jean Pierre de Caussade was one of the most remarkable spiritual writers of the Society of Jesus in France in the 18th Century. His death took place at Toulouse in 1751. His works have gone through many editions and have been republished...
  Inspirational/Religion Pages 400

- **Mental Chemistry** by *Charles Haanel* — ISBN: 1-59462-192-6 — **$23.95**
  Mental Chemistry allows the change of material conditions by combining and appropriately utilizing the power of the mind. Much like applied chemistry creates something new and unique out of careful combinations of chemicals the mastery of mental chemistry...
  New Age Pages 354

- **The Letters of Robert Browning and Elizabeth Barret Barrett 1845-1846 vol II** by *Robert Browning* and *Elizabeth Barrett* — ISBN: 1-59462-193-4 — **$35.95**
  Biographies Pages 596

- **Gleanings In Genesis (volume I)** by *Arthur W. Pink* — ISBN: 1-59462-130-6 — **$27.45**
  Appropriately has Genesis been termed "the seed plot of the Bible" for in it we have, in germ form, almost all of the great doctrines which are afterwards fully developed in the books of Scripture which follow...
  Religion/Inspirational Pages 420

- **The Master Key** by *L. W. de Laurence* — ISBN: 1-59462-001-6 — **$30.95**
  In no branch of human knowledge has there been a more lively increase of the spirit of research during the past few years than in the study of Psychology, Concentration and Mental Discipline. The requests for authentic lessons in Thought Control, Mental Discipline and...
  New Age/Business Pages 422

- **The Lesser Key Of Solomon Goetia** by *L. W. de Laurence* — ISBN: 1-59462-092-X — **$9.95**
  This translation of the first book of the "Lemegeton" which is now for the first time made accessible to students of Talismanic Magic was done, after careful collation and edition, from numerous Ancient Manuscripts in Hebrew, Latin, and French...
  New Age/Occult Pages 92

- **Rubaiyat Of Omar Khayyam** by *Edward Fitzgerald* — ISBN: 1-59462-332-5 — **$13.95**
  Edward Fitzgerald, whom the world has already learned, in spite of his own efforts to remain within the shadow of anonymity, to look upon as one of the rarest poets of the century, was born at Bredfield, in Suffolk, on the 31st of March, 1809. He was the third son of John Purcell...
  Music Pages 172

- **Ancient Law** by *Henry Maine* — ISBN: 1-59462-128-4 — **$29.95**
  The chief object of the following pages is to indicate some of the earliest ideas of mankind, as they are reflected in Ancient Law, and to point out the relation of those ideas to modern thought.
  Religion/History Pages 452

- **Far-Away Stories** by *William J. Locke* — ISBN: 1-59462-129-2 — **$19.45**
  "Good wine needs no bush, but a collection of mixed vintages does. And this book is just such a collection. Some of the stories I do not want to remain buried for ever in the museum files of dead magazine-numbers an author's not unpardonable vanity..."
  Fiction Pages 272

- **Life of David Crockett** by *David Crockett* — ISBN: 1-59462-250-7 — **$27.45**
  "Colonel David Crockett was one of the most remarkable men of the times in which he lived. Born in humble life, but gifted with a strong will, an indomitable courage, and unremitting perseverance...
  Biographies/New Age Pages 424

- **Lip-Reading** by *Edward Nitchie* — ISBN: 1-59462-206-X — **$25.95**
  Edward B. Nitchie, founder of the New York School for the Hard of Hearing, now the Nitchie School of Lip-Reading, Inc, wrote "LIP-READING Principles and Practice". The development and perfecting of this meritorious work on lip-reading was an undertaking...
  How-to Pages 400

- **A Handbook of Suggestive Therapeutics, Applied Hypnotism, Psychic Science** by *Henry Munro* — ISBN: 1-59462-214-0 — **$24.95**
  Health/New Age/Health Self-help Pages 376

- **A Doll's House: and Two Other Plays** by *Henrik Ibsen* — ISBN: 1-59462-112-8 — **$19.95**
  Henrik Ibsen created this classic when in revolutionary 1848 Rome. Introducing some striking concepts in playwriting for the realist genre, this play has been studied the world over.
  Fiction/Classics/Plays 308

- **The Light of Asia** by *sir Edwin Arnold* — ISBN: 1-59462-204-3 — **$13.95**
  In this poetic masterpiece, Edwin Arnold describes the life and teachings of Buddha. The man who was to become known as Buddha to the world was born as Prince Gautama of India but he rejected the worldly riches and abandoned the reigns of power when...
  Religion/History/Biographies Pages 170

- **The Complete Works of Guy de Maupassant** by *Guy de Maupassant* — ISBN: 1-59462-157-8 — **$16.95**
  "For days and days, nights and nights, I had dreamed of that first kiss which was to consecrate our engagement, and I knew not on what spot I should put my lips..."
  Fiction/Classics Pages 240

- **The Art of Cross-Examination** by *Francis L. Wellman* — ISBN: 1-59462-309-0 — **$26.95**
  Written by a renowned trial lawyer, Wellman imparts his experience and uses case studies to explain how to use psychology to extract desired information through questioning.
  How-to/Science/Reference Pages 408

- **Answered or Unanswered?** by *Louisa Vaughan* — ISBN: 1-59462-248-5 — **$10.95**
  Miracles of Faith in China
  Religion Pages 112

- **The Edinburgh Lectures on Mental Science (1909)** by *Thomas* — ISBN: 1-59462-008-3 — **$11.95**
  This book contains the substance of a course of lectures recently given by the writer in the Queen Street Hall, Edinburgh. Its purpose is to indicate the Natural Principles governing the relation between Mental Action and Material Conditions...
  New Age/Psychology Pages 148

- **Ayesha** by *H. Rider Haggard* — ISBN: 1-59462-301-5 — **$24.95**
  Verily and indeed it is the unexpected that happens! Probably if there was one person upon the earth from whom the Editor of this, and of a certain previous history, did not expect to hear again...
  Classics Pages 380

- **Ayala's Angel** by *Anthony Trollope* — ISBN: 1-59462-352-X — **$29.95**
  The two girls were both pretty, but Lucy who was twenty-one who supposed to be simple and comparatively unattractive, whereas Ayala was credited, as her Bombwhat romantic name might show, with poetic charm and a taste for romance. Ayala when her father died was nineteen...
  Fiction Pages 484

- **The American Commonwealth** by *James Bryce* — ISBN: 1-59462-286-8 — **$34.45**
  An interpretation of American democratic political theory. It examines political mechanics and society from the perspective of Scotsman James Bryce
  Politics Pages 572

- **Stories of the Pilgrims** by *Margaret P. Pumphrey* — ISBN: 1-59462-116-0 — **$17.95**
  This book explores pilgrims religious oppression in England as well as their escape to Holland and eventual crossing to America on the Mayflower, and their early days in New England.
  History Pages 268

www.bookjungle.com email: sales@bookjungle.com fax: 630-214-0564 mail: Book Jungle PO Box 2226 Champaign, IL 61825

BOOK JUNGLE

Bringing Classics to Life

www.bookjungle.com email: sales@bookjungle.com fax: 630-214-0564 mail: Book Jungle PO Box 2226 Champaign, IL 61825

QTY

The Fasting Cure *by* **Sinclair Upton**   ISBN: *1-59462-222-1*   **$13.95**
In the Cosmopolitan Magazine for May, 1910, and in the Contemporary Review (London) for April, 1910, I published an article dealing with my experiences in fasting. I have written a great many magazine articles, but never one which attracted so much attention... *New Age/Self Help/Health Pages 164*

Hebrew Astrology *by* **Sepharial**   ISBN: *1-59462-308-2*   **$13.45**
In these days of advanced thinking it is a matter of common observation that we have left many of the old landmarks behind and that we are now pressing forward to greater heights and to a wider horizon than that which represented the mind-content of our progenitors... *Astrology Pages 144*

Thought Vibration or The Law of Attraction in the Thought World   ISBN: *1-59462-127-6*   **$12.95**
by William Walker Atkinson   *Psychology/Religion Pages 144*

Optimism *by* **Helen Keller**   ISBN: *1-59462-108-X*   **$15.95**
Helen Keller was blind, deaf, and mute since 19 months old, yet famously learned how to overcome these handicaps, communicate with the world, and spread her lectures promoting optimism. An inspiring read for everyone... *Biographies/Inspirational Pages 84*

Sara Crewe *by* **Frances Burnett**   ISBN: *1-59462-360-0*   **$9.45**
In the first place, Miss Minchin lived in London. Her home was a large, dull, tall one, in a large, dull square, where all the houses were alike, and all the sparrows were alike, and where all the door-knockers made the same heavy sound... *Childrens Classic Pages 88*

The Autobiography of Benjamin Franklin *by* **Benjamin Franklin**   ISBN: *1-59462-135-7*   **$24.95**
The Autobiography of Benjamin Franklin has probably been more extensively read than any other American historical work, and no other book of its kind has had such ups and downs of fortune. Franklin lived for many years in England, where he was agent... *Biographies/History Pages 332*

Name	
Email	
Telephone	
Address	
City, State ZIP	

☐ Credit Card   ☐ Check / Money Order

Credit Card Number	
Expiration Date	
Signature	

Please Mail to: Book Jungle
                  PO Box 2226
                  Champaign, IL 61825
or Fax to: 630-214-0564

ORDERING INFORMATION

web: www.bookjungle.com
email: sales@bookjungle.com
fax: 630-214-0564
mail: Book Jungle PO Box 2226 Champaign, IL 61825
or PayPal to sales@bookjungle.com

Please contact us for bulk discounts

DIRECT-ORDER TERMS

20% Discount if You Order Two or More Books
Free Domestic Shipping!
Accepted: Master Card, Visa, Discover, American Express

www.ingramcontent.com/pod-product-compliance
Lightning Source LLC
Chambersburg PA
CBHW082032230426
43670CB00016B/2634